# SHAKESPEARE AND THE USES OF ANTIQUITY

## An Introductory Essay

*Charles and Michelle Martindale*

London and New York

First published 1990
by Routledge
11 New Fetter Lane, London EC4P 4EE

Simultaneously published in the USA and Canada
by Routledge
a division of Routledge, Chapman and Hall, Inc.
29 West 35th Street, New York, NY 10001

© 1990 Charles and Michelle Martindale

Typeset in 10/12pt Garamond
and printed by
Redwood Press Limited, Melksham, Wiltshire

*British Library Cataloguing in Publication Data*
Martindale, Charles
Shakespeare and the uses of antiquity: an introductory
essay on Shakespeare and English Renaissance classicism.
1. Drama in English.   Shakespeare, William Shakespeare,
William.   Influence of Classical literatures
I. Title   II. Martindale, Michelle, *1951–*
822.3'3
ISBN 0–415–02388–2

*Library of Congress Cataloging in Publication Data*
Martindale, Charles.
Shakespeare and the uses of antiquity: an introductory essay on
Shakespeare and English Renaissance classicism / Charles and
Michelle Martindale.
p.   cm.
Includes bibliographical references.
ISBN 0–415–02388–2
1. Shakespeare, William, 1564–1616 – Knowledge – Literature.
2. Shakespeare, William, 1564–1616 – Knowledge – Rome.   3. Rome in
literature.   4. Civilization, Classical, in literature.
5. Mythology, Classical, in literature.   6. Classicism – England –
History – 16th century.   7. Shakespeare, William, 1564–1616 –
Knowledge and learning.   I. Martindale, Michelle, 1951–.
II. Title.
PR3037.M37   1990        89–71346
822.3'3 – dc20        CIP

For Gabriel and
Benjamin
*pignora*

It has always been admitted by competent opinion that Shakspere's education was a 'trivial' one. But exactly because it was a trivial one it was perhaps best adapted to the doing of trivial things – such as writing immortal plays.

(Baldwin, vol. 2, p. 674)

# CONTENTS

# PREFACE

The issues which most concern many Shakespearean scholars today are those raised by post-structuralism, cultural materialism or the new historicism, feminism and so forth. In other words Shakespeare is being used – as he has always been used – as cultural currency in our battles for meaning and self-understanding. But interesting, and modish, as these concerns are, there are other approaches which have the advantage of being closer to those of Shakespeare himself and of his original audiences. Shakespeare, though not a learned man, wrote in an age saturated with matters classical. To the Elizabethans education meant essentially the study of Latin; inevitably as a result much that was written and thought was dominated by the classical tradition. One third of Shakespeare's plays are set in the ancient world, and he has constant recourse to classical mythology and history, and to classical ideas. This is simply a matter of record. That so narrow an education must have been a disaster will be agreed by all; the only problem is that it provoked one of the two or three richest flowerings in the history of Western literature.

This study is not designed primarily to provide an account of Shakespeare's classical sources. Those who require extended details of echoes and borrowings must read Baldwin and others. We rather aim, in certain specific areas, to follow up the *critical* implications of our present knowledge of Shakespeare's classicism. Baldwin argues that his enquiries into the compositional methods of Renaissance poets have no such implications: 'the result cannot possibly make a line of their poetry ... either more or less great. It can merely throw interesting and important light on how they attained their results. On literary appreciation itself such matters have little or no direct bearing' (vol.2, p.453). Admittedly to say that 'dusky Dis' (*Tempest* IV.i.89) is Ovid's *niger Dis* (*Met.* IV.438) tells us nothing very

vii

exciting; but to see that the masque evokes an Ovidian world but in a curiously artificial style, and to link this with Prospero's dismissal of his art, is to move from source hunting to criticism.

We write on the assumption that the modern student requires something more sophisticated than J.A.K. Thomson's spirited but cheerfully philistine little book *Shakespeare and the Classics* with its no-nonsense neo-Farmerian thesis. Our aim is not to be novel, but to put the position as we see it (even if that position sounds old-fashioned). Whether there is anything both new and productive in our readings of Shakespeare, others more expert must be the judge. Since the steady professionalizing of English studies, there has been a flood of publications on most subjects and especially on Shakespeare: there are 2,487 items listed in Velz's *Shakespeare and the Classical Tradition* alone. No one, even if s/he wanted, could now read all that has been written on him. Wishing to retain our sanity, we had neither the time nor the inclination to do more than dip our feet into the water. One of us is a lecturer in Classics, the other a teacher of English at a school; neither is part of the world of professional Shakespearean scholarship.

We nevertheless hope to bring a fresh perspective. Most of those who write about Shakespeare assume – such is his cultural authority – that he is at all times necessarily superior to the classical poets he used. This is not always the case, and we have not been afraid to say so. For example, none of Shakespeare's early Ovidian works, not even the *Dream*, equals the quality of Ovid's *Metamorphoses*; Shakespeare matched Ovid in one scene in *Cymbeline*, and surpassed him in a speech in *The Tempest*. And although he read at least some of the *Aeneid*, and echoed it, his poetic encounter with Virgil was not a profoundly productive one, in contrast to Dante's or Milton's.

This book is not designed as a comprehensive treatment of Shakespeare's classicism. There is no systematic account of Shakespeare's use of classical rhetoric, although there is much in these pages that bears on the subject. The reason is partly tactical: the general modern distaste for rhetoric, at least in its traditional form (despite the sterling work of scholars like Brian Vickers), makes an oblique approach advisable. (In fact much fashionable critical theory is best regarded as a new rhetoric, and one quite as technical and pedantic as its predecessor.) There are numerous other omissions both great and small. The most substantial is any account of romance forms. Romance had its origins in antiquity, but few ancient critics would have taken the Greek prose romances seriously as literature, while

Greek works which moderns might regard as romances – the *Odyssey*, for example, or Euripides' *Alcestis* and *Ion* – were assigned to other genres. The importance of romance as part of high literary culture is thus largely a post-classical phenomenon, part of the story of the Middle Ages and of the vernaculars, not of the classical tradition more narrowly defined. (Significantly, in the Renaissance Heliodorus' *Aethiopica* was read as a kind of prose epic.) In any case treatment of Shakespearean romance, which would involve lengthy consideration of vernacular developments, would require another book as large as this one and quite a different sort of expertise. We might have included a chapter on Shakespeare's Greece, with *Timon of Athens* as the main illustrative text; but *Timon* is not studied in schools and hardly in universities, while what we would wish to say on this subject is mostly implied in our account of *Troilus and Cressida*, a greater and currently more popular play. Above all we have chosen to write about matters which particularly interest us.

In the introductory chapter we look at three long-discussed issues: the extent of Shakespeare's classical knowledge, the doctrine of imitation, and the influence of Seneca on English Renaissance drama; we resist the modern tendency both to exaggerate Shakespeare's learning and to downgrade the importance of Seneca. In chapter 2 we explore the world of classical mythology, which Shakespeare utilized throughout his career, and which was the subject of his favourite classical book, Ovid's *Metamorphoses*. Chapter 3 deals with the world of Troy which Shakespeare recreated from a variety of ancient, medieval and Renaissance sources; we argue for the greater importance of Chapman's *Seven Books* from the *Iliad*, and the notion of classical epic style embodied therein, than is usually allowed. In chapter 4 we look at Shakespeare's presentation of the Roman world, and we suggest that Shakespeare's reading of Plutarch in North's translation enabled him to create a more persuasive image of Rome than that found in other plays of the period. However, we make no attempt to offer detailed interpretations of the three Roman plays; and we do not discuss, in any systematic way, Shakespeare's adaptation of North. In chapter 5 we illustrate Shakespeare's use of ancient moral ideas by examining the role of the Stoic virtue of constancy in a number of plays; a pagan moral world provides a context for understanding, and responding to, a number of key scenes and speeches.

Here it is important to issue a caveat which applies to this book as a whole. All critical methods are necessarily partial, and this is a particular problem when one is dealing with a writer as protean as Shakespeare. We would not claim that our approach is better than any other, still less that it affords the only frame of reference for discussing his works. Thus there is no sense in which Stoicism provides a uniquely authoritative focus for responses to particular plays. All we claim is that on occasion some knowledge of Stoicism may sharpen our sense of a passage, or reveal a significant pattern (though it will only be one among many). In the same way our account of Shakespeare's Troy is not intended to constitute an exhaustive reading of *Troilus* (whose chivalric and medieval components are outside our subject), merely to draw attention to some features which have been, comparatively, neglected. The same general point should be borne in mind by the reader throughout. Shakespeare's procedures are constantly shifting, and critics – less fleet of foot – are forever pressing the plays too far in the direction of a consistently patterned and narrow purposefulness. It follows that authors of books on particular aspects, if they are to preserve a sense of proportion, need to keep an eye on the wider picture, and a book on Shakespeare and the Classics cannot, in that sense, avoid becoming in part a book on Shakespeare *tout court*. This is our justification for occasionally moving into a slightly different critical mode in which we offer analyses of Shakespearean passages which, while connected with his classicism, are not restricted to it (this is evident, for example, in our discussion of the style of the Roman plays).

The book is designed, in the first instance, for university students, both those reading Classics who wish to know something of the classical heritage in English literature, and those reading English who would like to understand more of the debt of Renaissance authors to the ancients. We hope that it will also be of use to advanced sixthformers and to their teachers, and that there will be some material to interest scholars, particularly those who are not Shakespearean specialists. It is planned as a successor to C.A.M.'s *John Milton and the Transformation of Ancient Epic*. Milton was a man of unusual learning, a scholar who devoted much of his life to emulating the poetic achievements of the ancients. Shakespeare, by contrast, received only an ordinary grammar school education, and was a popular professional playwright who had to please to live. By studying their works, so different in kind, we shall learn much about the place of the Classics in the imagination of early modern Europe as it is reflected by our two greatest poets in their Renaissance setting. The work of the co-authors is inextricably blended. C.A.M. undertook the research and reading of the secondary material, and was responsible for the overall drafting of the book to ensure a satisfactory measure of stylistic continuity. His hand predominates in chapters 1, 2 and 4; chapter 5 is a reworking of a paper written by M.A.M. and first delivered at the Renaissance Seminar of the University of Sussex.

We are grateful to all those with whom we have discussed Shakespeare over many years, including Barbara Everett, Gabriel Josipovici, Stephen Medcalf, Alan Sinfield and other members of the Renaissance Seminar, and to the following for reading the manuscript and helping us to improve it: David Hopkins, A.D. Nuttall, Joanna and Robert Parker (of course they do not necessarily share any of the views expressed); gratitude is also due to Eleanor Gibbins for typing it. We have not been able to take account of anything published after June 1989. Unless otherwise stated all texts and translations are of our own devising; line references for Shakespeare are to the Arden Editions.

C.A.M:M.A.M.
Shoreham-by-Sea, July 1989

# ACKNOWLEDGEMENTS

We have re-used some material from C.A.M.'s previous writings: part of the introduction to *Ovid Renewed*, Cambridge University Press, 1988, and of the chapter 'Latin and English poetry: Ovid, Horace and others', in *The Legacy of Rome: A New Appraisal* (ed. Richard Jenkyns) to be published by Oxford University Press.

# 1

# INTRODUCTION

## SMALL LATIN

It is customary to begin discussion of the extent of Shakespeare's classical knowledge with the opinions of Ben Jonson. So, for the sake of variety, let us open with some well-known lines by Milton, a devotee of Shakespeare but one who had no reason for partiality over the issue:

> Then to the well-trod stage anon,
> If Jonson's learned sock be on,
> Or sweetest Shakespeare, Fancy's child,
> Warble his native wood-notes wild.
>
> (*L'Allegro*, 131–34)

A careless reading of these lines, together with an anachronistic understanding of their key terms, has encouraged the picturing of Shakespeare as a purely spontaneous genius. In fact the distinction, which is not polemical, is between Jonson's 'learning', that is his assiduous imitation of classical models and insistence on their superiority, and Shakespeare's delight in a general ambience of English language and inspiration. The dominant contrast is not between Art and Nature, but between the classical and the 'native'; and that contrast involves a pastiche of the characteristic styles of the two authors, not surprising in a poem devoted to literary parody and allusion. In the lines on Jonson, where the vocabulary has a plain, hard-edged, concrete quality, 'sock' Englishes a Latin metonymy (*soccus*, the slipper worn by comic actors, for comedy), and there may be a punning jest by which the 'sock' could be either on stage or on Jonson's foot (cf. Jonson's 'Ode to Himself: On *The New Inn*', 37; Horace, *Ars Poetica*, 80). The lines on Shakespeare use suggestive

1

but somewhat unfocused metaphorical writing, with a distinct shift midway, as Shakespeare, first the child of a semi-personified Fancy, becomes a bird or rustic singer of the forest. 'Sweetest' hints at the Shakespearean style, described in his own time as 'sugared' and 'sweet'; it was the Shakespeare of plays like *A Midsummer Night's Dream* whom Milton especially favoured, and Shakespeare is anyway treated here as a writer of comedy only. Since these complimentary lines are couched in Shakespearean terms, we should take the key words in something of their Shakespearean sense. In particular, 'fancy' means imagination, and is not equivalent to 'nature', to which indeed it is sometimes opposed: for example in *Antony and Cleopatra* II.ii.200f. ('O'er-picturing that Venus where we see/The fancy outwork nature') fancy, man's creative faculty, amounts almost to art, or at least to an aspect of art. That Shakespeare is 'Fancy's child' does not mean that he is Nature's child, untutored and artless, but that he is a great exponent of the powers of the imagination. The passage thus has no bearing on the question of how much ancient literature Shakespeare had read, even if Milton is nodding, with some wit, at the tradition already established by Jonson. Milton is certainly not trying to score points for Jonson against Shakespeare, or vice versa.

Let us return to Jonson and his celebrated tribute from the First Folio 'To the Memory of My Beloved, The Author, Mr. William Shakespeare, And What He Hath Left Us' (1623). Dryden – who should have known better – called it 'an insolent, sparing, and invidious panegyric', apparently supposing that Jonson was criticizing his rival.[1] However, the hesitations of the opening lines testify not to genuine dubieties but to a conventional awareness of the dangers inherent in eulogy, while in the body of the poem the 'Swan of Avon' is presented as the ideal poet combining Nature and Art in his 'well-turned and true-filed lines' (68). (Admittedly Jonson, in combative mood, expressed a different opinion to the Scottish poet William Drummond: 'Shakespeare wanted art'.[2]) Despite his lack of classical knowledge – 'And though thou hadst small Latin, and less Greek' (31) – Shakespeare surpassed not only all previous English poets, but also all the classical writers both of tragedy and of comedy – from Jonson a remarkable compliment. The tone is judicious – Jonson will not deny what is known to all – but whatever reservations the private man may have had about Shakespeare's 'art', the public poet shows none. If Jonson had made his well-known comment privately, he might have meant by it 'virtually no Latin and no Greek at all', but in this wholly eulogistic context the words should be taken without irony. In consequence 'less Greek' should imply that Shakespeare had some Greek, perhaps enough to struggle through easy texts like the New Testament. According to Nicholas Rowe's *Life* (1709), Shakespeare went to 'free-school' 'for some time', but was withdrawn because of his father's straitened circumstances;[3] so it was at 'free-school', probably Stratford Grammar School, that he learned his small Latin. There is also a story reported by John Aubrey, deriving from William Beeston, the son of one of Shakespeare's fellow actors, that Shakespeare had been a schoolmaster in the country, which showed that 'he understood Latin pretty well'. Whether true or false, it has little bearing on the question of Shakespeare's Latinity; a country schoolmaster could pass muster with very small Latin indeed.

The argument about the extent of Shakespeare's classical knowledge thus started in his own day and has continued until ours. Contributors to it are often arguing at cross purposes. For example, Housman contrasts the disciplined Milton, 'steeped through and through with classical literature', with the unlearned Shakespeare, who constantly descends into what (in Housman's view) is atrocious Elizabethanism.[4] Chesterton by contrast argues that 'Shakespeare was every bit as classical as Milton', citing some famous lines from Othello's speech before he kills Desdemona:

> If I quench thee, thou flaming minister,
> I can again thy former light restore
> Should I repent me; but once put out thine,
> Thou cunning'st pattern of excelling nature,
> I know not where is that Promethean heat
> That can thy light relume.                          (V.ii.8–13)[5]

In one version of the Prometheus myth he is the giver of fire, in another the instigator of human life itself. Shakespeare's allusion possibly fuses these two ideas, so that 'Promethean heat' comes to mean something like 'vital spark' or 'flame of life'; or it may simply give a sense of 'original fire', a fire that kindles where no fire exists. The striking reference is embedded in a smoothly-rolling classicizing period, culminating in a fine Latinism 'relume'. Chesterton comments:

> the classical spirit is no matter of names or allusions ... this
> profound resonance, striking such echoes out of such hollows

3

and abysses, could not thus be achieved without a very deep understanding of classical diction. It could not be done without the word 'Promethean'; ... without those rolling polysyllables that are the power of Homer and Virgil. In one practical and prosaic sense, of course, a man might say what Othello says. He might say, 'If I kill this woman, how the devil am I to bring her to life again'; but hardly with majesty; hardly with mystery; not precisely with all those meanings and echoes of meanings which belong to a great line of verse.

*(Chesterton on Shakespeare*, 1971, pp. 17–18)

Granted their differences of taste and a shared tendency to exaggerate, Housman and Chesterton are not so much at odds as might appear. Housman was right to claim that Shakespeare did not imitate – and probably could not have imitated – 'the dignity ... the unfaltering elevation of style, the just subordination of detail' of Virgil in Milton's way. But Chesterton was right to argue that Shakespeare was part of the general culture of Western Europe descending from Rome (unlike, say, Langland). As Chesterton puts it, 'the classical tradition ... was the popular thing, the common thing; even the vulgar thing'.

The argument is seldom conducted in a neutral or disinterested spirit. All too often one can hear the sound of the grinding of axes. To some readers, particularly in the eighteenth century, it seemed that the honour of England required the demonstration of Shakespeare's classical learning. To others Shakespeare's very lack of it was testimony to his greatness. Often the matter became entangled in the question of the rival merits of Shakespeare and Jonson and of the superiority of original genius to stale imitation. For example, Leonard Digges wrote in 1640:

> Next Nature only helped him, for look through
> This whole book, thou shalt find he doth not borrow
> One phrase from Greeks, nor Latins imitate,
> Nor once from vulgar languages translate...
> So have I seen when *Caesar* would appear...
>            how the audience
> Were ravished, with what wonder they went thence,
> When some new day they would not brook a line
> Of tedious, though well-laboured, *Catiline* ...

(Thomson, p. 25)

Passages like Prospero's renunciation speech show that Digges' first point is simply incorrect, and remind us of the tendentiousness of this whole tribute. In similar vein Rowe reports a conversation of the poets Suckling, Davenant, Endymion Porter, Jonson and John Hales, a Fellow of Eton College, at which Hales, in answer to Jonson's criticisms of Shakespeare, pointedly told him that 'if Mr. Shakespeare had not read the ancients, he had likewise not stolen anything from them' (Baldwin, vol. 1, p. 19). Dryden, in *Of Dramatic Poesy* (1668), enlisted Shakespeare in an antithetical division of poets, when he wrote that Shakespeare 'was naturally learned; he needed not the spectacles of books to read nature; he looked inwards, and found her there'.[6] Pope praised the supposedly untutored Homer in just these terms. Echoing Dryden he contrasted Homer's 'invention' with Virgil's 'judgement'.[7] Historical credibility is seldom reached in quite this way. Our own century is not free of such confusions. For example, the Leavisite school's determination to establish English as a separate discipline, wholly independent of Classics from which it had arisen, involved a perverse privileging of the supposedly 'native' over any foreign influences. For this 'Little Englandism' Shakespeare, clearly our supreme poet, had to be pressed into service and the undeniably classical Milton 'dislodged'. Today the position is reversed: within universities the institutional pressures to publish promote an endless search for fresh sources, and make belief in a learned Shakespeare advantageous to academics avid for job security.

A milestone in the history of the debate is Richard Farmer's *Essay on the Learning of Shakespeare* (1767), a brilliant intellectual achievement.[8] Farmer, who argues that Shakespeare had little knowledge of Latin works, was wrong in some of his conclusions but right in many of his methods; he was the first to address the problem as one of historical scholarship. He established the principle – still too often ignored – that it is not enough to point to an apparent similarity between a passage in Shakespeare and one in a classical writer.[9] It is necessary to know about Elizabethan and Jacobean literature (in which Farmer was remarkably well versed for the period), possible intermediate vernacular sources, the availability of translations and so forth. Farmer made one incorrect assumption; that if Shakespeare used a translation he cannot also have used the original. But, despite the defects and the maliciously triumphal tone, nothing better was written on the subject until Paul Stapfer's book *Shakespeare et*

*L'Antiquité*, translated into English in 1880. Many thought that Farmer had settled the matter. In the circumstances Dr. Johnson's conclusion was eminently reasonable (particularly if by 'easy perusal' he meant the sort of perusal of ancient texts which he himself could make):

> Jonson, his friend ... besides that he had no imaginable temptation to falsehood, wrote at a time when the character and acquisitions of Shakespeare were known to multitudes. His evidence ought therefore to decide the controversy, unless some testimony of equal force could be opposed ... It is most likely that he had learned Latin sufficiently to make him acquainted with construction, but that he never advanced to an easy perusal of the Roman authors.[10]
>
> (Dr. Johnson, *Preface to Shakespeare*, 1765, pp. 76–77)

Testimony for a more generous view of Shakespeare's 'small Latin' than Farmer's was eventually supplied by T.W. Baldwin, by means of a more rigorous and informed application of Farmer's own methods. Baldwin's argument is frequently misunderstood: so J.A.K. Thomson claims that Baldwin only 'tells us in very great detail what Shakespeare *could* have learned at school'.[11] But Baldwin proved his case rather in the sense that Darwin 'proved' evolution. He collected a vast number of tiny data which show that the classical knowledge displayed in Shakespeare's plays is exactly what one would expect of someone who had been to grammar school; of this the most economical explanation is that Shakespeare indeed attended grammar school, and accordingly learned there a certain amount of Latin, large by twentieth-century standards, but reasonably described as 'small' by the more learned Jonson. Baldwin also demonstrated that the vocabulary in Shakespeare's adaptations of Latin material is sometimes closer to the glosses in Cooper's *Thesaurus*, the standard Latin dictionary of the period, than to the available translations, which suggests that Shakespeare had recourse to the original, at least on occasion. Baldwin's two volumes are one of the supreme achievements of Shakespearean scholarship, but, prolix and overwhelming in their detail, they are not for the busy or the faint-hearted. Yet Baldwin is no mere pedant, rather a man of wisdom and even wit; we have lived long in his company while writing this book and have come to know and to admire him more and more.

It is worth reflecting briefly on the character of Shakespeare's education, based largely on the study of Latin texts. First, the reading was remarkably adult; boys of 9 and 10 or less would read 'Tully's *Offices*' (Cicero's *De Officiis*) in English. Juan Luis Vives (1492–1540), the Spanish educationalist, recommended the story of Lucretia in Livy for the young princess Mary both for delight and to teach her about life.[12] Secondly, it was intensely rhetorical. It was an Erasmian doctrine that language was the basis of knowledge; hence the focus on words and their arrangement and on *copia*, rhetorical fluency. Shakespeare's interest in the techniques of teaching is shown on a number of occasions in his plays. In *Merry Wives* IV.i.9ff. we have a basic grammar lesson drawn from William Lily's standard school grammar (first published in 1527) in which Sir Hugh Evans questions the boy William (sic). In *The Shrew* III.i.16ff. we see the method of construing Latin poetry (in this instance a couplet from Ovid, *Heroides* I.33f.), as a disguised Lucentio pretends to instruct Bianca in translation while using the lesson to pass her a message. In particular in *Love's Labour's Lost* Shakespeare gives us a rounded portrayal of the pedantic schoolteacher Holofernes, with his devotion to Ovid and fondness for using triplets: 'Let me hear a staff, a stanza, a verse; *lege, domine;*' (IV.ii.100)[13] – a fondness which produces a moment of some pathos during the 'pageant of the nine worthies' when he rebukes the mockers in his audience with the words 'This is not generous, not gentle, not humble' (V.ii.623). Shakespeare might laugh at his teachers, but, when it came to verbal fluency, he showed himself their star pupil.

There were obvious limits to Shakespeare's scholarliness. When he wrote his Roman plays he used as his basic source an English translation of Plutarch, whereas Jonson for his read through a whole range of classical sources in the original. On the other hand, Shakespeare's knowledge of mythology was far greater than that of most university students of Classics today. Admittedly he occasionally makes mistakes. In *2 Henry IV* II.ii.85–86 'Althaea dreamt she was delivered of a firebrand'. Althaea, who had a real brand on which the life of her son depended, is confused with Hecuba, who had just such a dream about Paris (whose seduction of Helen led to the burning of Troy). However it may not altogether be special pleading to suggest that the mistake could be the Page's, not Shakespeare's, since in *Troilus* II.ii.111 Shakespeare gets the story right ('our firebrand brother'). But certainly in *Troilus* V.ii.151 (if the text is correct) Arachne and Ariadne are conflated, presumably because of the similarity of names:

> the spacious breadth of this division
> Admits no orifex for a point as subtle
> As Ariachne's broken woof to enter.[14]

Yet, if Shakespeare's memory failed him here, his imagination did not. The passage combines the sense of a spider's web (since Arachne was turned into a spider) with that of a thread leading through the darkness of the labyrinth (as Ariadne led Theseus). Inaccuracies are not confined to mythology. A number of references show that Shakespeare believed that the Capitol was a building where the Senate met, and in which Caesar was assassinated. This was a belief shared by many contemporaries, the origin of which was probably Ralph Higden's *Polychronicon* and the *Memorabilia Urbis Romae*.[15] Thus Shakespeare cannot exactly be accused of ignorance. However, more learned men, including Jonson, knew better. Sometimes a 'mistake' must be put down to deliberate imaginative freedom. In dealing with *Antony and Cleopatra* IV.xiv.50–54

> Eros! – I come, my queen – Eros! – Stay for me,
> Where souls do couch on flowers, we'll hand in hand,
> And with our sprightly port make the ghosts gaze;
> Dido and her Aeneas shall want troops
> And all the haunt be ours,

the pedantic eighteenth-century scholar William Warburton changed Aeneas to Sychaeus,[16] since in *Aeneid* VI Dido is shown in the underworld with Sychaeus, her former husband. Dryden too in *All For Love* V.395ff. silently, and more tactfully, corrected the reference:

> While hand in hand we walk in groves below,
> Whole troops of lovers' ghosts shall flock about us,
> And all the train be ours.

However Shakespeare knew what he was about; the idea of a place for lovers in Elysium is first found in *Tibullus* I.3.57ff., and often features in neo-Latin poetry, but Shakespeare did not need a 'source' to weave his beautifully imaginative fantasy.

If Shakespeare was not a learned writer, it does not follow that he was not profoundly influenced by classical literature. For William Golding learning Greek and struggling through Homer was a formative experience, the fruits of which we can see in *Pincher Martin* and elsewhere, but this does not make him a Greek scholar. Learning is anyway a relative matter. The university man Marlowe, the whole of whose output is witness to his classical enthusiasms, and who knew enough Latin to translate Ovid's *Amores* and Lucan's first book, made many a howler. For example, in *Amores* III.10(9).39 he translates (evocatively) *canebat frugibus Ide* as 'Ida, the seat of groves, did sing with corn'; unfortunately he is confusing *cānere*, 'to be white' ('Ida was white with corn') with *cănere*, 'to sing'. Similarly one scholar argues that Chaucer was not the excellent Latinist he is often supposed to have been.[17] In *Aeneid* IV.180 *Fama* flies 'on swift wings' (*pernicibus alis*); in *The House of Fame* 1391f. Chaucer translates this as 'partridge's wings'. Perhaps his manuscript had the impossible *perdicibus*, but no scholar would have been fooled. Yet Chaucer was clearly inspired by Latin poets, in particular by Ovid, his ancient *alter ego*. One must also understand the state of scholarship in his own day. For example, when he renders *Aeneid* IV.169f. *ille dies primus leti primusque malorum/causa fuit* by 'this was the firste morwe/Of hire gladnesse, and gynning of hire sorwe' (*Legend of Good Women*, 1230f.), confusing *letum* 'death' with *laetum*, neuter of *laetus* 'joyful' (usually spelt *letum* in medieval manuscripts), he was following a widespread misinterpretation – Gavin Douglas, a better scholar, makes the same mistake in his translation. These points apply to Shakespeare with still more force. Shakespeare's relative lack of classical learning makes the extent to which his imagination was fired by Graeco-Roman mythology and history, and the prevalence of Greek and Roman settings among his works, all the more remarkable. It reminds us of the degree to which Western culture was saturated in the classics, so that by losing them – as now seems not unlikely – we shall be cutting ourselves off from much that is best in 'the mind of Europe'.

Intertextuality is a fashionable word. But C.S. Lewis – no post-structuralist – long ago gave a magnificent statement of the interconnectedness of Western literature:

> Arnold gave me at once ... a sense, not indeed of passionless vision, but of a passionate, silent gazing at things a long way off. And here observe how literature actually works. Parrot critics say that *Sohrab* is a poem for classicists, to be enjoyed only by those who recognize the Homeric echoes. But I ... knew nothing of Homer. For me the relation between Arnold and Homer worked the other way; when I came, years later, to read the *Iliad* I liked it partly because it was for me reminiscent of *Sohrab*. Plainly, it does not matter at what point you first break

into the system of European poetry. Only keep your ears open and your mouth shut and everything will lead you to every-thing else in the end – *ogni parte ad ogni parte splende*.

(C.S. Lewis, *Surprised by Joy*, 1955, p. 56)[18]

When a poet echoes an earlier poet, who in turn echoed an earlier poet, and so on, he becomes part of that system. In the words of Charles Trinkaus, 'In the history of culture, nothing is truly original, but nothing is ever the same'.[19] If you read through the specialist journals, you constantly encounter articles proposing new sources for Shakespeare, some of them examples of what might be termed 'the Fluellen fallacy' ('there is salmons in both')[20], but many, even if improbable as sources, useful analogues, pointing to the system and its unity. A textual system is thus often a more helpful concept than the idea of unprovable sources or allusions; if Shakespeare had read all that is proposed for him, he would not have found time to write many plays. For example, one can cite numerous possible English 'sources' for Shakespeare's mythology, but Ovid is usually the author whom Shakespeare designs to evoke. In other words, a great deal of the material he uses is commonplace.[21] In the poems this can be a weakness, but in the plays it does not matter, since these are mimetic of actions and persons, and most people's 'ideas' and preferences are in fact commonplaces.

Shakespeare used to be presented as a systematic conservative moralizer, with a unified 'world picture'. This view is now somewhat passé, but many new images – Shakespeare as meticulous organizer of imagery; Shakespeare as complete humanist; Shakespeare as feminist or radical; Shakespeare as thorough-going sceptic – are no less un-convincing. Shakespeare, in Frank Kermode's words 'a person of enormously superior intelligence',[22] was clearly well-read – how else could one account for his richness of vocabulary? – but opportunistic in his reading, always on the look-out for material he could use for his own work. He knew some foreign languages, but often preferred to use translations; he did not necessarily read books all the way through; like all his contemporaries – like most scholars even – he used short-cuts to knowledge. Totalizing readings of his works are always suspect – all too clearly he is being made in the image of modern scholars or critics, as they conceive themselves to be in their ideal moments. To make these old-fashioned points, to argue, in other words, for a return to something more like the Shakespeare of Ben Jonson and Samuel Johnson, is to invite a charge of philistinism.

It should not do so. Shakespeare again and again dipped casually into other men's work and turned their dross to gold. Everyone has their own image of Shakespeare. It would be better if more often it was made explicit. This, at any rate, is ours.

What, in view of the situation we have sketched, do the ideal investigators of Shakespeare's classicism need to know? First, obviously, they must be intimate with Shakespeare's works, and sensitive critics of them. Secondly, they must be equally familiar with the classics themselves and with the standard Renaissance editions and commentaries. Thirdly, they must have a full knowledge of Renaissance literature in both English and Latin. Fourthly, they must be familiar with all the grammar school material: Lily's *Grammar*; Cooper's *Thesaurus*; the encyclopaedias and handbooks in common use; Aphthonius' rhetorical exercises; neo-Latin poems like those of Mantuan, the hero of Holofernes, and Palingenius, possibly the source for 'All the world's a stage'[23]; the fables of Camerarius, where Shakespeare first found the fable of the belly and the members used in *Coriolanus*, with its trite moral *contra seditionem*; and much else.[24] Obviously such a paragon has never arisen (Baldwin comes nearest, but he is no literary critic), and, if present educational trends continue, will probably never arise. In the meantime we must muddle through as best we can.

To conclude, the investigations of Baldwin (even if he is rather too inclined to see definite connections between Shakespeare's writings and Latin works) confirm the evidence of Rowe and indeed the view of Jonson when put in its proper context. Shakespeare went to grammar school, where he spent a good deal of time, by modern standards, learning Latin. But he did not proceed to university, and he did not make any private, systematic study of the ancients in the manner of Ben Jonson. However, his 'small Latin' (as Jonson saw it) would have allowed him to read Latin books, if they were not too difficult, without a translation where necessary. If he had any Greek, it was quite insufficient to read the great works of archaic and classical Greece, even had he wanted to do so – but there is no reason to think that he did.

## IMITARI IS NOTHING

Dr. Johnson, like Leonard Digges, supposed that Shakespeare did not directly imitate the ancients. Baldwin has shown that this view is incorrect. Shakespeare 'knew thoroughly the fundamentals of com-

11

position as they were taught in his day', involving him in 'selecting and recombining materials and models'[25] (although he does so in a way less exact than Jonson's, so that the model is frequently invisible). This was a typical Renaissance procedure, even though, in Shakespeare's case the result was a miracle we cannot explain; the effect of his ever-changing mastery of language certainly cannot ultimately be accounted for in *purely* rhetorical terms. The doctrine of imitation (itself of classical origin) was of course at the heart of much Renaissance thinking about literature, and is eloquently expounded by Jonson in *Discoveries*. One learned to write by imitating the 'best' authors, that is the most admired classical writers. This idea, which held sway for so long, is often found unexciting or objectionable today. But it had the solid virtue of being practical, and can more than justify itself by its results. The change in attitude reflects the decline of the assumption that the principal aim of literary study is to learn to write well. Modern scholars often treat imitation primarily as a species of allusion, eager perhaps to make it more acceptable to post-Romantic sensibilities, and implying that knowledge of the original context of any reminiscence is an indispensable component of meaning. This is misleading, for the traditional metaphors used in discussions of imitation suggest rather creative assimilation than allusion. The process resembles the way bees make honey from flower nectars, or the relationship between father and son. The result is a fresh creation deriving from, but independent of, the original.

Kipling ends one of his finest stories, 'The Gardener', with an allusion to St. John's Gospel ('she went away, supposing him to be the gardener'); the reader who misses this cannot properly interpret. The allusion suggests that the heroine has encountered a supernatural figure, even Christ Himself, or at any rate someone with a Christ-like ability to see into men's souls and create a moment of revelation and self-realization. By contrast, if we take Jonson's touching imitation of one of Martial's most touching epigrams, a knowledge of the original, while a source of pleasure to the learned and a useful tool for the critic, is not an *essential* requirement in a reader:

> To you, Fronto father, mother Flaccilla, I commend this girl, my sweetheart and darling, that tiny Erotion may not shudder at the black shades and the Tartarean hound's huge jaws. She would have completed only her sixth cold winter, had she not lived as many days too few. Beside protectors so old let her play friskily, and prattle my name with lisping tongue. Let not the

clods cover hard her soft bones, and do not be heavy on her, earth; she was not so on you.

(5.34: Loeb adapted)

'On My First Daughter'
Here lies to each her parents' ruth
Mary, the daughter of their youth;
Yet, all Heaven's gifts being Heaven's due,
It makes the father less to rue.
At six months' end she parted hence
With safety of her innocence;
Whose soul Heaven's queen (whose name she bears)
In comfort of her mother's tears,
Hath placed amongst her virgin-train;
Where, while that severed doth remain,
This grave partakes the fleshly birth,
Which cover lightly, gentle earth.

(*Epigrams*, 22)

Jonson, seeking to write an epitaph for his baby daughter, remembered an authoritative exemplar in Martial's epigram commemorating a dead slave girl. Intractably Roman detail is ignored, including the picture of Erotion recoiling from the huge dog Cerberus, a detail pathetic yet playful in tone, since nobody took the traditional mythology of the Underworld literally. The gap is filled with Christian elements, in particular the reference to the Virgin (Jonson was a Catholic at this date). Martial concludes with the traditional request that the earth should not lie heavy on the dead, which has a special gracefulness in a poem about a child: 'mollia non rigidus caespes tegat ossa nec illi,/terra, gravis fueris: non fuit illa tibi'. So too Jonson's poem wheels round finally, not bitterly but with a soft sadness, to the small grave on earth, and a version of the *topos*, but with a Christian twist: Mary Jonson's soul is in heaven, so it is only her body in the ground. The poem's pathos comes in part from Jonson's acquiescence in divine justice and his acceptance that his 'ruth' derives from a return of dues (another *topos* of classical origin). Various elements in Martial's poem (a father and a mother, the age of the dead girl, her destiny in the afterlife, the prayer to the earth) have been re-used, and its tone, pathos and smooth-running elegance wholly assimilated into a fresh and English creation.

For Thomas Greene, Renaissance imitation 'opens a distance, sketches a significant itinerary' in a way that combines 'reverence'

13

and 'rebellion'. He argues that writers of the period experienced a sense of cultural distance and loss, in connection with antiquity, and that the essential difference between medieval and Renaissance imitation is that there is no 'strain of disjuncture' in the former.[26] But, as he himself admits, this analysis has little application to English literature of the late sixteenth century. In England at least the main distinction between medieval and Renaissance practice is a different and a simpler one: where the medieval poet made relaxed use of the original as a mine for material, his Renaissance successor engaged in more self-conscious stylistic imitation and emulation (this is an argument for treating Chaucer as medieval, and Spenser as Renaissance). There is little sense of strain in a poet like Spenser, rather a relaxed fusion of earlier vernacular and newer humanist traditions. There was less melancholy about the loss of antiquity than in Italy or France, partly because there was no poet writing in English as learned as Petrarch, at least before Milton (who certainly sometimes felt the disjunction Greene describes), and no Rome and few Roman ruins to remind writers of a more glorious past. Significantly, the most obvious exception, Spenser's *Ruins of Rome*, is a translation from the French of du Bellay, though Spenser also builds his lachrymose *Ruins of Time* around the vanished glories of the Roman city of Verolanium, which he had read about in William Camden's *Britannia*. Equally important was the prestige of Chaucer, to Spenser 'well of English undefyled' (*Faerie Queene*, IV.ii.32). It is partly because of a native classical tradition, which begins with Chaucer and precedes the humanist flowering of the sixteenth century, that Shakespeare is able to be so free and relaxed in his use of classical material. For example, in *Winter's Tale* IV.iv.27–30, where Shakespeare elaborates a bald sentence from his source, Greene's *Pandosto* ('Neptune became a ram, Jupiter a bull, Apollo a shepherd') into

> Jupiter
> Became a bull and bellowed; the green Neptune
> A ram and bleated; and the fire-robed god,
> Golden Apollo, a poor humble swain,

the combination of bold exuberance and homely wit is a long way from the studied neo-classical manner of continental humanism.[27] Even with Jonson, perhaps the first unambiguously Renaissance figure in English literature, we encounter no melancholy, no great recognition of a gulf to be bridged, but rather a robust type of classicism which cements Rome on to the vernacular. In the remain-

14

der of this section we will look at some examples of different types of imitation in Shakespeare.

## Imitatio of Plot

It is well known that *The Comedy of Errors*, a 'learned' play of a kind to appeal to the students and lawyers of the Inns of Court, imitates the plot of Plautus' *Menaechmi*. Shakespeare complicates that plot, with a pair of servants also identical (on loan from Plautus' *Amphitruo*), by extending the love interest, and by giving the whole a romance framework deriving ultimately from the tale of Apollonius of Tyre.[28] The conflation of farce and romance is not in itself original, since Plautus had done the same in *Rudens*, a play with which *The Tempest* has some obvious affinities. Nevertheless, we have a case of *aemulatio* (the overgoing of the model) as well as of *imitatio*. What we do not find is any close *stylistic* imitation of Plautus' highly distinctive writing. Different kinds of verse are decorously handled, but without the Plautine virtuosity of style and metre. Shakespeare could have written the play from a translation alone. Perhaps he did: William Warner's version of *Menaechmi*, the first in English, had not yet been published, but Shakespeare might have seen it in manuscript, or a friend could have provided him with a crib. Of the two plays Plautus', with its coherence of manner and tone, and its skilful plot with the various 'errors' carefully analysed by Lambinus in the standard Renaissance edition, is surely the more assured; Shakespeare's hints at a promise of greater things. There is a pre-echo of that fuller sense of psychological readjustment in those characters who are involved in recognition, of the sea – cruel or kind – as a place of trial where men are lost and found, characteristic of later and greater comedies.

## Imitatio of Classical Loci

Local imitations of brief passages from the Classics are frequently encountered in English Renaissance literature. They do not prove that the author had read through the whole of the original work, since anthologies of passages helpful for composition were in widespread use. For example

>           – the innocent sleep,
> Sleep that knits up the ravelled sleave of care,
> The death of each day's life, sore labour's bath,

Balm of hurt minds, great Nature's second course
Chief nourisher in life's feast…

(*Macbeth* II.ii.35ff.)

relates to two passages of Latin poetry, in which personified Sleep, given a list of attributes, is invoked:

Somne, quies rerum, placidissime, Somne, deorum,
pax animi, quem cura fugit, qui corpora duris
fessa ministeriis mulces reparasque labori.

(Ovid *Met*. XI.623–625)

*(Sleep, rest of the world, Sleep, gentlest of the gods, peace for the mind, whom care flees, who soothest bodies tired with hard tasks and refreshest them for work.)*

                    tuque, o domitor,
Somne malorum, requies animi,
pars humanae melior vitae,
volucre o matris genus Astraeae,
frater durae languide Mortis,
veris miscens falsa, futuri
certus et idem pessimus auctor,
pater o rerum, portus vitae,
lucis requies noctisque comes,
qui par regi famuloque venis
pavidum leti genus humanum
cogis longam discere noctem.

(Seneca, *Hercules Furens*, 1065ff. [text uncertain])

*(And thou, Sleep, conqueror of ills, rest of mind, better part of human life, winged son of mother Astraea, soothing brother of harsh death, mixing false with true, certain and likewise worst presager of the future, o father of the world, harbour of life, rest from day and companion of darkness, who comest equally to king and to pauper, and forcest the human race fearful of death to know its long night.)*

Shakespeare could have found both quotations together in Mirandula's popular quotation book *Illustrium Poetarum Flores*,[29] or in the more substantial compilation of the *Polyanthea*, which included prose excerpts as well as verse. The latter's entry under *Somnium, Somnus*, in an early seventeenth-century edition, gives a definition and etymology, followed by excerpts from the Bible, the Church

Fathers, the poets (Homer, Menander, Plautus, Tibullus, Virgil, Horace, Ovid, Seneca, Claudian and Thomas More) and the philosophers (here including Petrarch) as well as apophthegms (pithy maxims), similitudes, adages (proverbs) and *exempla*.[30] This massive compendium could help writers to appear considerably more learned than they were. Ovid was one of Shakespeare's favourites, but even so the quotation books could help to jog his memory. The Ovid passage is characterized by gentle sounds suggesting sleep; by contrast, in the Seneca there is a more powerful accumulation of appositional phrases which is closer to both the structure and the mood of Shakespeare's lines – and, as we shall see, there are signs that Shakespeare had Seneca in mind when composing *Macbeth*, and in particular may have read through *Hercules Furens* in Latin. Shakespeare concentrates, more exclusively than Seneca, on sleep as a healer of men's troubles, which he expresses through a series of ostensibly unrelated images, several of them vague or difficult in expression, and all piled up as passionately high utterances. The speech, interrupted though it is by Lady Macbeth, has much of the quality of a soliloquy, as Macbeth's speeches so often do, even when he is not alone. Although the metaphorical murdering of sleep is obviously connected with the actual murder of Duncan, it is above all for *himself* that he is concerned; in the phrase 'the innocent sleep', the adjective glances at the murder of the innocent Duncan, but in a way that is characteristically depersonalized and generalized – Macbeth's sense of pathos focusses more easily on abstractions than on persons. In the following line the 'ravelled sleave' primarily means something like the frayed filament of a whole thread, but the entire phrase has a characteristic obscurity, not least because of the slipperiness of the genitive, all part of the dark, deconstructive intricacy with which Shakespeare presents Macbeth's musings. The implication may be that care is like a frazzled thread, a suggestive picture of jangling nerves; or perhaps care may rather be equivalent to the process, the ravelling, than to the sleave or the whole thread. It is a repeated feature of Macbeth's speeches that the openings are particularly hard to understand (no wonder Lady Macbeth responds by asking 'What do you mean?'). The attributes 'bath' and 'balm' relate to a thread of medical imagery in the play, while in the phrases 'great Nature's second course' and 'chief nourisher in life's feast' there is a combination of the grandiose and the abstract with a curiously precise domestic image, of which the overall effect is again vague and elusive. The passage is a fine example of creative imitation as the Renaissance understood it, with the classical material adapted to its new context and conformed to the character of the speaker.

A few lines later we come to another probable Senecan imitation:

> Will all great Neptune's ocean wash this blood
> Clean from my hand? No, this my hand will rather
> The multitudinous seas incarnadine,
> Making the green one red.

$$(59-62)$$

Twice in his plays Seneca uses the motif, once in *Hippolytus* and once in *Hercules Furens*, where it is given to Hercules on learning that he has killed his children. It is perhaps the latter passage which Shakespeare is imitating, though if he had a commentary it would probably have pointed him to the parallel:

> Quis Tanais aut quis Nilus aut quis Persica
> violentus unda Tigris aut Rhenus ferox
> Tagusve Hibera turbidus gaza fluens
> abluere dextram poterit? Arctoum licet
> Maeotis in me gelida transfundat mare
> et tota Tethys per meas currat manus,
> haerebit altum facinus.

$$(1323-1329)$$

*(What Tanais or what Nile or what Tigris violent with its Persian wave or warlike Rhine or Tagus flowing turbid with its Spanish treasure* [i.e. golden sand] *will be able to clean my hand? Should cold Maeotis pour the northern sea over me, and all Tethys* [sea] *run through my hands, the deep crime will stick.)*

Similarly, *Hippolytus* 725–728 runs

> Quis eluet me Tanais aut quae barbaris
> Maeotis undis, Pontico incumbens mari?
> Non ipse magnus Oceano pater
> Tantum expiarit scelus.

*(What Tanais or what Maeotis with barbaric waters falling on the Pontic sea will wash me clean? The great father himself* [Neptune] *with his ocean could not expiate such a crime.)*

Shakespeare substitutes for the specifically named seas the grand sweep of 'all great Neptune's ocean' (possibly suggested by *magnus Oceano pater* in the *Hippolytus*). In 'making the green one red', where 'one' seems to hover between the two boldly splashed colours, Shakespeare turns adjectives into nouns, a Latinate device. Critics talk glibly of guilt and conscience, and there is an upper crusting of moral language and thought in *Macbeth*, and a handful of references which work overtime to illustrate it. But the play has less to do with good and bad than with fair and foul, something less elevated and cerebral, and Macbeth's conscience focusses almost exclusively on the damage he has brought to his own well-being. This point is almost invariably sanitized. It is easier on the feelings to think about a good man ruined, and to impose a conventional pattern, than to plumb the murky depths of a murderer's mind. Macbeth concentrates on cleansing the blood rather than on the question of guilt, and, by a somewhat hysterical inversion, on the pollution of the ocean which his bloodstained hand will cause. The sense of sin gives way before the heightened power and glamour of the words, as the objective reality of the matter retreats before Macbeth's overpowering tendency to look into the texture of his thoughts and see only what lies there. His regret or anxiety is not focussed on anything outside himself, but participates in a surrealist vision in which a green ocean – and why specify green, if only the purifying properties of water are involved? – turns red. Editors apparently think that Shakespeare did not know what 'incarnadine' meant ('to make pink', not 'to make bloody'); but perhaps it refers to the earlier part of the process in which the blood and water are mingled, whose result is the 'one red'. The massive 'multitudinous' ('enormous', but hinting at the many creatures in the sea which the blood will destroy) is in tension with the monosyllabic 'one'. There may well be a reference, in so religious a play, to the plague of blood in *Exodus*, with perhaps further eucharistic overtones.

Shakespeare's imaginative power is brought out if we compare another use of the same Senecan motif from *The Insatiate Countess* V.i.40–44, perhaps by Marston:

> What Tanais, Nilus, or what Tigris swift,
> What Rhenus fiercer than the cataract,
> Although Maeotis cold, the waves of all the Northern sea,
> Should flow for ever through these guilty hands,
> Yet the sanguinolent stain would extant be.[31]

This is much closer to Seneca, and much more explicitly concerned with the indelibility of guilt, but the overall effect is merely clumsy and bombastic. Yet it is worth noticing that Shakespeare's language is more, not less hyperbolical; Shakespeare has learned to use such extremism. The high-flown, imaginative, metaphorical nature of Macbeth's words contrasts beautifully with his wife's practical response: 'A little water clears us of this deed'(66).

## Imitation of a Speech out of Ovid

Pupils at Westminster had to memorize Ovid at the rate of twelve lines a week.[32] So perhaps Shakespeare might have learned Medea's speech in *Metamorphoses* VII.192ff. when at Stratford (there was something of a 'national curriculum' in Tudor schools):

> 197   auraeque et venti montesque amnesque lacusque,
>       dique omnes nemorum dique omnes noctis adeste,
>       quorum ope cum volui ripis mirantibus amnes
> 200   in fontes rediere suos, concussaque sisto
>       stantia concutio cantu freta, nubila pello
>       nubilaque induco, ventosque abigoque vocoque,
> 203   vipereas rumpo verbis et carmine fauces,
>       vivaque saxa sua convulsaque robora terra
>       et silvas moveo, iubeoque tremescere montes
>       et mugire solum manesque exire sepulchris;
> 207   te quoque, Luna, traho, quamvis Temesaea labores
>       aera tuos minuant, currus quoque carmine nostro
> 209   pallet avi, pallet nostris Aurora venenis...

*Ye breezes and winds and mountains and rivers and lakes, and all ye gods of groves and all ye gods of night, be present, by whose aid, when I have wanted, as the banks marvelled, rivers have returned to their sources, by my charm I still the shaken seas and shake the stilled, the winds I both drive away and summon, I break the jaws of snakes with my words and spells, I move living rocks and oaks uprooted from their own soil and woods, and I bid the mountains tremble and the ground moan and the ghosts come out of their graves; thee too, Moon, I drag down, although the bronzes of Temesa lessen your eclipse; the chariot of my grandfather [the Sun] pales at my spells, Aurora pales at my poisons.*

This may not be the greatest poetry, but it is accomplished writing, whose technique would have been well worth studying. It evinces a combination of fluid verse movement marked by varied pauses (indicated in our punctuation by the commas) and enjambment (absence of pauses at verse ends) in six lines with a certain formality: for example, the five separate nouns in polysyndeton (the repeated use of conjunctions) in 197, or the two balanced grouped phrases with reinforcing alliteration in 198. There are three antithetical clauses in 200–202, each taking a slightly different form: the first employs polyptoton (two words deriving from the same root, *concussa, concutio*), alliteration of c and s, and a patterned word order (past participle, verb: present participle, verb – at the same time *concussa* corresponds to *concutio* and *sisto* to *stantia* in a chiastic order ABBA); the second uses the word order ABAB again with repetition of *nubila*; the third has a single object for both verbs, this time linked by double -*que*. The whole complex forms a diminishing tricolon of six, four and three words respectively. The tension of 204 is sustained by separating words in grammatical agreement (hyperbaton: *sua ... terra*); in 207 apostrophe is used for both variety and climax in the reference to Medea's power to draw down the moon. Shakespeare would have been required to subject such passages to just this sort of minute grammatical and rhetorical analysis, with considerable benefit when he came himself to write.

Shakespeare imitated these lines of Ovid when he composed Prospero's speech of renunciation in *The Tempest* (V.i.33–57):

> Ye elves of hills, brooks, standing lakes, and groves
> And ye that on the sands with printless foot
> Do chase the ebbing Neptune and do fly him
> When he comes back, you demi-puppets that
> By moonshine do the green sour ringlets make
> Whereof the ewe not bites, and you whose pastime
> Is to make midnight mushrooms, that rejoice
> To hear the solemn curfew, by whose aid –
> Weak masters though ye be – I have bedimmed
> The noontide sun, called forth the mutinous winds
> And 'twixt the green sea and the azured vault
> Set roaring war; to the dread rattling thunder
> Have I given fire and rifted Jove's stout oak
> With his own bolt, the strong-based promontory
> Have I made shake and by the spurs plucked up
> The pine and cedar; graves at my command
> Have waked their sleepers, oped and let 'em forth
> By my so potent Art. But this rough magic
> I here abjure, and when I have required

21

> Some heavenly music, which even now I do,
> To work mine end upon their senses that
> This airy charm is for, I'll break my staff,
> Bury it certain fathoms in the earth,
> And deeper than did ever plummet sound
> I'll drown my book.

Shakespeare seems also to have glanced at Golding's translation, although similarity with Golding may sometimes be due simply to the use of the same dictionary and translation methods:[33]

> Ye airs and winds, ye elves of hills, of brooks, of woods alone,
> Of standing lakes, and of the Night, approach ye everyone;
> Through help of whom (the crooked banks much wondering at
>   the thing)
> I have compelled streams to run clean backward to their spring;
> By charms I make the calm seas rough, and make the rough seas
>   plain,
> And cover all the sky with clouds and chase them thence again;
> By charms I raise and lay the winds, and burst the viper's jaw,
> And from the bowels of the earth both stone and trees do draw;
> Whole woods and forests I remove, I make the mountains
>   shake,
> And even the earth itself to groan and fearfully to quake;
> I call up dead men from their graves, and thee, o lightsome
>   moon,
> I darken oft, though beaten brass abate thy peril soon;
> Our sorcery dims the morning fair and darks the sun at noon...

Golding's version is lively but very crude in comparison with the original, while Shakespeare, by contrast, matches and even surpasses Ovid's variety of verse movement, while increasing both structural complexity and richness of language. The speech is as electrifying as anything in English poetry. The invocation does not reach the expected climax in a prayer or demand – this is relegated to a series of subordinate clauses and turns out to be merely a request for background music – but leads instead to a resignation of magical powers (the details of the invocation being dismissed, with some irony presumably, as 'rough magic'). Prospero switches from energy, enthusiasm and increasing exultation in his powers – powers reflected in the power of language – to a wistful weariness; the syntax (the invocation never coming to a proper conclusion) is oddly unsettling, even dizzying. If not Shakespeare's farewell to the stage, at any rate the passage has a valedictory quality, and Prospero's Art is not only that of the magician, but also, as the play's language strongly suggests, of the poet and playwright.

Before that Art is abjured, it is celebrated in a passage of breathtaking virtuosity. The verse line is elastic whilst under an extraordinary control, and gives an impression that it is only just within the parameters of blank verse in rhythm and sound (the unusual frequency of enjambments, elisions and especially feminine endings should be noted). In line 33 the monosyllabic words run helter-skelter, skipping from the fifth syllable, against the grain of the metre, the plurals making the line a mouthful of sound; a lighter, more regular line follows, befitting the lovely detail of elvish lightness – 'with printless foot'. In line 35 the extra syllable 'him' (as with 'magic' in 50) creates a slight rhythmic hiccup, while there is a fleeting glimpse of elves running out and back by the shore, at once playful children and disturbing powers. The beginning of line 38, in addition to the monosyllables, has the powerful compression of 'not bites' (for 'does not bite'), whereby the English is given something of the solid presence of Latin (translators from Latin often complain about the mass of little auxiliary words in English). The light lithe patter of language which dominates in the lines about the elves now modulates, via the romantic 'solemn curfew' – the sort of touch which haunted Milton in his early poetry – to a grandeur which, after onomatopoeia for the thunder, ends in abruptly stifled near-ranting. Look, the passage seems to be saying; look at what can be done by a supreme master. And then, with a change of register and a hard-won simplicity, Prospero says farewell to his magic, and Shakespeare to his Ovid. In this instance it should be plain that the use Shakespeare is making of Ovid is imitative, not allusive; educated members of the audience would recognize the presence of Ovid, but there is no question of any such complex interplay between the divergent meanings of the two texts as our more ingenious critics so often suppose. Our concern should rather be with *style*, where a comparison can highlight what is distinctive in Prospero's speech.

### Imitatio or furtum? Cleopatra's barge

Comparing the description of Cleopatra's barge with its source in Plutarch and its later adaptation by Dryden in *All For Love* has become something of a stock rhetorical exercise, but the task cannot be shirked because it tells us so much about Shakespeare's's method of imitation.[34]

> She disdained to set forward otherwise, but to take her barge in the river Cydnus, the poop whereof was of gold, the sails of purple and the oars of silver, which kept stroke in rowing after the sound of the music of flutes, hautboys, citherns, viols and such other instruments as they played upon in the barge. And now for the person of herself – she was laid under a pavilion of cloth of gold of tissue, apparelled and attired like the goddess Venus commonly drawn in picture; and hard by her, on either hand of her, pretty fair boys apparelled as painters do set forth god Cupid, with little fans in their hands, with the which they fanned wind upon her. Her ladies and gentlewomen also, the fairest of them, were apparelled like the nymphs Nereids – which are the mermaids of the waters – and like the Graces, some steering the helm, others tending the tackle and ropes of the barge, out of the which there came a wonderful passing sweet savour of perfumes, that perfumed the wharf's side, pestered with innumerable multitudes of people. Some of them followed the barge all along the riverside, others also ran out of the city to see her coming in; so that in the end there ran such multitudes of people one after another to see her that Antonius was left post alone in the market-place, in his imperial seat, to give audience: and there went a rumour in the people's mouths that the goddess Venus was come to play with the god Bacchus, for the general good of all Asia.
>
> (Plutarch, *Life of Antony*, 26, translated by Thomas North, 1579)

> The barge she sat in, like a burnished throne,
> Burned on the water; the poop was beaten gold,
> Purple the sails, and so perfumed that
> The winds were love-sick with them; the oars were silver,
> Which to the tune of flutes kept stroke, and made
> The water which they beat to follow faster,
> As amorous of their strokes. For her own person –
> It beggared all description: she did lie
> In her pavilion – cloth-of-gold, of tissue –
> O'er picturing that Venus where we see
> The fancy outwork nature; on each side her
> Stood pretty dimpled boys, like smiling Cupids,

With divers-coloured fans, whose wind did seem
To glow the delicate cheeks which they did cool,
And what they undid did ...
Her gentlewomen, like the Nereides,
So many mermaids, tended her in the eyes,
And made their bends adornings; at the helm
A seeming mermaid steers; the silken tackle
Swell with the touches of those flower-soft hands
That yarely frame the office. From the barge
A strange invisible perfume hits the sense
Of the adjacent wharfs. The city cast
Her people out upon her; and Antony,
Enthroned in the market-place, did sit alone,
Whistling to the air, which, but for vacancy,
Had gone to gaze on Cleopatra too
And made a gap in nature.
        (Shakespeare, *Antony and Cleopatra*, II.ii.191–218)


          To clear herself
For sending him no aid she came from Egypt.
Her galley down the silver Cydnus rowed,
The tackling silk, the streamers waved with gold,
The gentle winds were lodged in purple sails.
Her nymphs, like Nereids, round her couch were placed,
Where she, another sea-born Venus, lay ...
She lay, and leant her cheek upon her hand,
And cast a look so languishingly sweet
As if, secure of all beholders' hearts,
Neglecting she could take 'em. Boys, like Cupids,
Stood fanning, with their painted wings, the winds
That played about her face; but if she smiled,
A darting glory seemed to blaze abroad,
That men's desiring eyes were never wearied,
But hung upon the object. To soft flutes
The silver oars kept time, and while they played
The hearing gave new pleasure to the sight,
And both to thought. 'Twas heaven, or somewhat more,
For she so charmed all hearts that gazing crowds
Stood panting on the shore, and wanted breath
To give their welcome voice.
        (Dryden, *All for Love*, III.i. 161–182)

25

Shakespeare adheres more closely than Dryden both to the details in North's Plutarch and to their order. On the other hand he adds a dimension of wit, imagination and romantic conceitedness which is absent from the source. Dryden has virtually nothing of this, and concentrates on Cleopatra's 'womanly' allure. The passage of Plutarch is of course part of a historical narrative; the dramatists inevitably have to alter its impact by giving it to a character, Shakespeare to the plain man Enobarbus, who is gossiping with the two cronies from the opposite political camp, which allows for the possibility of a certain detachment, Dryden to Antony himself, which removes any element of irony.

In Plutarch the scene is part of a political manoeuvre. Cleopatra uses her opulent trappings to create a public image. She affects a certain nonchalance, making light of Antony's summons and setting out to meet him in a blaze of wealth and glamour, designed to set off her own still greater allurements. The vocabulary of magic – 'the charms and enchantment of her passing beauty and grace' – does not hint at anything beyond her natural attractiveness, although it may have suggested to Shakespeare more complex possibilities. Cleopatra's disguised attendants are part of a theatrical performance, and the comparisons with painting are purely descriptive and clarificatory. There is no interest in the subtleties of the relationship between nature and art, and no suggestion of the lurking presence of divinity. The association of the lovers with Venus and Bacchus is simply a popular rumour, from which author and reader alike are distanced.

Enobarbus' connoisseur's account flickers between admiration and amusement. The phrasing is at times almost disconcertingly close to North's (for example, in the distinctive and rather obscure 'cloth of gold of tissue'); minor adjustments (like the metaphorical 'burned') simply make the account more perfumed. But the description is also mythologized and eroticized; there is an interest in the interplay of art and nature and a concern with paradox; and shimmering through the whole is an ambiguous sense of wonder and comedy. It is the inanimate elements, partially personified, which become the focus for erotic feeling – the winds love-sick with the scented sails, the amorous longings of the water (with the pun on 'strokes'). Shakespeare develops North's straightforward comparison of Cleopatra to a painting of Venus into a remarkably compressed paradox about art and nature, where we have to envisage two stages of 'outdoing' (North does not even suggest one). Great Renaissance

26

paintings were commonly praised for surpassing nature herself; but here, in a breathtakingly quick leap, we are told that Cleopatra in her own nature outdoes the outdoing splendours of fancy. Shakespeare does not even tell us whether she is dressed like Venus, as in Plutarch, or simply has the aura of the goddess. The lines pre-echo the later, still more extreme ontological speculations of Cleopatra (V.ii.96–100), when she tells Dolabella that her imaginings about Antony soar far beyond anything which could be merely imaginary:

> if there be, nor ever were one such,
> It's past the size of dreaming. Nature wants stuff
> To vie strange forms with fancy, yet to imagine
> An Antony were nature's piece 'gainst fancy,
> Condemning shadows quite.

In Plutarch, Cleopatra carefully devises a sumptuous pageant with disguised attendants; in Shakespeare, Cleopatra's motives are not directly related to the mysterious and indefinite phenomenon of the barge with its artistic effects like the mermaid-gentlewomen who 'made their bends adornings'. Elegant paradoxes abound, including the cool air which performs the effect of heat, where the whole phrase is poised on the ambiguous atmosphere established by the word 'seemed'. Shakespeare retains from the source the detail that Antony was left alone in the market-place, which he nudges towards a fuller sense of comedy by adding the heartily naturalistic picture of the nonplussed Antony 'whistling to the air' (twiddling his thumbs as it were); then Enobarbus, with a change of tone, develops, as a fancy, the thought that even the air would have gone to look at Cleopatra 'but for vacancy'. He does not commit himself to belief in such a disruption in natural laws, but toys with the possibility to demonstrate the apparent powers of Cleopatra as a goddess operating within nature and presiding over it. Enobarbus, tactfully and unlike Dryden's Antony, avoids direct description of Cleopatra's person; rather she is described in terms of her impact on nature. The environment is the actor, Cleopatra the force omnipresent but almost unseen which motivates it. It is not even said that the people poured out of the city, but the 'The City cast/Her people out upon her'.

Dryden, returning to Plutarch, removes most of these elements of fancy, mystery and wit. In his version Cleopatra is again merely a woman, though with a powerful erotic allure, given to obvious 'wiles', and her action has a precise political motivation. The barge's trappings are sumptuous, but there is no metaphorical or romantic fancy. The attendants do not merge with the world of nature-spirits. Some conceits (for example 'the winds/That played about her face', 'the hearing gave new pleasure to the sight,/And both to thought') suggest that Dryden had observed, and wished to retain, something of the exhilaration which Shakespeare's outdoing paradoxes convey, but more 'decorously' and without philosophic complexity. Cleopatra's power is not over inanimate nature but over men's hearts, as the best lines in the passage show:

> A darting glory seemed to blaze abroad
> That men's desiring eyes were never wearied
> But hung upon the object.

When Antony says of her ''Twas heaven, or somewhat more', although there is less mockery than in Enobarbus' account, 'heaven' casts a hint of the commonplace over the proceedings; Dryden's Cleopatra is not a goddess, and the word seems to be taking on some of its modern, shallower meaning. By and large we have tried to keep this comparison at the level of description, not evaluation. It would be pointless to set out, solemnly, to demonstrate Shakespeare's superiority to Dryden. It is better to observe that Dryden's version, in spirit closer to Plutarch's, is effective enough in its own way.

It remains to ask whether Shakespeare's use of North in this instance constitutes proper imitation as the Renaissance understood it. Shakespeare's procedure here is essentially like the other examples we have analysed, but Jonson clearly assumed that the imitator of classical material read it in the original language. Donald Russell argues that there were five criteria for successful imitation presupposed in most ancient discussions, which he gives as follows:

(i) The object must be worth imitating.
(ii) The spirit rather than the letter must be reproduced.
(iii) The imitation must be tacitly acknowledged, on the understanding that the informed reader will recognize and approve the borrowing.
(iv) The borrowing must be 'made one's own', by individual treatment and assimilation to its new place and purpose.
(v) The imitator must think of himself as competing with his model.[35]

(Donald Russell, 'De imitatione', p. 16)

Of these criteria Shakespeare meets the second, fourth and (perhaps) fifth. But it is not clear that the first or third are satisfied. In particular it is doubtful whether the passage from North would be in the majority of the audience's repertoire. Some of the more learned might even be misled into thinking that Shakespeare was adapting Plutarch's original Greek. Perhaps then an ancient critic would have characterized this passage as *furtum* (theft), or, as we would say, plagiarism. It is unlikely that any of this would have bothered Shakespeare in the least; he knew a good passage when he saw one, and knew too how to improve it and make it his own. To transfer to Shakespeare Dryden's famous words about Jonson, 'what would be theft in other poets is only victory in him'.[36]

## SENECA BY CANDLELIGHT

The battle over the question of Seneca's influence on English Renaissance tragedy continues to rage. For some time the anti-Senecans have held the field, but there are signs that their opponents are regrouping and beginning a counter-attack. G.K. Hunter, in two influential and closely argued essays, has trenchantly put the case against widespread Senecan influence. He concludes that 'we are left with a few well-worn anthology passages and a few isolated tricks like stichomythia (and even that occurs outside tragedy) as relics of the once extensive empire of Seneca's undisputed influence'. Hunter sees a direct line of descent running from medieval drama through the Tudor interludes to the developed popular theatre with little room left for Seneca: 'If Seneca's tragedies had not survived, some details would have had to be changed – but the overall picture would not have been altered.'[37]

Some of Hunter's arguments are persuasive. The Elizabethans did not have to resort to Seneca to find the traditional 'Senecan' ingredients of tyrants, ghosts, horrors, rant and bombast, since the vernacular tradition supplied these in plenty. It is anyway wholly unsatisfactory to characterize Seneca in this way. Likewise five-act structure came principally from Terence, as Baldwin has demonstrated,[38] not from Seneca, and in general Seneca's formal influence on popular drama was small. The more thorough-going English Senecans, like Thomas Hughes, author of *The Misfortunes of Arthur* (1587), almost a patchwork of Senecan phrases,[39] were of no great importance for mainstream developments. Hunter is also right to insist that a bare list of parallels proves little about significant affinities. But some of his other points do less to establish his case. It is true that Seneca's tragedies were not an essential part of the normal school curriculum (although we know, for example, that they were studied at Westminster in the sixth form[40]), and that the complete translation of 1581 was never reprinted. But dramatists would naturally be particularly interested in Seneca as the most available and prestigious ancient tragedian – after all there were no published English versions of Greek tragedies at all, except *Jocasta* by Kinwelmersh and Gascoigne, which derived at two removes from Euripides' *Phoenissae* – and yet English Seneca must soon have seemed old-fashioned and unsatisfactory to a poet like Marlowe who would have preferred to use the original. Likewise it is true that 'Senecan' qualities can be found in other Latin poets, in particular Ovid, the favourite of the age. But popular as was Ovid's 'sweet', witty, conceited style, there were other weightier rhetorical traditions which were exploited by the dramatists, particularly at moments of the highest tragic intensity.

Hunter observes that much Elizabethan literature was only superficially classical, with a 'Gothic' (that is medieval) structure underneath, and that in consequence Seneca was frequently misunderstood or accommodated to Christian belief. For example, Dean Nowell of Westminster particularly admired *Hippolytus* because of its similarity to the Biblical story of Joseph and Potiphar's wife.[41] We can see this accommodation affecting the translators both in their conception of the plays and in the actual texture of their versions. But if the Elizabethan Seneca was not the same as ours – and ours too is no doubt partly formed by our local beliefs and preoccupations – this does not mean that he was not influential; rather the accommodation precisely helped to make him more assimilable.[42]

On the one hand it is wrong to make too sharp a distinction between the native and classical traditions; on the other it should be acknowledged that there is a gap between the interludes and the developed drama which is partly the result of a more precise use of classical models including Seneca, and the ability to transfer into the vernacular aspects of their styles. From the early sixteenth century onwards classical influences were at work even in popular entertainments. For example, the interlude *Jack Juggler* (composed before 1562/3) was based on Plautus' *Amphitruo* and designed for an audience familiar with the original, but it also shares many qualities with other interludes.[43] R.B.'s *A New Tragical Comedy of Appius and Virginia*, its story probably taken from Chaucer's 'Physician's tale', postdates *Gorboduc* (1562), which Sidney at least thought Senecan, and could have been influenced by it.[44] It is larded with classical

references; for example, the tyrant Appius justifies his desire for
Virginia with an allusion to the rape of Lucretia:

Well now I range at large, my will for to express,
For look how Tarquin Lucrece fair by force did once oppress.

(557f.)

and refers to a series of Ovidian lovers, including Pygmalion and
Salmacis (357, 361). The stylistic crudities make these classical
touches sound unconvincing (we are inevitably reminded of the play
of Pyramus in the *Dream*):

Come, Ventus, come, blow forth thy blast,
Prince Eol [= Aeolus], listen well.
The filthiest fact that ever was
I, Rumour, now shall tell.

(736–739)

Elements in the popular drama (the vigorous use of the vernacular,
the mixing of high and low, of serious and comic, the Christian and
moralizing schemes) survive into the later dramatic tradition, but the
authors of the interludes have no command over the elaborate rhetorical sentence structures – or the sense of personality which accompanies this high rhetoric – employed by Shakespeare's
generation, which have a different pedigree. *Macbeth* may not closely
resemble Seneca's *Thyestes*, but it has even less of the flavour of
*Appius and Virginia*. So too stichomythia (alternating lines for two
speakers) is found in the vernacular tradition, but hardly the intense
verbal parrying characteristic of Seneca in which 'language itself
becomes the battlefield' and the exchange is 'a test of ... self-possession', not a conversation.[45] Two other works which have been seen
by the anti-Senecans as bridging the gap between medieval and
Renaissance drama tell a similar story. John Pickering's *Horestes*
(1567), treating Orestes' vengeance on his mother, takes its plot from
Lydgate's Troy Book; like *Appius and Virginia* it has a key role for
the Vice, and the mythological and other classical references which
decorate the speeches (in fourteeners) of the 'high' characters are used
largely in the old medieval way. The gulf which divides this interlude
from later tragedy is shown by the inclusion of a love duet, sung to a
popular tune, for Clytemnestra and Aegisthus, and by the banality of
much of the poetry; thus Idumeus (Idomeneus) says to Menalaus
(sic): 'Horestes, he is young of years, and you are somewhat old'
(1010). Thomas Preston's *Cambyses, King of Persia: A Lamentable*

*Tragedy, Mixed Full of Pleasant Mirth* (before 1569/70), a much less lively piece, has similar stylistic defects; Preston tries, unsuccessfully, to raise the tone of the king's speeches by some Latinate vocabulary: 'With all festination your offices to frequent' (1104).[46]

In all these works there is no consistent effort to naturalize in English a high tragic rhetoric modelled on classical poetry. This was largely the achievement of the tragedians of the 1580s and 1590s, and in that achievement Seneca, along with Virgil and Ovid, played some part. The beginnings of that rhetoric are first heard in the obviously classicizing *Gorboduc* with its *nuntius* and moralizing lyric choruses dividing the acts:

> O cruel fates, o mindful wrath of gods,
> Whose vengeance neither Simois' stained streams
> Flowing with blood of Trojan princes slain,
> Nor Phrygian fields made rank with corpses dead
> Of Asian kings and lords, can yet appease,
> Ne slaughter of unhappy Priam's race
> Nor Ilion's fall, made level with the soil,
> Can yet suffice, but still continued rage
> Pursues our lives and from the farthest seas
> Doth chase the issue of destroyed Troy.
>
> (III.i.1–10)

Here we find a cumulative rhetorical structure, with delayed verbs and balanced clauses, introduced by negatives (a scheme of which Seneca is fond, e.g. *Thyestes* 344–8; 350–68). Admittedly this rhetoric is still under an imperfect control – the expected prayer to the fates never materializes[47] – but we are already far from the language of the interludes. Likewise there is an accurately modern use of classical names, with no medieval 'quaintness'.

Hunter in effect requires us to be able to isolate a distinct Senecan strand in the plays of which we can say that 'here is the true Seneca, pure and unalloyed, embodied in English writing'. In consequence he can argue that even the stylistic significance of Seneca has been exaggerated, since the great Elizabethans did not reproduce the 're-petitive cleverness' and 'compression' of the original: 'Seneca's rhet-oric', he claims, 'is used to distance from us the highly-charged events described, and continuously resolves them into wit and abstraction', a description that makes Seneca sound more Ovidian than he is and underestimates his effectiveness in moving the passions.[48] Certainly the lack of narrative, of social context, of much sense of individual 'personality' as we understand it, gives a particular flavour to Seneca's rhetoric. But Hunter's argument proves too much. On this basis it could be claimed that Horace had no real influence on Jonson, or Ovid on Spenser, since the differences in style and ethos in either case are great. Such differences are inevitable when a change of language is involved. Neo-Latin writers could reproduce the Senecan style closely, and did so even when translating Greek plays. By contrast any imitation in another language will always involve substantial stylistic alterations, particularly if the writer aims to create original work. Nevertheless some Senecan stylistic features are represented in English drama; as Wolfgang Clemen modestly puts it, Seneca 'endorsed and reinforced the already existing tendency to express whatever has emotional potentialities in speeches of a heightened poetic quality'.[49] And Seneca was the most immediate classical model for declamatory verse, aside from the speeches in epic.

Certainly the Elizabethans themselves did not share Hunter's view. Polonius, whose opinions are unlikely to be other than conventional, saw Seneca as the prime model for tragedy, and in particular emphasized the importance of his style: 'Seneca cannot be too heavy, nor Plautus too light' (*Hamlet*, II.ii.396).[50] Sidney praised Gorboduc for 'climbing to the height of Seneca his style'.[51] William Webbe wrote of *Gismond of Salerne* (1567–1568), a tragedy written for the Inns of Court, that it was 'of all men generally desired as a work either in stateliness of show, depth of conceit, or true ornaments of poetical art, inferior to none of the best in that kind, no, were the Roman Seneca the censurer'.[52] The popular dramatists, including Kyd, Marlowe and Shakespeare, cited Seneca in Latin, if only to flatter their audiences. In the Preface to Greene's *Menaphon*, Thomas Nashe criticizes ignorant poetasters forced to read Seneca in translation to compensate for their lack of knowledge of the original:

English Seneca read by candlelight yields many good sentences, as 'Blood is a beggar' and so forth; and, if you entreat him fair in a frosty morning, he will afford you whole *Hamlets*, I should say handfuls of tragical speeches ... Seneca, let blood line by line and page by page, at length must needs die to our stage.[52]

The verse Preface to Heywood's translation of *Thyestes* (1560) recounts how the poet in a dream saw a vision of a grave garlanded figure holding a book, who identifies himself as Seneca:

'O blissful day', quoth I, 'wherein returned is again
So worthy wight. O happy hour, that liefer is to me
Than life, wherein it haps me so that I should Senec see!
Art thou the same that whilom didst thy tragedies indite
With wondrous wit and regal style?'

(32–36)

At the very least all this evidence shows the prestige and cultural authority of Seneca, even if in part the aim was simply to validate theatrical enterprise by respectable classical precedent. And one should not forget the importance of Seneca in Italy and sixteenth-century France, or his dominance of neo-Latin tragedy, exemplified by the Scottish humanist, George Buchanan's celebrated *Jephtha*.

Shakespeare, much of whose work falls between the first full flood of Senecanism and the renewed early seventeenth-century interest, is now seldom credited with any special concern for Seneca. Certainly Senecan elements in his works are often the result of indirect influences. For example Cleopatra's

O sun,
Burn the great sphere thou mov'st in, darkling stand
The varying shore of the world

(*Antony and Cleopatra*, IV.xv.9–11)

ultimately derives from a Senecan *topos*, 'the prayer for universal extinction', but that *topos* had been used countless times by earlier English dramatists.[54] The same is true of the rhetorical flourish 'I am Antony yet' (III.xiii.93), although Shakespeare was surely aware of the most powerful Senecan usage of the figure (*Medea*, 165–167):

*Nurse*: nihilque superest opibus e tantis tibi.
*Medea*: Medea superest: hic mare et terras vides
ferrumque et ignes et deos et fulmina.
('*You have nothing left from your great resources.*'
'*Medea is left – in her you see sea, lands, sword, fire, gods and thunderbolts.*')[55]

Certainly Shakespeare seldom gives us Seneca in as pure a form as Chapman. For example *Bussy D'Ambois* not only affords a Herculean hero in imitation of *Hercules Oetaeus*, but catches the very essence of Senecan rhetoric at its most intensely poetic:

fly where men feel
The burning axletree, and those that suffer
Beneath the chariot of the snowy Bear.

(V.iii.151–153)

T.S. Eliot thought that 'the attitude of self-dramatization ... at moments of tragic intensity'[56] illustrated in the final scene of *Othello* derived from Seneca. Although Eliot also tried to forge a dubious link between the Stoic philosophy and Senecan tragic language, his intuition about Othello's rhetorical style is worth pursuing. Othello, 'great of heart' (*magnanimus*), as Cassius calls him after his death, is shown as a foreigner among Italians, as a man with an exotic history of adventures in distant lands, as a heroic character in contrast to the super-subtle Venetians, and accordingly aligned with an old-fashioned but still prized set of values, partly at odds with a prevailing, more politic ambience. His language, grand, musical, exotic and classicizing – of the classical references in the play six out of eleven, and these the most substantial, are put into his mouth[57] – is contrasted with Iago's plainer, blunter, more 'modern' and colloquial manner of speech. The play thus involves a clash of discourses, and it is a peculiarly scarifying moment when Iago temporarily slips into Othello's characteristic style, with its verbal music and balanced classical rhetoric, for 'not poppy, nor mandragora,/Nor all the drowsy syrups of the world ... ' (III.iii.335f.), where the evocative rolling sounds are organized into a tricolon crescendo. One can compare the four-fold crescendo (tetracolon) in Othello's richly orchestrated last speech, introduced by anaphora ('Of one'), with clauses of 9, 12, 17 and 22 words:

> then must you speak
> Of one that loved not wisely but too well,
> Of one not easily jealous but being wrought
> Perplexed in the extreme, of one whose hand
> Like the base Indian threw a pearl away
> Richer than all his tribe, of one whose subdued eyes
> Albeit unused to the melting mood
> Drop tears as fast as the Arabian trees
> Their medicinal gum.
>
> (V.ii.344–352)

Othello's earlier address to his soul (a section of which we have already discussed), 'It is the cause, it is the cause, my soul', is delivered with an acute consciousness on his part that it marks a grand moment. Othello addresses his soul – and later the stars, the light, the sleeping Desdemona – not as part of an inward psychological rumination but as elevated apostrophe. It is as if we are offered a series of publicly addressed comments at a moment of intense privacy. This form of outwardly turned introspection might well strike a Renaissance listener as Senecan, especially as self-apostrophe – to *animus, ira, dolor, furor* – occurs frequently in Seneca's tragedies.[58] Another grandly rhetorical moment is Othello's vow (III.iii.460–467):

> Like to the Pontic sea,
> Whose icy current and compulsive course
> Ne'er feels retiring ebb but keeps due on
> To the Propontic and the Hellespont,
> Even so my bloody thoughts, with violent pace,
> Shall ne'er look back, ne'er ebb to humble love,
> Till that a capable and wide revenge
> Swallow them up.

The geography comes from Pliny's *Natural History* (which Shakespeare read – or dipped into – in Philemon Holland's translation), with the Hellespont added for greater grandeur and resonance.[59] But Shakespeare of course is not evoking Pliny but high classical epic and tragedy; sources are not the same as style and effect. Both the fondness for geographical detail and the use of simile in a speech – omnipresent in Seneca but generally avoided in epic, where such similes are confined to the narrative for reasons of decorum – could be seen as Senecan (cf. e.g. *Medea*, 382–386; *Hippolytus*, 580–582), even though the style is more open-textured (the speech is too weighty for Ovid). The simile is of noticeably formal construction with a degree of systematic homologation not commonly found in the later Shakespeare. Most of the speech is missing from the first Quarto, and Pope thought the passage 'an unnatural excursion in this place', presumably because it is too formal for such a moment of intense passion and because it stands out stylistically from its surroundings.[60] (The use of sea-currents to illustrate human behaviour is like Thomas Fuller's comparison of the stoical Sir Horace Vere to the Caspian Sea, which 'doth never ebb nor flow'.[61]) Othello is striving to surmount the fluctuations of jealousy and to present himself as a man of fixed resolve; hence the somewhat strained pitch of the rhetoric, which nevertheless has a genuine ring of the high style. The final clause suggests an annihilation which will drive away all troubling thoughts, an attitude far removed from the detached calm of a true Stoic, but recalling the extremism of Seneca's tragic figures.

These arguments for a Senecan presence in *Othello* will obviously not convince a doubter. The indisputable case, to our mind, is

*Macbeth*. Even the sceptical Thomson accepts that Shakespeare probably read one or more of Seneca's plays (including *Hercules Furens*) in Latin before writing it.[62] The power of Seneca's plays lies partly in their sense that emotional desires, if released, can be like wild beasts, enabling human beings to make a grotesque hell of the world, a sense expressed through a glitteringly self-conscious language, pitched at an unrelenting level of intensity, capable of doing justice to this hothouse vision. It is no coincidence that they came back into fashion after Europe had experienced the monstrous excesses of totalitarianism, which made the Victorian charges of 'bad taste' in Seneca seem merely trivial. There are a number of features in *Macbeth* – the heated rhetoric, the brooding sense of evil, the pre-occupation with power, the obsessive introspection, the claustro-phobic images of cosmic destruction – which recall Seneca's manner and interests, together with an unusually high number of passages which seem to derive from his plays (we have already looked at two of them).[63] For example, Macbeth's soliloquy (V.iii.22ff.):

> I have lived long enough – my way of life
> Is fallen into the sere, the yellow leaf;
> And that which should accompany old age –
> As honour, love, obedience, troops of friends –
> I must not look to have...

probably comes from a passage in *Hercules Furens* (1258–1261) when Hercules confronts the ruin of his life:

> cur animam in ista luce detineam amplius
> morerque nihil est; cuncta iam amisi bona, –
> mentem, arma, famam, coniugem, natos, manus,
> etiam furorem.

*(There is no reason for me to hold my life longer in this light. I have lost all advantages, composure, weapons, fame, wife, children, hands – even my madness.)*

This is a typical piece of Senecan writing: the somewhat restricted and ordinary vocabulary, offset by rhetorical devices; the line-filling asyndeton of 1260 with its mixture of abstract and concrete words; the paradoxical point of the climax (it would be better for Hercules to be mad again). Shakespeare's lines are more meditative than Seneca's. The balanced rhetoric, which owes something to Seneca's syntactical arrangements, with the list of lost advantages in asyndeton – though

Shakespeare builds them up cumulatively with lengthening phrases – is used to convey a sense of part-weary, part-dignified contemplation. The speech ends with what is Macbeth's only honest perception of the feelings of others – 'mouth-honour, breath,/Which the poor heart would fain deny, and dare not'. The main glory of the lines, however, is the image of the autumn leaves with its sudden splash of colour.

It has also plausibly been argued that Lady Macbeth, who talks of a willingness to murder her children and is associated with witchcraft, may be designed to recall aspects of Seneca's Medea.[64] David Norbrook notes that George Buchanan, whose history of Scotland may have been consulted by Shakespeare, was a leading neo-Senecan dramatist.[65] No one of these factors alone would make the case; it is their accumulation that is convincing. Seneca's tragedies frequently focus on a bad woman or man, and the structure of *Macbeth*, whereby the choice of evil unleashes catastrophic consequences which infect the whole cosmos, is typically Senecan.[66] In I.vii, Macbeth starts to rethink his position, but is confirmed in his original intention by his wife, a Senecan sequence, although in Shakespeare there is a much fuller sense of contrasted personalities. In III.ii.16 Macbeth links an image of cosmic destruction with his own diseased thought; in II.iv the unnatural darkness of the world is related to the evils of the time, and the setting takes on the essentially rhetorical and symbolic function of descriptions in Seneca. Macbeth is also a tyrant, with a measure of classical ancestry. Emrys Jones suggests that Macbeth's apparent forgetfulness about Banquo's death can be seen as part of the typology of tyranny, since an analogous story is told of the Emperor Claudius in Suetonius' Life.[67] In a consciously Senecan play a tyrant is likely to have some flavour of Seneca, however many other precedents there may be in vernacular drama.[68] The structure of *Macbeth* also requires a degree of prior knowledge of the plot by the audience, and the role of the witches in revealing the future thus allows for the kind of ironies which we associate with Greek drama, and which Shakespeare presumably intuited from Seneca; the simplicity of the plot – if it is not, in part at least, the result of abridgement – has a classical concentration unique in Shakespeare.

More important is the play's focus on the mind of Macbeth. W.R. Johnson says of Seneca's Medea that:

> she is a state of mind, self-exulting, self-punishing, self-annihilating, and her voice and the voices of the phantoms who try to

question or comfort her, vague images of a world she has almost forgotten, reverberate from a vast depth of consciousness that is endlessly distant from the place and time in which she has her physical presence.[69]

Similarly Gordon Braden stresses Seneca's interest in 'the subjectivity of consciousness' (hence the almost complete absence of plot). Senecan characters are frequently isolated and prey to 'a fantasy of individual autonomy'; their rhetoric becomes 'the language of the self's autarceia', its selfhood and self-sufficiency.[70] Thus when Graham Bradshaw calls *Macbeth* unSenecan, because Seneca lacks 'that sense of the psyche as something stratified, vertiginous', which is Christian and Augustinian, and quotes Auerbach on 'the comparatively cool and rational procedure of the classical, and specifically of the Roman, style, which looks at and organizes things from above',[71] he is misdescribing Seneca, whose rhetoric, far from being cool, is frequently pitched at the edge of hysteria, and who was, in so many ways, the precursor of Augustine.

After the brief appearance of the witches, *Macbeth* begins with a fast-moving scene, in which a primitive heroic world is evoked with its grim humour (34f.), a world in which Macbeth's 'nobility' resides in his violent military valour (21f.) and supposed loyalty. In such simple heroic contexts Macbeth can impress us, as at the play's conclusion. The description of him as 'Bellona's bridegroom' (55) is an unexpected classical touch, reminding us how saturated Shakespeare's culture was with classicism, since it is not perhaps wholly appropriate to this northern world. The Arden editor describes the scene as 'one of the weakest' in the play.[72] Actually it is splendidly brisk, with some splendid writing. The context which the play provides for Macbeth's crazy criminality is a heroic world, historically differentiated to some extent from Jacobean society, with succession of kings by election and battles of dazzling ancientry: 'Where the Norweyan banners flout the sky/And fan our people cold –'. (50f.) But the scene is something of a deliberate false start. We expect a heroic play, but, instead of heroism, the strange psychological broodings of the protagonist are foregrounded, as he transfers the permitted violence of the loyal warrior into forbidden areas and so deforms it. As a result, in Bradshaw's words, Macbeth's 'asides and soliloquies show him dreaming an uninterrupted, unmanning nightmare while the rest of the play goes on elsewhere'.[73] The bizarre psychological language in which the first act soliloquies are couched attempts to picture not the decision-making process itself, but its much more unformed precursors. It is as if a Senecan consciousness is adrift in a world of action. Shakespeare seems less interested in *Macbeth* – at least in comparison with other plays – in creating a richly imagined background. That presumably is what Emrys Jones means when he observes that 'Shakespeare locates the action in a region deep in our minds', something no one would say of *Hamlet*.[74] This does not imply that *Macbeth* ultimately resembles a play by Seneca. For one thing it is Christian, both overtly and covertly. For another the language is of course not Senecan but Shakespearean, and is far richer in interlocking imagery and far more supple than Seneca's, whose characters, as T.S. Eliot observed, 'all seem to speak with the same voice, and at the top of it', producing 'a monotony of forcefulness'.[75] What it does mean is that Shakespeare reflected on the character of Senecan drama and was partly inspired by his reflections to write *Macbeth* in the form that he did. And that surely is precisely what we mean by 'influence' – an inflowing of one author into another to create a new work of art.

To illustrate the mood of Macbeth's broodings we may look at his night-piece from the dagger soliloquy (II.i.49–60), which combines introspection and atmospheric description in a manner reminiscent of *Thyestes*:[76]

> Now o'er the one half-world
> Nature seems dead, and wicked dreams abuse
> The curtained sleep; witchcraft celebrates
> Pale Hecate's offerings, and withered murder
> Alarumed by his sentinel the wolf,
> Whose howl's his watch, thus with stealthy pace,
> With Tarquin's ravishing strides, towards his design
> Moves like a ghost – Thou sure and firm-set earth,
> Hear not my steps, which way they walk, for fear
> Thy very stones prate of my whereabout,
> And take the present horror from the time,
> Which now suits with it.

Macbeth luxuriates in the sheer horror of things – that is of the atmosphere, not the murder itself, which to some extent he is shuffling from his mind. A sinister vagueness dominates, partly through the imprecisions of the personifications; for example, it is uncertain how far we should envisage 'withered murder' as an actual haggard figure creeping towards us. The wolf, of course, is pure atmosphere (no normal murderer wants an accompaniment of disturbing noises);

we are near the timbre of a werewolf story. The allusion to Tarquin the ravisher creates a mood of sinister stealth and monstrous violence. In the climactic apostrophe to earth, Macbeth glides weirdly from the practical point, however melodramatically expressed, of wishing the concealment of his murderous activities, to one far less rational; he wants silence and secrecy because these provide the most appropriate atmosphere for the deed. Macbeth, in other words, is interested in the aesthetics of evil. How far Shakespeare had travelled as a poet can be seen if we compare these lines with a stanza from *Lucrece* (162–168):

> Now stole upon the time the dead of night,
> When heavy sleep had closed up mortal eyes;
> No comfortable star did lend his light,
> No noise but owls' and wolves' death-boding cries;
> Now serves the season that they may surprise
> The silly lambs. Pure thoughts are dead and still,
> While lust and murder wakes to stain and kill.

It is in a sense arbitrary that the night of the rape should have this character, and there is none of the motivating force of Macbeth's conjuring imagination. The fusing of lust and murder foreshadows the inclusion, in *Macbeth*, of 'Tarquin's ravishing strides' in the evocation of an atmosphere of evil darkness accompanying murder. Macbeth's self-indulgent rhetoric verges on Senecan excess. But in such a passage Shakespeare goes beyond Seneca to imitate the complex workings of a singular human mind, something which, however, without Seneca before him, he might never have achieved.

Finally, a brief coda on Shakespeare and Greek tragedy. From time to time someone comes forward to propose significant links between them.[77] Any Greek language Shakespeare had would not have been sufficient to allow him to read the extremely taxing poetry of the fifth century BC. Renaissance culture remained primarily Latin-based; significantly, Sidney was advised that Greek was not a vital study.[78] If Shakespeare read any Greek plays, he will thus have read them in Latin (there were no published English translations except *Jocasta*, although Peele apparently translated an *Iphigenia*). The poet Thomas Watson, who was prominent in London literary circles, translated Sophocles' *Antigone* into Latin, and Latin versions of all the plays were available. Obviously one cannot prove a negative, but we can observe that if Shakespeare read them he gained little from the experience. Moreover, despite all efforts, no one has yet succeeded in producing one single piece of evidence from the plays to make any such debt certain, or even particularly likely. The reference in *Titus* I.i.379 to the story of the burial of Ajax does not prove that Shakespeare read Sophocles' play: all the information is to be found in a note on Horace's *Satires* II.iii.187 in Lambinus' edition, which was a standard school textbook, and doubtless in many other places.[79] Indeed to argue that Shakespeare had read the *Ajax* is to convict him of wasting his time if this is all the fruit it bore.

We should remember that the Renaissance canon of classical texts was different from the modern canon. When Shakespeare wrote *Timon of Athens*, with its Greek setting, he used Plutarch's *Lives* and possibly the dialogue *Timon the Misanthrope* by Lucian (second century AD), which he would have read in French or Italian, or in Erasmus' Latin version. Lucian, little studied today, was a particular favourite of the Renaissance. Shakespeare's road to Greece (a Greece where, in *Timon*, Athens has a Senate and most of the characters have Latin names) was thus through post-classical authors and through the late romances, which gave indirect access to features of Homer's *Odyssey* and Euripides' 'tragi-comedies', not through what we regard as the central texts. One cannot help feeling that the search for direct connections with Greek drama springs from the desire to draw together the two supreme tragic traditions, and from a dissatisfaction with the single influence of Seneca, a dissatisfaction compounded by the narrow and prescriptive attitudes of most classical scholars towards him. We must accept that in the Renaissance Seneca was admired by people of 'taste' and discrimination, sometimes above the Greeks – those who have no Latin and no Greek might reflect that their opinion on the matter is not likely to be of any great consequence. The elder Scaliger thought Seneca superior even to Euripides in polish and equal in majesty to any of the Greeks.[80] Giraldi Cinthio found him altogether superior because of his elevation of diction.[81] Even Roger Ascham, who in that brief early flowering of Greek studies in England preferred Greek tragedy, commended 'our' Seneca's 'elocution and verse'.[82] Milton, who in general favoured Greece above Rome, found Euripides more congenial than his predecessors, a perfectly normal taste for the period, Euripides being the most rhetorical and 'Senecan' so to say of the three tragedians. Tastes change, and, if we wish to understand past ages, we must not patronize their preferences, and might even try to see a little with their eyes. It is easy to understand why, to an age addicted to *copia*, Seneca, with his taut but repetitive verbal brilliance, should have made a strong appeal. Moreover, the freedom of his plays from opaque local particulars – creating that effect of voices verbalizing in empty space disliked by many moderns – made him more useful to writers who knew little of early Greek religion and culture. But a liking for Seneca needs no apology; he had a restricted but powerful genius.

By far the best case for Shakespeare's use of Greek tragedy has been made by Emrys Jones.[83] He argues that two of the Renaissance's favourite Greek plays (which happen not to be to modern taste), both turned into Latin by Erasmus, could have influenced Shakespeare. *Titus* with its dual movement – great suffering followed by revenge – has structural affinities with Euripides' *Hecuba*, while the similarity between the quarrel scenes in *Julius Caesar* and in Euripides' *Iphigenia in Aulis* was noticed as early as the seventeenth century. However, structural arguments alone are always insufficient to prove direct influence. If we need a parallel for the structure of *Titus*, we can find it in Ovid's story of Philomela. Two quarrel scenes composed independently are likely enough to have similarities, and similarities of structure exist between works which are clearly unconnected. To give a Shakespearean example, the last two acts of *Timon*, where a stationary Timon is approached by a number of visitors, bear a striking resemblance to the structure of Aeschylus' *Prometheus Vinctus*, and, to a lesser extent, that of Sophocles' *Oedipus Coloneus*, plays which we have no reason to believe Shakespeare knew.[84] Likewise there are similarities between *Lear* and *Oedipus Coloneus*, and between Sophocles' *Electra* and *Hamlet*, which are simply the result of chance and the continuity of European culture and sensibility. So too there are analogies between Coriolanus' soliloquy in IV.iv.12ff. and Ajax's 'deception speech' (646ff.); both heroes recognize, but prove reluctant to accept, the world's 'slippery turns'. But for Shakespeare there were more readily available models for such heroic intransigence, for example in the Achilles of Chapman's *Iliad*, or in Virgil's Turnus. The essential thrust of Farmer's argument, it will be recalled, was that it is never enough merely to point to apparent resemblances.

Jones has a further, more specific argument. In *Titus* I.i.135–138 (an act that some scholars credit to Peele) there is a reference to the blinding by Hecuba of the Thracian king Polymestor, murderer of her son, 'in his tent'. Ovid has an account of the story, but with no reference to a tent (*Met.* XIII.536ff.); the pair simply go *in secreta* (555), to a secret place of hoarded gold. In Euripides Hecuba lures her enemy into *her* tent. Shakespeare's reference, unless we emend the

43

text, is thus distinct from either version, but is rather closer to Euripides'. But this seems a slender peg on which to hang Jones's thesis that Shakespeare had read through the whole play carefully (and, if so, why had he forgotten so theatrically significant and memorable a detail?). Perhaps Shakespeare derived the information by an indirect route (for example a handbook or an Ovid commentary); perhaps a friend told him about a performance of Euripides which he had seen; or perhaps Shakespeare was unconsciously recalling the story of Judith and Holofernes. While we would obviously like to be able to adduce a specific source, the most plausible view remains that Seneca was the closest Shakespeare ever got to Greek tragedy, but, to a man who could always make a silk purse out of a sow's ear, that was quite close enough.

# 2

# SHAKESPEARE'S OVID

Ovid was Shakespeare's favourite poet.[1] As Baldwin puts it, 'Ovid was Shakespeare's master of poetry.... No other poet ancient or modern receives such attention'.[2] The cynical might suggest that this could be because Ovid is the most accessible of the major Latin poets for someone with small Latin, but in fact Ovid nourished not only Shakespeare's imagination but that of the whole age. Less easy for a modern to understand, despite Ezra Pound's eccentric description of it as 'the most beautiful book in the language',[3] is Shakespeare's evident enthusiasm for Arthur Golding's translation of the *Metamorphoses* (1567). The problem with this version is partly metrical: the ambling jog-trot of the fourteeners is hard for a modern ear to accept, but the Elizabethans must have felt differently, and, as late as the 1590s, Chapman thought the metre the best to represent the hexameters of Homer's *Iliad*. We are often presented with an Ovid whose main features are wit and irreverence, but the Elizabethans also emphasized a vein of pathos, glamour and romance. For example, in *Faerie Queene* III.vi.45:

> And all about grew every sort of flowre,
> To which sad lovers were transformd of yore;
> Fresh *Hyacinthus*, *Phoebus* paramoure,
> And dearest loue,
> Foolish *Narcisse*, that likes the watry shore,
> Sad *Amaranthus*, made a flowre but late,
> Sad *Amaranthus*, in whose purple gore
> Me seemes I see *Amintas* wretched fate,
> To whom sweet Poets verse hath given endlesse date

we have the pathos of the Ovidian transformations – 'sad', 'fresh', 'foolish' – rueful memories of distant untimely fatalities. The Ovidian

45

setting provides a context for the resigned grief for the recently dead Sidney, and the whole is suffused with a kind of sweet melancholy frequently found in such Ovidian imitations. Shakespeare often strikes a not dissimilar note:

> In such a night
> Did Thisbe fearfully o'ertrip the dew,
> And saw the lion's shadow ere himself
> And ran dismayed away.
> In such a night
> Stood Dido with a willow in her hand
> Upon the wild sea banks, and waft her love
> To come again to Carthage.
> In such a night
> Medea gathered the enchanted herbs
> That did renew old Aeson.

In *The Merchant of Venice* V.i, in alternating speeches, the lovers Lorenzo and Jessica relate the moonlit night in which they find themselves to episodes from four great love stories (Troilus and Cressida, Pyramus and Thisbe, Dido and Aeneas, Medea and Jason, the first from Chaucer, the remaining three Ovidian, though all also handled by Chaucer) before the mood evaporates into mild teasing. Since all four are in fact stories of tragic love, a modern critic might feel that Shakespeare is being wry or ironic at the expense of his complacent lovers (the following banter reminds us of the deception of Shylock), but the timbre of the verse lends little support to such a reading; the romantic sweetness has been isolated from stories which turn out tragic or squalid or sinister. The lines on Dido (which seem to derive from *Heroides* X, Ariadne to Theseus, as well as VII, Dido to Aeneas) in particular are beautifully modulated, with several romantic details, the willow branch of the forsaken lover, the wild sea bank, the word 'waft' suggesting gentle melancholy and yearning. As Matthew Arnold colourfully put it, the whole passage is 'drenched and intoxicated with the fairy-dew of . . . natural magic'.[4] Thus when Shakespeare looked at Ovid he could find romance, but not only that; he could also find mastery of rhetoric, wit, humour, skilful storytelling, a delight in human foibles, an interest in women and love, a sceptical temper, a refusal to take sides or seriously endorse political ideologies, 'negative capability'. It all paints a curiously familiar picture – of Shakespeare himself. Small wonder then that Ovid was his favourite.

It is well known that Francis Meres in 1598 compared Shakespeare directly to Ovid: 'As the soul of Euphorbus was thought to live in Pythagoras, so the sweet, witty soul of Ovid lives in mellifluous and honey-tongued Shakespeare, witness his *Venus and Adonis*, his *Lucrece*, his sugared sonnets'.[5] Such comparisons are commonplace enough in the period, and in general do not need to be taken overseriously. In Shakespeare's case, however, it does seem that he may have started his career with a deliberate attempt to present himself as something of an English Ovid. His sonnets endlessly reflect on the ravages of time, echoing more than once Pythagoras' speech on the perpetual changefulness of things, a theme also handled, majestically, by Spenser in the *Mutabilitie Cantos* of the *Faerie Queene*.[6] A number of his early plays, from *Titus Andronicus* to *A Midsummer Night's Dream*, owe a large debt to Ovid, and above all his two narrative poems directly treat Ovidian subjects. It is worth observing the adjectives Meres uses to characterize the similarity between the two writers, not all of which would occur most immediately to a contemporary critic. We shall in due course argue that, in certain important respects, the two narratives are unlike Ovid; it is thus as well to acknowledge at the outset that there may be a gap of perception, or at least a considerable difference of emphasis, between Elizabethan and modern views of Ovid.

## PHILOMELA IN *TITUS* AND *CYMBELINE*

One early work of Shakespeare's in which Ovid is an important informing presence is his first tragedy, *Titus Andronicus*, or, to give it its full title, *The most lamentable Roman Tragedy of Titus Andronicus*,[8] perhaps first composed in 1592 and published in revised form in 1594. *Titus* used confidently to be described as a Senecan play. Certainly Seneca is quoted (or rather misquoted) in Latin (IV.i.81f; cf.II.i.135); Titus' cosmic fantasy in IV.iii.65ff. has a Senecan ring; the depiction of uncontrolled emotion leading to catastrophic consequences is central to Seneca's interests and understanding of psychopathology. Especially close to *Titus* in atmosphere is *Thyestes* with its brooding sense of evil and its climax in a cannibal feast. But neither the language nor the dramaturgy of *Titus* owe much to Seneca.

*Titus* is an ostentatiously classical play,[9] even though no modern Roman historian would recognize the picture of Rome it presents. It is peppered with allusions to classical mythology (e.g. I.i.136ff., 316; II.iii.61ff.; V.iii.80ff.), mostly deriving from Ovid or Virgil, and to

47

Roman history (e.g. IV.i.90f.; V.iii.36ff.). Ovid and Horace, as well as Seneca, are quoted in Latin (IV.iii.4; IV.ii.20f.),[10] and a character refers to Cicero's *Orator* (IV.i.14). There is much Latinate diction, for example 'obsequious' (V.iii.152 = 'dutiful in performing funeral rites') or 'successantly' (IV.iv.113), as well as the use of actual Latin phrases including the climactic word *stuprum*, 'rape' (I.i.98,185; II.i.133–135; IV.i.78; IV.iii.53f.).[11] Indeed the extent of this classical colouring has been used as an argument against Shakespeare's authorship; but a tendency to sow with the sack rather than with the hand is characteristic also of the Ovidian narratives, and is probably just a mark of early date (few of the references require any special learning). Most of the writing in the play is classical in a generalized way, without owing anything directly to particular Latin writers. Much of the verse of the first act, for example, is plain and 'manly', and quite free from the rhetorical over-elaboration and Ovidian (or Senecan) 'decadence' of which the play is sometimes accused on the basis of certain untypical passages. Thus Titus' lament for his sons employs a simple but moving heroic rhetoric, based on anaphora and balanced clauses, and culminating in a rolling line of the kind we are apt to think of as Miltonic:[12]

> In peace and honour rest you here, my sons;
> Rome's readiest champions, repose you here in rest,
> Secure from worldly chances and mishaps.
> Here lurks no treason, here no envy swells,
> Here grow no damned drugs, here are no storms.
> No noise but silence and eternal sleep.
>
> (150–156)

Even in the scene of the cannibal feast there is none of the verbal dexterity and slick wit of Ovid (however for word play in pathetic writing see III.ii.29: 'O handle not the theme, to talk of hands'). *Titus* contains more eloquent writing than is usually recognized, but it is seldom nuanced or detached in the Ovidian way:

> For now I stand as one upon a rock
> Environed with a wilderness of sea,
> Who marks the waxing tide grow wave by wave,
> Expecting ever when some envious surge
> Will in his brinish bowels swallow him.
>
> (III.i.93–97)

For I have heard my grandsire say full oft
Extremity of griefs would make men mad,
And I have read that Hecuba of Troy
Ran mad for sorrow.

(IV.i.18–21)

The moving final cadence of the second passage (another reference to Ovid's *Metamorphoses*) has more than a hint of Shakespeare's later verse mastery.

But if Ovid's influence should not be exaggerated, neither should it be downplayed. Ovid operates in *Titus* in two quite distinct ways. First, he provides a stylistic model for certain speeches. Secondly, his version of the story of Tereus, Philomela and Procne (*Metamorphoses* VI.424ff.) lies behind the play's action, and helps to characterize and control it. The story, one of violent rape and equally violent revenge, is perhaps the grisliest in the entire *Metamorphoses*. Tereus, the Thracian king, falls in love with his wife's sister Philomela, rapes her and cuts out her tongue. She contrives, nonetheless, to get a message, by means of a woven tapestry, to her sister Procne, who rescues her, and the two plot revenge. They cut up Tereus' son Itys and serve him to his father; when Tereus asks for Itys, the sisters reveal their plot. As he pursues the pair, they are all turned into birds, he into a hoopoe, they into a swallow and a nightingale. The story is told at length, in leisurely epic style, but probably also brought to its original readers memories of the more gruesome Republican tragedies, particularly those of Accius. There is considerable emphasis on tragic suffering, pathos and violent action, with many atmospheric and intensifying details. But aspects of Ovid's familiar virtuosity remain to undercut, distance, or complicate, from time to time, the reader's response, and puzzle us about the episode's tone. For example, when Philomela first appears radiant in both beauty and attire, she is compared, in an epic simile, to naiads and dryads stepping in the midst of woods, 'should one only give them refinement and clothing like hers' (451–454). The lightly pedantic qualification underlines the artificiality of the traditional form of the simile (where normally not all details correspond), and momentarily distracts us from the story and our 'natural' (or stereotyped) emotional responses to it. Neat Ovidian formulations, like the syllepsis *flagrat vitio gentisque suoque* (460: 'Tereus burns with both his own vice and that of his race'), or the paradox *perque suam contraque suam petit ipsa salutem* (477: 'Philomela asks [to visit her sister] by her own welfare and against it') are surprisingly pat for their contexts. While

49

Philomela's angry reaction to her rape is in general powerful enough, her ingenious paradoxes, framed in an elegant tricolon, *paelex ego facta sororis,/tu geminus coniunx, hostis mihi debita Procne* (537f: 'I am rendered my sister's rival, you a double husband, Procne a justified enemy to me') might seem over-ingenious for the situation. Violence horrifically described is part of the epic tradition from the *Iliad* onwards, but Ovid's polished description of the severed tongue of Philomela quivering on the ground, and in particular the un-expectedness but exactitude of the simile used to describe it, creates a certain aesthetic detachment, even pleasure, which co-exists with the horror:

> radix micat ultima linguae;
> ipsa iacet terraeque tremens immurmurat atrae,
> utque salire solet mutilatae cauda colubrae,
> palpitat et moriens dominae vestigia quaerit;
> hoc quoque post facinus (vix ausim credere) fertur
> saepe sua lacerum repetisse libidine corpus.
>
> (557–562)

*(The root of the tongue twitches, while the tongue itself lies there and quivering murmurs into the dark earth. Just as the severed tail of a snake is apt to twitch, it palpitates and dying seeks its mistress' feet. Even after this crime – I would scarcely dare believe it – Tereus, it is said, often repeated his characteristic lustful treatment of the mangled body.)*

The lightly interjected doubt about the final multiple rape of the mutilated girl is again puzzling in tone; is it genuine dubiety, or rhetorical intensification, or does it hint that we are engaged in a kind of prurient collusion with Tereus' action? Ovid's 'wit out of season', as Dryden termed it, is also evident in the cannibal feast. Tereus 'gorges his own flesh into his stomach' (651: *inque suam sua viscera congerit alvum*), and – improving upon the traditional conceit of a man-eating animal as 'the living tomb' of his victim – he describes himself as 'the wretched tomb of his own son' (665). When he asks for Itys, Procne taunts him with a grisly pun 'you have within (i.e. inside the room, or inside your stomach) the one whom you seek' (655: *intus habes quem poscis*). The final metamorphosis transposes the verbal ingenuity into a different key to create a mood of fantasy. The warrior Tereus, pursuing with his helmet and spear, becomes the crested hoopoe with its long beak, and there is word-play (probably

50

involving supposed etymology) in *vertitur in volucrem, cui stant in vertice cristae* (672: 'he turns into a bird, whose crest stands out on his head').

It could be argued that Shakespeare aims at similarly sophisticated effects, but – like the too easy association of *Titus* with the modern Theatre of Cruelty or of the Absurd – such a response may well be anachronistic. In all probability many Elizabethan readers saw nothing in Ovid's story but suffering, pathos and vengeance, merely intensified by Ovid's stylistic virtuosity and brilliant rhetoric. Certainly it was the pathos and tragic power of *Titus* – not some sophisticated ambivalence – that seems to have made it a long-lasting favourite with audiences. When the body of Bassianus is found in a pit (II.iii.231f.), Martius describes the corpse with an allusion to the *Metamorphoses*: 'So pale did shine the moon on Pyramus,/When he by night lay bathed in maiden blood'. The Ovidian evocation with its timbre of sweet romanticism – and how Shakespearean it is – is typical, as we have seen, of the Elizabethan response to the *Metamorphoses*, and would be more at home in one of the early romantic comedies. In this context it is likely to strike a modern as inappropriate – like Quintus' question which comes as near to unintentional farce as anything in the play: 'If it be dark, how dost thou know 'tis he?' (225) – but this is presumably the result of a failure of decorum, not of artful and deliberate disjunction, or of a controlled disproportion of style and matter, in Ovid's way. Closer to our Ovid – the post-modern Ovid, let us call him – is the description of Lavinia's severed tongue (III.i.82–86):

> O, that delightful engine of her thoughts,
> That blabbed them with such pleasing eloquence,
> Is torn from forth that pretty hollow cage,
> Where like a sweet melodious bird it sung
> Sweet varied notes, enchanting every ear.

But even here there is none of the disconcerting precision and coolness of Ovid, much more an emotional intensification.

All this has bearing on the much discussed speech of Martius when he finds the mutilated Lavinia (II.iv.11–57):

> Speak, gentle niece, what stern ungentle hands
> Hath lopped and hewed and made thy body bare
> Of her two branches, those sweet ornaments,
> Whose circling shadows kings have sought to sleep in...

51

Alas, a crimson river of warm blood,
Like to a bubbling fountain stirred with wind,
Doth rise and fall between thy rosed lips,
Coming and going with thy honey breath.
But sure some Tereus hath deflowered thee,
And, lest thou shouldst detect him, cut thy tongue...
And, notwithstanding all this loss of blood,
As from a conduit with three issuing spouts,
Yet do thy cheeks look red as Titan's face,
Blushing to be encountered with a cloud...
Fair Philomel, why she but lost her tongue,
And in a tedious sampler sewed her mind;
But, lovely niece, that mean is cut from thee.
A craftier Tereus, cousin, hast thou met,
And he hath cut those pretty fingers off.

Wolfgang Clemen criticizes the 'unsuitable and inorganic' images of the speech with their 'almost wanton playfulness',[13] which echoes similar criticisms of Ovid both in antiquity and thereafter, most notably perhaps in Dryden's comparison of Ovid and Chaucer.[14] Clearly Shakespeare has Ovid in mind, since Martius draws a careful parallel between the fates of Lavinia and Philomela. But the effect, as we read it, is not flippant or disorientating, but rather one of pathos and sorrow; a pathos reinforced, not undercut, by the rich, heady sweetness which modern audiences tend to find so disgusting when conjoined with violence. The style may derive from Ovid, but its impact is different. We cannot find here the tone of detachment of which some critics speak.

Another speech arguably designed to recall Ovid is Tamora's attempt to seduce Aaron, in which she presents a picture of a blissful summer landscape, a *locus amoenus* ripe for love (II.iii.10ff.):[15]

10    My lovely Aaron, wherefore look'st thou sad,
      When everything doth make a gleeful boast?
12    The birds chant melody on every bush,
      The snake lies rolled in the cheerful sun,
      The green leaves quiver with the cooling wind,
      And make a chequered shadow on the ground.
      Under their sweet shade, Aaron, let us sit...
21    And after conflict such as was supposed
      The wandering prince and Dido once enjoyed,
      When with a happy storm they were surprised,

24  And curtained with a counsel-keeping cave,
    We may, each wreathed in the other's arms,
    Our pastimes done, possess a golden slumber –,
    Whiles hounds and horn and sweet melodious birds
    Be unto us as is a nurse's song
    Of lullaby, to bring her babe to sleep.

There is some grace and charm in the diction. This is 'sweet' writing
which Elizabethans probably thought of as Ovidian, and which can
be compared to such things as Ovid's description of the morning air
and the birdsong as he lies in bed with his girl (*Amores* I.13.5–8). It is
true that the only allusion is to Virgil *Aeneid* IV, as Tamora relates the
nearby hunt to the one which brought Dido and Aeneas into their
intimacy in the cave.[16] The allusion is confidently made in the form of
a decorative parenthesis, and it is not really integral to her argument,
although it supports her amorous hints and supplies some poetic
grandeur. The style, however, is anything but Virgilian: 'conflicts'
presumably refers to the *militia amoris*, the warfare of love found in
love elegy; 'happy storm' is a paradox of an Elizabethan/Ovidian
kind; and the excessive alliteration of line 24 is more characteristic of
Elizabethan rhetorical schemes than of Virgil. In fact Shakespeare has
little of the Virgilian sensibility, and frequently Ovidianizes Virgilian
matter in this way. J.W. Velz's claim that a full study of Virgil and
Shakespeare is a key desideratum is thus misplaced;[17] we at least
would rather be spared it.[18] Tamora's 'sugared' style, the style of an
alluring seductress, means that there is no hint of her wickedness and
cruelty, and this again can puzzle readers used to Shakespeare's later
manner of characterization. Two points can be made. First, the mode
can be related to the later baroque 'affekt' approach to character; it is
emotions rather than personalities that are being imitated, as in a
Handel opera. It is indeed plausible that there is no difference between the expression of love or anger by a good man and by a bad. In
contrast to Tamora's lyricism Aaron is thinking only of his greed and
ambition, violent thoughts reflected in the change of timbre:

> Madam, though Venus govern your desires,
> Saturn is dominator over mine . . .
> Vengeance is in my heart, death in my hand,
> Blood and revenge are hammering in my head.

                                                            (30ff.)

It makes one think of Bottom's literary views: Aaron is speaking, like

Ercles, in 'a tyrant's vein', whereas Tamora, here dominated by Venus, is, like the lover, 'more condoling'. In general we have what we might call a typology of language, rather than the more complex relationship of character and language which Shakespeare later developed. Secondly, atmosphere is anyway more important here than character; later in the scene the same wood becomes a place of hellish horror to provide a backdrop for murder (91ff.).

More significant than these points of language and diction is Shakespeare's use of the Philomela story to provide a typology of action for his own plot. What is surprising here is the manner in which the characters themselves see the story in these terms. In a more sophisticated drama, this would give a flavour of extreme literariness, but here in *Titus* the effect remains fugitive and perverse. It is not just that Shakespeare is imitating, and trying to outdo, Ovid by 'improving' on the Philomela story (thus Lavinia has her arms cut off as well as her tongue so that she cannot send, like her predecessor, a message by means of a sampler), but that his characters sometimes use their knowledge of the story to plan their next actions. It is thus appropriate that Lavinia employs a copy of the *Metamorphoses* itself to reveal what has happened to her (IV.i.40ff.). The reference back to the model provides a curious mirror image of the proceedings; this is probably being used to intensify the pathos and the classical atmosphere, but it has possibilities of complexities not yet dreamed of, but realized, as we shall shortly see, in a famous scene in *Cymbeline*. So too Titus' choice of revenge is suggested to him by Ovid's story (V.ii.195f.), and, when he kills Lavinia to put her out of her shame, he relates his action to that of Virginius, who killed his daughter when she was threatened with rape by the tyrant Appius (V.iii.35–47). Traditional moral readings of Ovid's story are also relevant to Shakespeare's concerns in *Titus*; as Alexander Ross puts it in his discussion of the myth, 'there are two violent affections which make men shake off all humanity: the one is impotent [i.e. uncontrolled] lust, the other inordinate desire of revenge'.[19]

We have suggested that Shakespeare – like many of his contemporaries – may have read the Ovidian myth of Philomela differently from modern critics. One counter-argument would be that, when years later, in *Cymbeline*, he re-used some of the material we have been examining, the results were – in the modern sense – more genuinely Ovidian in the curious mixture of tones. (We would rather suppose that Shakespeare's conception of Ovid matured as he grew older.) In a remarkable *coup de theâtre* Iachimo emerges from a trunk to record the details of Imogen's chamber and of her person, so as to win his wager with Posthumus that she has been corrupted (II.ii). A number of motifs from *Titus* re-appear. Before falling asleep, Imogen has been reading 'The tale of Tereus' (a story clearly chosen for thematic reasons, not as characterization), stopping at the point 'Where Philomel gave up', that is just at the moment of the rape (45f.). Iachimo implicitly presents himself as a rapist –

> Our Tarquin thus
> Did softly press the rushes, ere he wakened
> The chastity he wounded
>
> (12–14)

– an Ovidian story (which Shakespeare treated in *The Rape of Lucrece*) evoked with unusual delicacy and understatement to reinforce the sense of stealth. His opening words have a brooding, *Macbeth*-like intensity (11f.: 'The cricket sings, and man's o'er-laboured sense/Repairs itself by rest'). There is a strong emphasis on female sexuality with the woman as victim. Of course no actual rape occurs, and the spirited Imogen, a girl who takes her future firmly into her own hands, is no passive instrument of male lust like the gentle Lavinia. But Iachimo's sophisticated wit associates the (male) audience with him in voyeurism and a prurient fascination at how far he will go (in the event he may possibly kiss her, and he closely inspects her left breast). The chamber itself, as later described to Posthumus, has an Ovidian opulence, with a silk tapestry showing the story of 'proud Cleopatra, when she met her Roman', and a chimney piece with 'chaste Dian, bathing' naked (perhaps putting us into the position of a peeping Actaeon[20]), as well as 'two winking Cupids/Of silver' (II.iv.66ff.), and there is too an Ovidian stress on the lifelike artistry of the work. Leonard Barkan has argued that Shakespeare, in *Titus*, shapes the story of Philomela around the issue of communication, a view of it shared by T.S. Eliot, who brooded on Ovid and Shakespeare when introducing the myth into *The Waste Land*: 'The change of Philomel, by the barbarous king/So rudely forced' (99f.). In *Cymbeline* too interpreting signs and relating them to reality is a central concern. In manner Iachimo's speech incorporates elements from earlier styles, and looks back, as scholars have demonstrated, to the lavishly conceited lyricism of *Venus and Adonis*, which again suggests a distinct Ovidian preoccupation:[21]

55

the flame of the taper
Bows towards her, and would under-peep her lids
To see the enclosed lights, now canopied
Under these windows, white and azure laced
With blue of heaven's own tinct.

(19–23)

By transposing the story into a tragi-comic mode, Shakespeare creates an effect which matches the tonal complexities of the *Metamorphoses*. *Cymbeline*, which wears its absurdities so archly on its sleeve, is too often stigmatized as experimental, or even incompetent. In reality Shakespeare wrote little to match its slick assurance, the highest of sophisticated high camp. A characteristic scene, which owes nothing directly to Ovid, but which Ovid might surely have applauded, is Imogen's discovery of the dead body of Cloten, which she mistakes for that of Posthumus. She is deeply moved, and in part moves the audience, but not only the obvious irony but also the intrinsic absurdity of some of her more extravagant verbal gestures, 'sincere' as they are, create a partly nervous reaction of laughter:

A headless man? The garments of Posthumus?
I know the shape of's leg; this is his hand,
His foot Mercurial, his Martial thigh,
The brawns of Hercules, but his Jovial face
– Murder in heaven! – How – ? 'Tis gone.

(IV.ii.308–312)

This superbly decadent mannerism is a very different sort of Ovidianism from the enchantments of the *Dream*, but one equally authentic.

## OVIDIAN NARRATIVE

In the 1590s there was a vogue for short mythological narrative poems in imitation of Ovid, sometimes today called *epyllia*, a term unknown to the Renaissance.[22] These examples of a sophisticated minor genre are the poetic equivalents, though inferior in both execution and power, to Titian's mythological *poesie*, which display a fully revived paganism, freedom from allegory, art for voluptuousness's sake, and powerful emotional complexity. For example 'The Rape of Europa', now in Boston, combines in a single image qualities not often found together in painting: it is erotic (as the girl's body is displayed to our gaze), witty (the knowing eye-contact by the bull with the (male?) viewer, the careering Cupids), but it has undercurrents too of menace in the dark clouds above, the dangerous romantic landscape, and the tempestuous seas ahead. The incorporation of these tonal complexities into an image of swirling motion constitutes an extraordinary pre-echo of the baroque mode.[23] None of the English narratives is in the same class, but the most accomplished and assured of the group, and the one which is most obviously a sophisticated Renaissance production in the new Italianate neo-classical manner, is undoubtedly Marlowe's *Hero and Leander*, which may well have pre-dated *Venus and Adonis* and set the fashion for the whole mini-genre.

Shakespeare wrote his two elaborate Ovidian narratives in 1593 and 1594 when the theatres were closed because of the plague.[24] They were something of a bid for fame and poetic seriousness. Plays were generally little regarded by the cognoscenti, and Shakespeare's reputation in his own lifetime rested in some circles more on the narratives than on any of his other works. There were no less than ten editions of *Venus and Adonis* and six of *Lucrece* by 1617. Shakespeare used a quotation from Ovid's *Amores* as an epigraph for *Venus and Adonis*: *vilia miretur vulgus; mihi flavus Apollo/Pocula Castalia plena ministret aqua* (1.15.35f.) (Let the crowd wonder at cheap things; for me let yellow-haired Apollo give cups full of the water of Castalia). The quotation was so well known that it does not prove that Shakespeare had read through *Amores* I in Latin.[25] The implicit claim to inspiration and the elitist contempt for the mob, together with the dedication to Southampton, show that Shakespeare was bidding high. In 1591 there had appeared a moralizing neo-Latin poem entitled *Narcissus* by one John Clapham, with a dedication to Southampton modest in tone, which plays on the notion of the poem as an *umbra* like Narcissus' reflection.[26] The modesty is justified, for *Narcissus* exemplifies Elizabethan classicism at its worst, suffering in particular from uncertainties of style and tone. For the opening allegorical sequence, in which Narcissus visits Cupid's palace, Clapham employs an epic manner with some Virgilian phraseology, which frequently sounds absurd in its new context; it is hard to believe that the foolish echo of the Sibyl's famous words about Hades, 'night and day it stands open', can be defended as wit. There are many further inept touches like the comparison of the lovers first to doves and then to crows looking for dead bodies. There is a lurch to a more Ovidian tone for Cupid's cynical advice on how to succeed in love, and for an abbreviated and moralized encounter between Narcissus and Echo, where Clapham attempts to overgo his original with elaborate echo effects. Ovidian turns are employed when Narcissus falls in love with his own image in the pool. For the death of Narcissus Clapham introduces details not in Ovid: when the image disappears at the coming of night, Narcissus drowns himself in the brook. (Shakespeare refers to the drowning in *Lucrece* 265f., and it is commonly encountered in Renaissance versions of the story.) We return to a more solemn manner for the final sequence, in which Venus pities Narcissus and arranges for him to be metamorphosed into a flower. Clapham cannot decide whether he requires pathos or moralizing, and in general he fails to integrate the Ovidian stylistic features with the moral and didactic tone. Incompetent as the poem is, it is likely (in view of the date and the dedication) that it provided the occasion for Shakespeare's decision to attempt an Ovidian mythological poem of a far more artistic and sophisticated kind. He may even have made use of the odd detail from Clapham, for example Venus' lament for Narcissus' beauty, and his transformation: the fair youthful Narcissus becomes a flower sacred to youth (*flos Iuventuti sacer*), illustrating the lot of the unfortunate lover. In this instance Shakespeare may thus have been able to use his small Latin to transform the basest of base metals into something rich and strange.

The story of Venus and Adonis is told briefly by Ovid in *Metamorphoses* X (510–559; 705–739), so that Shakespeare's poem represents a massive expansion of the original (*amplificatio*), something designed to show mastery of *copia*,[27] a quality which could be illustrated from Ovid himself, who frequently makes the same point twice or several times in different words (the speech of Hecuba in *Metamorphoses* XIII.494ff. was a stock example in the Renaissance). Shakespeare reproduces in a single work a multiplicity of tones, not necessarily found in every Ovidian story, but characteristic of the *Metamorphoses* as a whole, from near-farce to near-tragedy. Everywhere we find witty strokes, together with not infrequent touches of a broader kind of comedy, often signalled by jaunty rhymes which look forward to those in Byron's *Don Juan*, like 'For all my mind, my thought, my busy care,/Is how to get my palfrey from the mare' (383f.). But there are also passages of sensuous lyricism, most notably one that employs an image, derived from Ovid, of white on white (*Metamorphoses* IV.354f.):

> Full gently now she takes him by the hand,
> A lily prisoned in a gaol of snow,

Or ivory in an alabaster band –
So white a friend engirts so white a foe.

(361–364)

Shakespeare goes more deeply than Marlowe into the contradictions and complexities of sexuality, from the erotic topography of Venus' body (228ff.), a passage suggestive of Donne, at one extreme, to the hard pathos of her desperate 'motherly' search for her lover at the other: 'Like a milch doe, whose swelling dugs do ache,/Hasting to feed her fawn hid in some brake' (875f.). Shakespeare makes us sympathetic with Venus in her loss, even if he retains what Coleridge called his 'utter *aloofness*' of feeling;[28] not without reason has her 'For he being dead, with him is Beauty slain,/And Beauty dead, black chaos comes again' (1019f.) reminded many of *Othello*.[29] Ovidian too are the sudden shifts of tone within stanzas (e.g. 61–66), which complicate our response even to single moments in the story. What Shakespeare does not yet match is Ovid's delicacy. He handles the metamorphosis deftly so that, by a kind of elegant ring-composition, Adonis, described at the beginning by Venus as 'the field's chief flower' and 'more white and red than doves or roses are' is transformed at the end into a red flower 'chequered with white' (8–10; 1168–1170). But there is none of the wistful understated pathos of Ovid's picture of the windflower: '... *nimia levitate caducum/excutiunt idem, qui praestant nomina, venti*'(738f.) ('the same winds that give it its name shake off the flower, easily falling through its excessive fragility'). Shakespeare is not yet a poet like that.

The controlling image of Shakespeare's poem develops a metaphor from the *Metamorphoses*, found, for example, in the story of Apollo and Daphne – the opposition between hunting and love. The conceited description of the fatal wound, with its implication of sexual union, constitutes a kind of resolution: 'nuzzling in his flank the loving swine/Sheathed unaware the tusk in his soft groin' (1115f.).[30] In Ovid there is no suggestion that Adonis is an unwilling lover, but Shakespeare's reversal of the normal sexual stereotype, so that the woman becomes the predatory wooer and the man the reluctant object of her attentions, is entirely Ovidian in spirit, and indeed may well derive from the story of Salmacis and Hermaphroditus (*Metamorphoses* IV.285ff.), where we find a similar pattern, and which Shakespeare on a number of occasions fused with that of Venus and Adonis.[31] An active Venus is found in Spenser, Marlowe and other Renaissance poets, so that Shakespeare had simply to change a passive Adonis into a positively reluctant one. Hunter and hunted in the hunt of love, Shakespeare's pair are compared to wild animals, Venus, a woman large enough to pluck Adonis from his horse and tuck him under her arm (30–32), to an eagle and a vulture, the stripling Adonis to a netted bird, a dive-dapper and a roe (55ff.; 551ff.; 67,86,560ff.). Various details in the poem suggest that Shakespeare may have prepared himself by reading through the whole *Metamorphoses* in Golding's version. Thus his description of the boar echoes Golding's translation of Ovid's lines on the boar of Calydon, while Venus rushing entangled through the bushes recalls the flight of Daphne (619–630 = *Metamorphoses* VIII.281ff.; 871–84 = *Metamorphoses*. I.508f.).

But, while Ovidian in these respects, *Venus and Adonis* is also unOvidian in others. Whereas Marlowe's polished couplets allow him to match Ovid's style and attitude, Shakespeare's stanza, which wheels round upon itself, makes more difficult the achieving of an Ovidian manner. The poem moves slowly, and is encrusted with ornament, and it is almost a compendium of conceits and extended rhetorical tropes, which are both more elaborate than Ovid's and which impede narrative momentum. Ovid, of course, was admired for his stylistic virtuosity and witty rhetoric, so that Elizabethan readers may not have been alert to these differences. Indeed this manner was, for better or worse, part of Ovid's legacy. Again, unlike Marlowe, Shakespeare both shifts Ovid's story to England and emphasizes the natural setting, a combination which we shall meet again in his work, and which links the poem to a native tradition going back through Spenser to Chaucer, where the classical and the English meet on equal terms. There are brilliant vignettes (admired by Coleridge) – a hare pursued (679ff.), a snail retreating into his shell (1033ff.), a lark ascending:

> Lo, here the gentle lark, weary of rest,
> From his moist cabinet mounts up on high,
> And wakes the morning, from whose silver breast
> The sun ariseth in his majesty,
> Who doth the world so gloriously behold
> That cedar-tops and hills seem burnished gold.
>
> (853–858)

Shakespeare also replaces the expected mythological inset-narrative, typical of the genre, with the episode of the horse and the jennet (259ff.), which is presumably designed to show the 'normal' relation-

ship between male and female, and in which we find a characteristically 'English' feeling for equine beauty. (The commonplace source
for the description is Virgil, *Georgics* III, 75–94, although this does
not make the passage 'Virgilian'.[32]) Shakespeare's poem, opening
windows on to a wider world than Marlowe's, might have suggested
to the prescient that a greater than Marlowe was here, but the various
elements give the impression of being under a not quite perfect
control, and the whole is not without its longueurs. Marlowe's poem,
more limited in some ways, is more stylistically coherent and more
completely achieved, although his failure to finish it could suggest
that he sensed problems about incorporating the tragic sequel.

Despite any defects *Venus and Adonis* is one of the most glamorous productions of the English Renaissance, which deserved its high
reputation with contemporaries and which Ovid would surely have
been glad to have acknowledged as his offspring. By contrast many
modern readers feel that *The Rape of Lucrece*, presumably the 'graver
labour' referred to in the dedication to *Venus and Adonis*, is not a
success, despite its intriguing anticipations of later work, especially
*Macbeth*.[33] The reason, we would suggest, is that a fully tragic mode
does not suit an Ovidian poem, which calls rather for a mixed
serio-comic manner, something which Shakespeare subsequently
seems to have realized. There is a small army of interpreters eager to
find outstanding merits in Shakespeare's minor works, but it is
doubtful whether a failure to distinguish the great from the second-
rate serves anyone's interests. There are finer Elizabethan poems than
*Lucrece* which nobody except a few specialists bothers to read because they are not by Shakespeare, which might better be recommended to lovers of poetry. The problem with *Lucrece* is not
really its lack of unity (the switch from Tarquin to Lucrece), or
Lucrece's 'remorseless eloquence',[34] tedious though this is at times,
or the poem's prolixity (for this is true in a measure of *Venus and
Adonis*), or any confusion of Christian and pagan moral universes; it
is simply the fact that so little of the writing is especially distinguished. If Shakespeare had composed more lines like 'To stamp
the seal of time in aged things' (941) or (above all) 'she despairing
Hecuba beheld,/Staring on Priam's wounds with her old eyes'
(1447f.), we would be dealing with a poem of very different quality,
but it would not be an Ovidian poem.

Shakespeare seems to have prepared himself conscientiously for
his task, although (fortunately for him) the principal classical sources
were short and only two in number: Ovid, *Fasti* II, 685–852, which

Shakespeare presumably read in Latin (almost certainly in the standard edition of Paulus Marsus) because there was no published English translation at this date; and Livy I.57–60, which he probably read together with Painter's near-translation in *The Palace of Pleasure*. Marsus in his commentary correlated Ovid's version with Livy's, and comparing the two accounts was then – as now – a standard exercise.

It should be said immediately that Ovid's version is a superb example of his maturest art, and superior in every way to Shakespeare's. It has pace, elegance, economy, with details carefully selected to present clear, vivid scenes.[35] There are considerable technical problems about telling a story in elegiac couplets, particularly of the closed, polished Ovidian kind – significantly for the *Metamorphoses* Ovid employed hexameters – but he overcame them effortlessly; one may note, for example, the skilful use of the pluperfect tense as a means for moving from one discrete scene to the next. There are numerous elegances of style deployed with a lightness of touch which never interferes with the movement of the narrative. Ovid's Lucretia, surprisingly, far less rhetorical than Livy's and not given to the long, passionate outbursts of many of Ovid's heroines (in 825f. the repetition of *eloquar* mirrors her reluctance to speak), is presented, sensitively, as a tender woman led to suicide by shame; in his seemingly unreserved sympathy for her, Ovid is for once more like Gower than Chaucer. Ovid here eschews not only much of the complexity of tone with which he tends to treat such stories in the *Metamorphoses*, but also any hint of a high tragic manner. Despite the political context, the treatment of Lucretia takes us into an elegiac world of gentle pathos, not one of tragic or heroic gestures. Nothing is overdone, not even the villainy of Tarquin. It is an unusual, and yet unusually successful, example of Ovid's mature narrative art.

Despite some trivial verbal reminiscences (730; 409), Shakespeare shows no signs of trying to imitate the special qualities of the *Fasti* narrative. *Lucrece* is Ovidian in a more generalized way, employing a similar style to *Venus and Adonis* but transposed into a tragic key. Lucrece's complaints can be linked, to an extent, with the outbursts of various Ovidian heroines, like 'Ariadne passioning/For Theseus' perjury' mentioned in *Two Gentlemen of Verona* IV.iv.165f. (cf. *Heroides* X). Her address to Philomela (1128ff.) recalls a favourite story from the *Metamorphoses*. Tarquin's shifting thoughts may owe something to the divided monologues of such Ovidian heroines as Myrrha, reduced to turmoil and self-division over her desire for her

father. Ian Donaldson comments correctly that 'no other version of
the Lucretia story explores more minutely ... the mental processes of
the two major characters, their inconsistent waverings to and fro',
but his claim that Shakespeare found 'a new interior world of shifting
doubts, hesitations, anxieties, anticipations, and griefs'[36] ignores the
wider influence of Ovid (not to mention Euripides and Seneca), in
whom such shiftings are standard. There is also an aetiology (1747–
1750), and paradoxes, indecorous in this context, are thrown off
exuberantly in the manner of Ovid's Narcissus (*Metamorphoses*.
III.466ff.): 'But, poorly rich, so wanteth in his store/That, cloyed
with much, he pineth still for more' (97f.); 'And for himself himself
he must forsake' (157), together with one (730) possibly suggested by
a line in the *Fasti* (811): 'A captive victor that hath lost in gain'. More
significant, perhaps, is the *ecphrasis* (formal description) of the
painted hanging (or tapestry) depicting the sack of Troy and its
betrayal by Sinon, which Lucrece views after the rape, arguably the
finest continuous passage in the poem.[37] While the material for this
comes in the main from the *Aeneid* and *Metamorphoses* XIII, the idea
was perhaps suggested by the *Fasti*, where Ovid clearly forges a
thematic link between Tarquin's treacherous sack of Gabii and the
rape. Likewise Renaissance commentators compare Tarquin with
Sinon, relating the sack of Gabii to Virgil's narrative of the fall of
Troy. Shakespeare links Lucrece's body with a city under siege
(468f.:'This moves in him [Tarquin] more rage and lesser pity,/To
make the breach and enter this sweet city'). While *ecphrasis* is found
throughout ancient literature, and there are notable examples in the
*Aeneid*, Renaissance readers might still have thought first of Ovid.
Spenser had naturalized the Ovidian tapestry *ecphrasis* in English in
the *Faerie Queene*, and the emphasis on art – though characteristic of
the form as a whole – was rightly perceived as a particular Ovidian
concern. Moreover the *ecphrasis* constitutes a quasi-narrative 'digres-
sion' within the main story, which, as we have seen, is an Ovidian
feature of the genre.

   *Lucrece*, then, owes a good deal to Ovid. But brooding over it is the
dreary influence of the *Mirror for Magistrates* and the complaint
tradition, unintegrated with the more Ovidian elements. The address
to Night (771f.: 'O hateful, vaporous and foggy Night!/Since thou
art guilty of my cureless crime') makes one think all too quickly of
Pyramus' 'O grim-looked Night! O Night with hue so black,/O
Night, which ever art when day is not' (*Dream*, V.i. 168–169). The
extreme prolixity combined with lack of variety makes Ovid at his

most verbose seem economical. Passages of long straight moralizing, in the tradition of the moralized Ovids of the Middle Ages, replace the deft and frequently ironic comments of the narrator in the *Metamorphoses*, whose effect is so brilliantly captured by Marlowe – or rather by the fictional narrator – in *Hero and Leander*. The long conceited and prurient description of Lucrece in bed (386ff.) seems misjudged in this serious and tragic context; as we have seen, Shakespeare learned how to use this kind of material in *Cymbeline*. The fundamental mismatch of Ovidian style and tragic content in *Lucrece* repeats the failure of *Titus*. It was not a mistake which Shakespeare was to make again.

## OVID IN FAIRYLAND

We have argued that the two narrative poems, though they have Ovidian features, seem heavy-footed indeed when set alongside anything from the *Metamorphoses*. Paradoxically Shakespeare had to get further from Ovid to become more like him, and to achieve a deftness which is wholly Ovidian in a whole work. It is well known that *A Midsummer Night's Dream* (1596) follows no single source, and, in his Arden edition, Harold Brooks surveys, magisterially, a spectrum of sources and influences, probable and possible. We have nothing to add to his comprehensive list (though we might wish to subtract some items), but Brooks underestimates the central importance of Ovid.[38] The *Dream* is focussed on Ovidian concerns – metamorphosis, love and sexuality, identity and self-knowledge, art and illusion – which justify one classical scholar's description of it as 'Shakespeare's *Metamorphoses* – the most magical tribute that Ovid was ever paid'.[39] There are at least seven Ovidian features to the play.

### Metamorphosis

First and most immediately, there is metamorphosis itself, both literal and figurative, linked, as so often in the *Metamorphoses*, to erotic experience. At the centre is the transformation of Bottom. No one in Ovid is metamorphosed into an ass (although Midas receives ass's ears for his poor musical taste), so that it was probably from Apuleius' novel, *Metamorphoses* (usually known as *The Golden Ass*) that Shakespeare got the idea; even if – which is hard to believe – he had not read the Adlington translation of 1566, he was unlikely to have been ignorant of the story's principal motif.[40] Bottom's is only a partial transformation; this is presumably due mainly to theatrical convenience, but it also relates to a well-known iconographic type with which audiences would have been familiar. Actaeon, for example, is regularly represented in art not as a stag but as a man with a stag's head. In Titian's horrific painting of the death of Actaeon, now in the National Gallery in London, Actaeon is shown set back on the right of the picture, with a human torso but a stag's head and antlers, attacked by his dogs, while the left foreground is filled with the massive figure of Diana shooting an arrow and staring ahead of her unremittingly, pitilessly indifferent to his fate, an overwhelming image of divine power. The element of cruelty is as great as in Ovid's original narrative, and the depiction of the victim as half-man, half-beast increases the bizarre atmosphere of nightmare horror. What is removed – as generally with Bottom – is the full sense of what it might be like to be an animal which Ovid, whose Pythagoras in *Metamorphoses* XV is a defender of vegetarianism, sometimes explores. When the changed Actaeon 'casts his looks as if they were his arms round the dogs, like someone beseeching' (*Metamorphoses* III.240f.), we have an accurate picture of a stag at bay as well as of the pleading gestures of the doomed Actaeon. It is true that Bottom is given certain animal tastes; in particular in IV.i.32f. he expresses 'a great desire to a bottle [i.e. truss] of hay', but he asks for it politely, even diffidently, in a way that is wholly human (but for the joke it might as well be a mug of ale).

Metamorphosis in Ovid is of varying significance. Sometimes it is a reward, sometimes a punishment or at least a resolution of an intolerable dilemma; sometimes it confirms a person's fundamental character, sometimes it involves a more mysterious and genuine change of nature. For example Lycaon, whose wolf-like character is suggested by his name, is turned into a wolf (Greek *lykos*), but there is no such connection between Callisto's 'fault' in becoming pregnant and her transformation by Juno into a bear, which rather prepares for her stellification as the Great Bear (I.218ff.; II.409ff.). The exegetical tradition tended to simplify the picture by stressing the degrading effects of sin and passion as the root cause of downward metamorphosis; so, in the story of Pyramus and Thisbe, the staining of the mulberry could be read as the corruption of love by passion. One could argue, on a crude level, that Bottom's character as an ass is confirmed by his physical transformation. But, whereas there is nothing more to Lycaon than his wolfish nature, Bottom is far too richly characterized to be merely an embodiment of asininity.

During his period of change (about which he understands little) he remains gloriously himself, ridiculous, vain, cocksure, ebullient, kindly, an inspirer of affection in others, a source of life and delight.

By contrast the lovers and Titania undergo psychological change. Titania is degraded (even if in the long term this does not seem greatly to matter), but ultimately for the lovers metamorphosis proves a healing process, an exploration of their identity and sexuality as a preparation for marriage. Bottom's literal metamorphosis thus underpins transformations of other kinds, the various plots being cunningly intertwined, a common Shakespearean feature brought to its highest pitch of art in *Twelfth Night*. Recent critics rightly stress the erotic nature of the play (the salacious speculate on whether or not the doting Titania actually copulates with Bottom); in the end the misdirected eroticism is redeemed by a movement towards harmony, marriage and fertility. By contrast in Ovid there is a strong emphasis on rape and various forms of perverse sexuality, and there are surprisingly few children of sexual union. In that sense the *Dream*, like the *Faerie Queene* to which it is perhaps indebted and which celebrates the chaste union of lovers in marriage, might seem anti-Ovidian as well as Ovidian, although it is doubtful whether Shakespeare is taking this stance as consciously as the more explicitly philosophical and 'intellectual' Spenser. In Bottom's well-known speech after his restoration (IV.i.199ff.) there is also a hint of mystical experience by a holy fool, however comic his language and however garbled the quotation from Corinthians. In particular the sentence 'It shall be called Bottom's dream, because it hath no bottom' is not only humorous in its general absurdity and abuse of a famous philological joke (*lucus a non lucendo*), but hints at the possibility that his dream – like the play as a whole – has a bottomless profundity (the 1557 Geneva New Testament actually has the phrase 'the bottom of God's secrets' in I Corinthians 2 v.10).[41] Similarly, when Demetrius says of the lovers' experience in the forest 'These things seem small and undistinguishable,/Like far-off mountains turned into cloud' (IV.i.186f.), the language looks forward to later and greater images of insubstantiality and flux in *Antony and Cleopatra* and *The Tempest*, passages which suggest that the things of this world pass away – the insubstantiality of fantasy mirrors the insubstantiality of the whole sublunary world.

## Art

The doctrine that all art is about itself holds widespread sway in the academy. Impatience with it should not prevent us acknowledging that some works of art reflect on their fictional status.[42] The concern of the *Dream* with art and illusion links with a central preoccupation of the *Metamorphoses* and of Ovid's poetry generally. In *Amores* III.12 and *Ex Ponto* IV.8 Ovid praises the transforming power of the imagination. It is poets who create the world of myth, even in a sense, the gods themselves (*Ex Ponto*, IV.8.55f.). The *Metamorphoses* is much more than a poem about writing poetry, but art and artists are certainly central to it. Indeed this may help to explain Ovid's choice of subject; for, as one critic puts it, 'What is poetry but a metamorphosing power, turning fantasy to shapes and giving what is mortal a kind of immortality?'[43] In *Tristia* II.64 Ovid gives the subject of the *Metamorphoses* as 'bodies changed in an incredible manner' (*in non credendos corpora versa modos*), and in antiquity metamorphosis was a byword for unreality. Hence the challenge of the subject for a poet: metamorphosis was chosen as a theme so unreal that only the poet's art could give it substance. A number of stories directly concern artistic creation (Arachne, Marsyas, Orpheus, Pygmalion), while others could be seen in this light, for example that of Icarus who has been taken as a type of the aspiring artist. In the *Dream* art is primarily that of the actor and the playwright, and the actors presenting the play to us are mirrored by Bottom and his friends within the action. At the beginning of the play love and imagination are linked, and various other themes adumbrated, in Egeus' description of Lysander's courtship of his daughter:

> Thou, thou, Lysander, thou hast given her rhymes,
> And interchanged love-tokens with my child;
> Thou hast by moonlight at her window sung
> With faining voice verses of feigning love,
> And stol'n the impression of her fantasy
> With bracelets of thy hair, rings, gauds, conceits.
>
> (I.i.28–33)

Here we have the moon, lovers, art capturing the imagination, love and art stigmatized for their deceitfulness. The well-known exchange between Theseus and Hippolyta (V.i.1ff.) makes explicit much that until then has been hovering just below the surface of our consciousness.[44] Theseus, whose sceptical character had already been partly established in the tradition by Chaucer, doubts the story of the lovers. To him such strong imagination has little authority; it simply creates untruths in lunatic and in lover. Nevertheless his description of poetry, even if in its context intended as largely dismissive, grants it considerable power:

> The poet's eye, in a fine frenzy rolling,
> Doth glance from heaven to earth, from earth to heaven;
> And as imagination bodies forth
> The forms of things unknown, the poet's pen
> Turns them to shapes and gives to airy nothing
> A local habitation and a name.
>
> (12–17)

In a more tentative way Hippolyta replies that the story, even if outside normal experience, has a consistency which suggests reality. If we take this exchange purely within the drama Theseus is clearly wrong: the lovers have not just been dreaming, for we have seen the activity of the fairies with our own eyes. If, on the other hand, his is taken as a general comment on art and poetry, or as a comment from within on the *Dream* itself, the question becomes more complicated. The dialogue then obliquely raises the issue of the truth and value of fictional enterprises, of theatrical performance, of fantasy. A later comment by Theseus moderates, somewhat, his position. To Hippolyta's description of the play of Pyramus as 'the silliest stuff that ever I heard' (207), Theseus replies 'The best in this kind are but shadows, and the worst are no worse if imagination amend them'. Thus, although he continues to insist on the unreality of art, if with more metaphysical subtlety, he allows the imagination of the recipient a more constructive role. The epilogue continues to play on the question of the 'shadowy' quality of fictions, linking the status of the fairies with that of art, and on the need for the audience and actors to co-operate:

> If we shadows have offended,
> Think but this, and all is mended,
> That you have but slumbered here
> While these visions did appear;
> And this weak and idle theme
> No more yielding but a dream,
> Gentles, do not reprehend;
> If you pardon, we will mend.
>
> (409–416)

## Pyramus and Thisbe

The preoccupation with the art of the actor and writer links with one of the principal sequences in the *Dream*, the preparation and performance of a play and one which furthermore is shaped around the issue of illusion and dramatic representation, its subject taken directly from Ovid's *Metamorphoses* (IV.55ff.). On a first reading the romantic story of Pyramus and Thisbe, of young love thwarted leading to tragedy, which resembles in so many ways that of Romeo and Juliet, appears, despite the somewhat declamatory style of some of the speeches, largely free from the witty strokes that complicate the story of Philomela. But when we reach the death of Pyramus we encounter a surprising simile (probably with sexual implications) which compares the blood spurting from his wound as he lies on his back to water bursting out of a lead pipe (a simile echoed by Shakespeare, in a tragic context, in *Titus* II.iv.30). This apparent touch of grotesque wit, while it may undercut, does not destroy the pathos of the story as a whole, which certainly does not merely parody tragic love. On the other hand, on subsequent reflection, we may decide, in the light of the simile, that there are other details – the lovers kissing through the wall, or talking through the chink – which have a comic potential, even if the poet has not chosen to develop it very far; so, as also happens with Chaucer, even in seemingly 'serious' writing the overall tone remains curiously elusive. At the very least we may say that there is a potential element of absurdity in Ovid's story – even more marked in Golding's translation of it [45] – which Shakespeare has chosen to exploit. In the Middle Ages and thereafter it became a set vehicle for rhetorical display, and Shakespeare is also commenting on that tradition. Peter Quince's play is an affectionate portrayal, by a supreme professional, of amateur theatricals – the abrasive Jonson, always contemptuous of theatrical incompetence, would have made something very different of such a scene – and perhaps too, one might guess, of school performances, particularly if Shakespeare had indeed been a schoolmaster. It is not difficult to imagine what a class of schoolboys might make of Ovid's story, and 'Ninny's tomb', in particular, sounds like a schoolboy joke, one given extra point, perhaps, by Golding's tendency to anglicize Latin names to produce such oddities as 'Orphey' and 'Tarpey' (Orpheus and Tarpeia). Even in Ovid's Latin a schoolboy could find obscene possibilities in the *rima tenuis* (65), Shakespeare's 'crannied hole or chink' (157:

'cranny' is Golding's word), and Shakespeare locates suitable *double entendres* in the business, like Thisbe's words to the wall 'My cherry lips have often kissed thy stones' (188). All this is mere speculation, but Shakespeare's sense of amateur performances and performers, for example Bottom's desire to play all the parts (I.ii.16ff.), or the tendency of amateurs to return to their old mistakes in the stress of the moment (compare III.i.92 with V.i.200), is extraordinarily persuasive. Scholars have adduced a considerable number of works which Shakespeare could have been parodying,[46] but it might be better to regard them as sources for particular verbal follies rather than as direct objects of parody. Experience shows that audiences will laugh at burlesques without looking for a specific target, while the crucial point in any performance of the *Dream* is the contrast between the ridiculous and old-fashioned rhetorical texture of the 'stage' play and the stylistic assurance of the rest.

The mechanicals employ an extraordinary stylized manner of representation, in which actors impersonate inanimate objects; and everything that occurs is constantly explained to the audience. The irrepressible Bottom twice breaks vital theatrical convention by responding to the comments of the lovers on what is happening in the performance. And yet the mechanicals are convinced that it will be difficult for their audience to distinguish art and life. Accordingly in the rehearsal scene (III.i.8ff.) Bottom recommends that in order that the ladies should not be frightened, a prologue should explain that no one is actually killed and even that Pyramus is only Bottom the weaver. Yet paradoxically the more crazy their views on art and the more creaky their play, the easier it is for the theatre audience to accept the reality of the mechanicals themselves. Bottom, by being a bad actor in his own play, becomes outside it more than just an actor. There is a further paradox. Foolish as it is, the play allows the main features of Ovid's narrative – the wall, the moon, the lion, the bloodied garment – to retain their haunting presences. The play's very richness of nonsense makes the brittle and patronizing comments of the stage audience seem thin, trite and reductive. This is a familiar trick of Shakespeare's. In *2 Henry IV* (II.iv), a hidden Hal and Poins mock the aged Falstaff and Doll as they exchange words of love, but the more expressive texture of Falstaff's language turns the tables on the youthful mockers, so that it is they who are trivialized. Even Theseus' comment 'That is hot ice and wondrous strange snow' on the foolishly paradoxical title 'A tedious brief scene of young Pyramus and his love Thisbe, very tragical mirth' is curiously double-edged. 'Icy fire' is one of the great central metaphors of Petrarchan love poetry, an oxymoron which had been used to explore the contradictions of erotic experience. Theseus' superior 'How shall we find the concord of this discord?' (60) could thus be answered: in love, in poetry, in religion, in all those areas where the literal meaning of words is inadequate to express experiences beyond them and which our new pedants term 'mystifications'. Theseus chooses the play of Pyramus from among a selection of four subjects, of which two more – the battle of the Centaurs and Lapiths, a particularly disastrous wedding feast, and the dismemberment of Orpheus by the Bacchantes – come from Ovid. The love story is chosen for reasons of decorum, but the other subjects remind us of different, more violent aspects of the *Metamorphoses*, and thus may be an acknowledgement by Shakespeare that the enchantments of the *Dream* reflect in the main only the milder, less cruel aspects of Ovid's world.

## The Style of the Lovers' Couplets

For the speeches of the lovers Shakespeare used generally end-stopped rhyming couplets instead of blank verse. Here again there is an Ovidian connection, this time not with the *Metamorphoses*, but with the elegiacs of the love poetry. Marlowe had used heroic couplets, as the best English equivalent for Latin elegiacs, for his influential translation of the *Amores*, and Michael Drayton, in his modernizing of the *Heroides* in *England's Heroical Epistles* (1597), achieved at times a remarkable anticipation of Augustan practice. The couplet, with its potential for balance, antithesis and pointing, underwent a process of continual refinement throughout the seventeenth century, in preparation for the packed crystallizations of Pope. By contrast Shakespeare's couplets seem to a modern ear distinctly stiff, but certainly they aim to achieve an Ovidian effect in their use of obtrusive rhetorical figures and schemes, their antitheses and word-plays. For example in 'The one I'll slay, the other slayeth me' (II.i.190) the words are arranged in a pattern around a strong central caesura, 'the one' balancing 'the other' and the remainder forming a chiasmus (ABBA) 'I'll slay . . . slayeth me', with antithesis (reversal of subject and object, I/me) and variation of the same word ('slay'/'slayeth'). Helena's speech (I.i.181–185):

> Call you me fair? That fair again unsay!
> Demetrius loves your fair; o happy fair!

Your eyes are lode-stars, and your tongue's sweet air
More tuneable than lark to shepherd's ear,
When wheat is green, when hawthorn buds appear,

with the pleasing variety of its final triplet, manages to achieve a
measure of sweet lyricism and delicate feeling, but similar ostentatious 'elegances' are still employed for our delectation: balance
(strong central caesuras in four out of five lines); word play (the four
times repeated 'fair', 'air'/'ear'); chiasmus ('call fair … fair unsay');
antithesis ('eyes … tongue').[47] The couplets can be seen as part of the
creation of an Ovidian perspective, at once beautiful and comic. But
Ovid devoted much of his life to refining the elegiac couplet, so it is
small wonder if, beside him, Shakespeare appears somewhat of a
tyro. Ovid's influence proved happier in the blank verse and lyric
sections of the play.

## Faerie

The fairies in the *Dream* can in part be seen as a modernization of
Ovid's gods.[48] There was a tradition equating the classical gods with
the world of faerie. In the Middle English lay *Sir Orfeo* Heurodis (=
Eurydice) is not snatched away by Pluto but disappears into fairyland. More witty and self-conscious is the conflation in *The Merchant's Tale*, where Pluto and Proserpine are king and queen of the
fairies – and live at the bottom of Januarie's garden – and yet many of
the details of the classical myth are retained:

in that gardyn, in the ferther syde,
Pluto, that is kyng of Fayerye,
And many a lady in his compaignye,
Folwynge his wyf, the queene Proserpyna,
Which that he ravysshed out of Ethna
Whil that she gadered floures in the mede –
In Claudyan ye may the stories rede,
How in his grisely carte he hire fette –
(*Canterbury Tales* IV.2226ff.)

Similarly, when Chaucer translated Virgil's picture of Venus in the
guise of a hunting nymph (*Aeneid* I.319) *venatrix dederatque comam
diffundere ventis* as 'goynge in a queynt array/As she had ben an
hunteresse,/With wynd blowynge upon hir tresse' (*House of Fame*,
I.228–230), he takes Venus, in the words of one scholar, 'as the kind

of spirit he understands', and makes her into 'one of the faery hunt'.[49] As we have seen Shakespeare in the same vein turned Medea's gods into English elves for Prospero's speech of renunciation. The name Titania (daughter of Titan) suggests a classical goddess, and is presumably taken from the *Metamorphoses*, where it is used of both Circe and Diana. (This is usually regarded as proof that Shakespeare read Ovid in the original, since Titania does not appear in Golding. The argument is less than decisive, since Shakespeare could have come across the name in some dictionary or handbook, although admittedly it does not appear in Cooper's *Thesaurus*.) Like Ovid's gods, Shakespeare's fairies are menacing and powerful, with a control over nature and men, even if they are ultimately more benign. Titania and Oberon, whose quarrel resembles to an extent those of Ovid's Jupiter and Juno, have a double function, as presiding orderly powers and as forces more disruptive and irrational. In general Shakespeare again softens the picture in Ovid, which stresses the gods' cruelty and heartlessness.

## Aetiology

Many of the stories in the *Metamorphoses* are aetiological, that is, like Kipling's *Just So Stories* they give the *origins* of a particular phenomenon. For example the story of Salmacis and Hermaphroditus explains the enervating powers of a pool in Caria, while that of Phaethon, who set the world on fire, contains a witty incidental aetiology when he turns the Ethiopians black. Spenser had been the first poet to naturalize the Ovidian aetiological narrative in English in the *Faerie Queene*, and numerous poets soon followed in his footsteps. Oberon's account of the origins of love-in-idleness with its power to induce love at first sight (II.i.148–174) is an *aition* in the form of a short self-contained narrative, except that the brief exchange with Puck gives it a dramatic context and immediacy. In the first part Oberon gorgeously sketches in a dreamy, romantic nightscape for his account of Cupid's flight, with numerous exotic details: himself listening enchanted on a promontory, the mermaid on a dolphin's back calming the sea, while the stars, in contrast stimulated into wilder motion, shoot madly from the sky to listen to her song. The story of the origins of the flower proceeds with a certain briskness and despatch, though each gesture and moment is sharply drawn. The slickness and economy of the style has an Ovidian ring, combining a hint of sophisticated detachment from the story with a romantic, sweet melancholy about the flower:

> Yet marked I where the bolt of Cupid fell:
> It fell upon a little western flower,
> Before milk-white, now purple with love's wound,
> And maidens call it 'love-in-idleness'.

(165–168)

The staining of the flower is probably taken from the story of Pyramus and Thisbe, where the dying Pyramus stains the formerly white mulberry red with his blood, which was frequently, as we have seen, taken as an image of the effects of passion.

## Echoes

Finally, there are a number of direct verbal echoes of Ovid and Golding. For example, 'night's swift dragons' (III.ii.379) probably derive from Medea's chariot (VII.218f.) and Theseus' hunting speech (IV.i.118ff.) owes something both to Actaeon's hounds and to the bulls of Colchis driven by Jason. The most interesting of these echoes occurs in what is perhaps the finest speech in the play and one of the most classicizing, Titania's account of the 'distemperature' in nature caused by her quarrel with Oberon, which culminates in a surreal vision of confusion in the seasons, a version of the impossibility *topos* (*adyneton*), a figure common in classical poetry (II.i.103–117):

> hoary-headed frosts
> Fall in the fresh lap of the crimson rose;
> And on old Hiems' thin and icy crown
> An odorous chaplet of sweet summer buds
> Is, as in mockery, set; the spring, the summer,
> The childing autumn, angry winter, change
> Their wonted liveries.

(107–113)

The lines have their background in Spenser and Ovid/Golding (the four seasons in the palace of the Sun, *Metamorphoses* II.27–30; and in Pythagoras' speech, XV.199–213), with a further possible link with Medea's alteration of the seasons in *Metamorphoses* VII.[50] The 'hoary-headed frosts' are not quite the figures of a Spenserian procession, although they are fleetingly so: the lines oscillate between a personification of aspects of nature, with erotic overtones, involving a weird but vigorous union of youth and age, and a description, of some precision, of a phenomenon in nature. Similarly the masque-like figure of Hiems as an old man covered in ice but wearing a garland of roses partly dissolves into a description of a wintry scene; for the words 'thin and icy' do not properly cohere with the depiction of the head of a fully anthropomorphized figure (hence, perhaps, the First Quarto's 'chin' for 'thin'). The trick is typical of Ovid; in XI.157ff. Mount Tmolus is at one moment a fully anthropomor-phized god, at the next the mountain itself with its nodding trees. For the description of Hiems Shakespeare remembered both Ovid's La-tin and Golding's translation. Golding has Winter, not Hiems (who, incidentally, is a female, not a male figure in Ovid), but his elab-oration of Ovid's line *glacialis Hiems, canos hirsuta capillos* ('icy winter bristling with white hair') into

And lastly quaking for the cold, stood Winter all forlorn
With rugged head as white as dove and garments all to-torn,
Forladen with the icicles that dangled up and down
Upon his grey and hoary beard and snowy frozen crown,

has obviously left its mark on Shakespeare's phrasing.

Ovid in sum is the author most insistently evoked in the *Dream*, but, as we have seen, generally in a partly romanticized form. That is Shakespeare's way, at this stage of his career, with other classical authors as well. From the dry, matter-of-fact list of Theseus' amours in North's translation of Plutarch's *Life of Theseus*, he produced a passage where the rich orchestration of classical names combines with the night-time, moonlit setting to create an opulently suggestive picture:

Didst not thou lead him through the glimmering night
From Perigouna whom he ravished,
And made him with fair Aegles break his faith,
With Ariadne and Antiopa?

(II.i.77–80)

Similarly the Ovid of the *Dream* is one largely, though by no means wholly, purged of the elements of cruelty, sadism and perversion which run, with a thread of violence, through the *Metamorphoses*. We have, in other words, an enchanted version of Ovid.

Twice in subsequent plays we again find Shakespeare with Ovid in fairyland. In *The Merry Wives of Windsor* (V.v) at midnight in the forest Falstaff, disguised as Herne the Hunter, and wearing the horns which make him into a comic Actaeon, an icon of lust, is burned and beaten, with surprising violence, by the 'fairies'. Yet, as Barkan suggests, the 'mythic picture' means that Falstaff is able to pull 'from the jaws of degradation something of Bottom's visionary glory'.[51] In *The Tempest* Ovid is more deeply concealed. In fact there is a whole trail of references to Virgil's *Aeneid*, which critics in vain have tried to make into a significant pattern:[52] the storm (though the main source here is the *Naufragium* from Erasmus' *Colloquies*), Ferdinand's meeting with Miranda recalling Aeneas' with Venus, the obscure jokes about 'widow' Dido, the Harpies, Iris and Juno in the masque (I.i.; I.ii.424ff.; II.i.73–97; III.iii.52; IV.i.60ff. and 102); perhaps too there are Virgilian resonances in Prospero's quasi-epic account of his exile, in particular I.ii.128f. 'one midnight/*Fated* to the purpose'. Yet the Virgilian material is firmly adapted into an Ovidian romance mode, where the magic island sets the dominant tone, and where we re-encounter the familiar Ovidian concern with art and illusion. The betrothal masque (IV.i), classical in manner, is written in a highly artificial verse style, typical of masque, stately and static, which creates a sense of distance and unreality. Perhaps it is in part a pastiche of Shakespeare's sense of the popular Ovidian poetry of his youth, now seen as a faraway memory, beautiful but outdated and fragile. Certainly some of the details, for example Juno's peacock-drawn chariot or Ceres' reference to 'dusky Dis' and his rape of her daughter, could come from Ovid, and if the stilted style seems remote from Ovid's polish, the masque nevertheless richly evokes the glamorously peopled world of an anglicized *Metamorphoses*:

> You nymphs, called Naiades, of the windring brooks,
> With your sedged crowns and ever-harmless looks,
> Leave your crisp channels, and on this green land
> Answer your summons.

> (128–131)

Thus perhaps it is not surprising that shortly afterwards – and we are here making a point about the play, not about Shakespeare's life-history – Shakespeare, through Prospero, says a last lingering farewell to his Ovid, and through him to the world of high fantasy and imagination in which both of them had so revelled.

# PYGMALION IN *THE WINTER'S TALE*

Occasionally Shakespeare uses a story pattern out of Ovid as a basis for a sequence of his own, without attempting a recognizably Ovidian tone (for example, Richard II seems to be modelled to some extent on Narcissus[53]). The most familiar example of the technique occurs in the final scene of *The Winter's Tale*, which is partly patterned on Ovid's story of Pygmalion (*Metamorphoses* X.243–297: the statue does not feature in *Pandosto*, the main source.)[54] This is one of the finest stories in the poem, and as fine an example of Ovid's mythopoeic powers as the familiar account of Orpheus' loss of Eurydice through a fatal backward glance is of Virgil's. In both cases modern readers often assume that this is the original version of the myth, whereas in fact – in these their classic formulations – they are creations of the Augustan poets. The story which Ovid remodelled apparently concerned a king of Cyprus who had sexual intercourse with a statue, an action which perhaps constituted a 'sacred marriage' with the goddess Aphrodite. It was Ovid who made Pygmalion a sculptor and the statue his creation, eventually brought to life and marriage by Venus. In this form the story has the inevitability and shapeliness which we associate with the great myths. Ovid has retained from his source a strongly erotic character, which he never quite pushes firmly in the direction of definite sexual perversion. Even his arch comment that the statue looked as beautiful naked as adorned (266) does not destroy the unexpected, underlying sense of innocence: the description of Pygmalion's actions as the statue's lover, suggestive of the world of Roman love elegy (the winning words; the bringing of gifts, including shells, birds and flowers; the kissing and fondling) is witty and touching rather than merely salacious. In the final metamorphosis joy and a sense of miraculous release as stone becomes flesh prevails against any encroachment of the grotesque. The atmosphere is wholly different from that of Marston's *The Metamorphosis of Pygmalion's Image*, a poem by turns satiric, voyeuristic and lubricious, based on Ovid's story and published in 1598.

Like so many Ovidian stories, this one can be taken purely as narrative, or it can be expounded in some sense which could be called allegorical. Modern readers – influenced in part no doubt by *The Winter's Tale* itself and by the nineteenth-century popularity of the story as a fable about art – normally treat it as an exploration of the relationship between art and life. Although such a reading ignores, or

77

downplays, the prevailing eroticism – which is seen merely as a source of wit in the telling – it seems to make sense of several features of the story: the fact that Pygmalion is an artist, the emphasis on his skill, the comment that the statue seemed to live and to wish to move, so much did the artistry conceal itself by artistry (252: *ars adeo latet arte sua*). Oddly enough readers and commentators in the Middle Ages and Renaissance seem in general to have taken the story differently. Pygmalion was seen either as an example of the devoted lover, as he is by the indulgent Gower (*Confessio Amantis*, IV.371–450), or as a warning against misplaced passion. Thus Golding, in his verse *Epistle*, claims that

> The tenth book chiefly doth contain one kind of argument,
> Reproving most prodigious lusts of such as have been bent
> To incest most unnatural.

(213–215)

However he does not explain how, in this light, he would read the Pygmalion story itself, with its happy dénouement, so different from the fate of the incestuous Myrrha in the one which follows. George Sandys, whose substantial commentary, published with his translation of the *Metamorphoses* in 1632, contains much tralaticious lore relevant to the earlier period, also seems ill at ease with Pygmalion.[55] After observing, with some banality, that it is not 'extraordinary for excellent artisans to admire their own skill', he suggests of the statue that 'the life which was given it by the goddess was no other than the grace and beauty of the figure'. He then offers a different allegorization of the kind known as 'historical', that the statue 'may be some virgin on whom Pygmalion was enamoured, who, long as obdurate as the matter whereof she was made, was mollified at length by his obsequiousness'. Such allegories may again be coming into fashion. Jasper Griffin has recently suggested that Pygmalion should be regarded as a Roman bridegroom gently moulding his bride to be a wife and mother.[56] A less conservative, feminist variant sees the story as an illustration of the way that perfect images of the female are constructed by men as objects of desire. In other words Sandys splits apart the questions of art and life, and does not propose an interpretation which links them. Finally he observes, perhaps rather gleefully, that there is evidence that people in ancient times did fall in love with statues: *autres temps, autres moeurs*.

Even if the Pygmalion story is taken as a meditation on life and art, very different interpretations might still be made of it. It could be read as a fable about the artist's power to improve on humdrum reality and to give to airy nothings a habitation and a name. Or it might suggest that life is superior to art (since only when the statue becomes a woman can Pygmalion be satisfied); or that the artist must not try to possess his work completely but must let it go; or that love is the force which allows the artist to create something, ultimately, separate from himself. Or, if we think all this rather high-minded – as Ovid might surely have done – we may prefer to say that Ovid is simply following through, with perverse literalness, the implications of a cliché about the lifelikeness of great works of art: what if a statue which looked like a living person actually came alive? Something like this, we suspect, was in Ovid's mind, as was a desire to write a dextrous erotic parody – in the Narcissus story he showed how a man falls in love with himself, here how a man makes love to a statue. But as he wrote, the story of itself carried him into richer and less cynical possibilities. As always, we should trust the tale, not the teller.

However that may be, Shakespeare's sense of the story, as one about nature and art, is unusual for his time (it thus links with the debate between Perdita and Polixenes in IV.iv). Shakespeare proves to be – as we might have suspected – an independent-minded and attentive reader, not a slavish follower of commentators and traditions.[57] (There is a moral here for scholars.) Before the final 'transformation' there is an intense and sustained emphasis on the statue's apparent status as a work of art. Paulina, it seems, keeps an art 'gallery' (the very word used), in which are displayed 'many singularities' (10–12). The statue is supposedly the work of the Italian master Giulio Romano, described in the previous scene as Nature's 'ape' (IV.ii.99), and famous for his illusionist effects. The verisimilitude of the statue, while necessary for Paulina's plan, must be taken seriously, at the level of ideas, since it relates to a central preoccupation of Renaissance aesthetics, deriving from antiquity. Only if such verisimilitude is accepted as a criterion of great art, can the wonder of the onlookers be kept directed to the statue's extraordinary beauty; in other words, this view of art is necessary to the type of illusion, or state of wondering confusion, which Paulina initially seeks to create. There is also a tension, in the reference to Hermione's wrinkles, between two potentially conflicting ideals of Renaissance aesthetics, verisimilitude and idealism.[58] When Leontes observes that the statue represents an older woman than the Hermione he remembers of sixteen years before, Paulina replies that this only demonstrates the skills of the artist. This, partly a necessary ploy to allay doubt, also suggests that art can capture important truths which might not otherwise be observed. Leontes is brought to see the real and present Hermione initially through sight of a work of art, presented as one of the ways of bridging the gap in time. In Leontes' comment 'The fixure of her eye has motion in't,/As we are mocked with art' (67f.), there is a play on the different senses of 'fixure', both colouring or carving and fixedness, the second meaning providing a paradox with 'motion'. The art 'mocks' Leontes, because, while only art, it gives the impression that the real Hermione has been restored to him (58).[59] When Leontes, encouraged by Paulina, pursues his 'fancy' that the statue is alive and appears to breathe, again the presentation focusses sharply on the language of artistic appreciation, as Shakespeare strains his own art to its highest pitch of paradox: 'What fine chisel/Could ever yet cut breath?' (78f.). But now the time has come for Paulina to move her designs from the sphere of art to that of magic and miracle. The early part of the scene is thus saturated with a certain kind of language about art, and the idea of art presupposed in it – one which is now held only by the unsophisticated and even by them in a much etiolated form – must be recovered if it is to retain its proper impact. It is remarkable how Shakespeare builds up tension with variations of ever-increasing complexity on the same basic idea – an idea implicit in Ovid but not given this degree of emphasis – to prepare for the climax of the statue's revivification. Whether he has succeeded or not partly requires the test of the theatre.

The dramaturgy of the scene is in fact unique in Shakespeare. In Ovid the statue actually comes to life – which determines the character of the story. In Shakespeare Hermione has presumably never died, although the audience has been misled about the matter and is never given a full account, and the revivification is stage-managed by Paulina. (It is just possible that Hermione has been in some state of suspended animation.) To that extent the episode parallels various closing scenes in Shakespeare where a person believed dead by others returns to them, sometimes after a piece of stage-management. The strong sense of resurrection in these scenes does not reside in any sense of the supernatural, rather it has to do with the psychological impact of the event on those who have passed the boundary of acceptance that the person concerned is dead. In these plays the reactions of the characters in their ignorance are readily seen by the audience to be misprision, but, despite this apparent distancing, the scenes of reunion are intensely moving, as the audience is strongly exposed to the emotions felt on stage. In *The Winter's Tale* by contrast, just possibly to achieve an effect closer to Ovid's, Shakespeare contrives to make his audience share *directly* in the experience of the stage characters without the complications of superior knowledge. However – for we must speak as we find – paradoxically this direct participation does not, in the event, make for a more powerful emotional experience. Even on the most rational explanation Hermione's concealment is on a different level of oddity from anything in the parallel plays, and the whole business has a degree of artifice which risks an emotional vacuum. Shakespeare does not attempt a poignancy of writing like 'Of charity, what kin are you to me?/What countryman, what name, what parentage?' (*Twelfth Night* V.i.228f.). Instead he relies on the action of Hermione in descending from the pedestal and on the accompanying music.[60] It may be that he is trying to do too much: hence the deliberate ambiguity about the status of the 'miracle', so that a presumably explicable occurrence can be invested with the quality of the supernatural in an artificial world which unites, in romance time, the Delphic oracle with the art of Giulio Romano. In this perilous conjuncture of myth and reality, of nature and miracle, it is required we do awake our faith, so that a pagan mystery can be metamorphosed into spiritual renewal, in which the gods look down and from their sacred vials pour their graces.

The descent of Hermione has an elemental flavour of myth beyond Ovid's description of the metamorphosis of the statue. This is not – or not merely – because of any supposed Christian undertones in Shakespeare's play, since the closest parallel to the effect of the scene – and one which has indeed been claimed as a direct source – occurs in another pagan work, Euripides' *Alcestis*.[61] This was one of the plays which Buchanan chose to translate into Latin, and there were other Latin versions available, but we have already expressed scepticism about the idea that Shakespeare read Greek plays in Latin translations. Any similarity is thus in our view likely to be fortuitous. Euripides' play is the closest in feeling of all his untragic tragedies to one of Shakespeare's late romances. Alcestis dies in place of her husband Admetus to secure the future of the household after obtaining a promise that he will never remarry. Out of hospitality Admetus entertains Hercules during the mourning period; when Hercules learns the truth he goes to wrestle with Death and restore Alcestis. In the final scene he returns with a veiled woman whom he presses, with almost violent insistence, on Admetus, as a new wife. In the end Admetus agrees to take the woman into his home; the moment when he lifts the veil to find his wife corresponds to the descent of Hermione. We said that the similarity with Shakespeare was fortuitous, but this may not be quite right. Rather it could be said to illustrate Shakespeare's ability to discern, behind the generally commonplace romance materials he was directly using, the possibilities of patterns of actions and emotion which had in fact resided in the great poetry of classical Greece which he had never read.[62] So too on occasion he was able to use Ovid's sophisticated literariness as a gateway to a different and more elemental treatment of myth.

## MYTHS OUT OF OVID

Shakespeare's most obvious debt to Ovid – and, to a lesser extent, to Virgil – is the whole system of Graeco-Roman mythology to which he had constant recourse throughout his career. R.K. Root – whose study of the subject, published in 1903, still remains the standard work – argues, in a way which derives from Victorian assumptions about Shakespeare's 'development', that there are three phases in Shakespeare's use of mythology.[63] In the early plays the allusions are marked by their graceful charm. In the second phase, beginning with *As You Like It*, they either become more playful and satiric, or are used very sparingly, especially in the great tragedies. In the final group of plays mythology is revived, but with 'deeper' meanings predominating, and a stress on divinity, nature myth, and 'types of qualities, physical or moral'. The explanation of these changes, Root argues, resides in Shakespeare's recognition of 'the insincerity of the Ovidian system'. 'Serious' plays and scenes do not contain mythological allusions, so that, during his middle period, they become less frequent as Shakespeare's art becomes more profound. Root has sufficient confidence in his scheme to use it to resolve problems of disputed dates and authorship. In the general picture that emerges of the frequency and character of Shakespeare's mythology there is clearly truth, though also a measure of simplification, compounded by a certain circularity of method (plays are excluded from the authentic canon, and their exclusion is subsequently justified by the pattern which emerges without them). Root's explanation of the shifts, however, is quite implausible. It rests on the assumption that Ovid's *Metamorphoses* is a trivial work, without 'spiritual significance'. There is absolutely no reason to suppose that Shakespeare ever lost his taste for Ovid, or that the shifting use of mythological material in his plays can be related to changes in his estimation of the *Metamorphoses*. Indeed the most extended allusion to it – the one which comes nearest to direct translation – occurs in *The Tempest*. A more plausible explanation lies in changes of taste and fashion among audiences, for which Shakespeare always had keen antennae. Thus in the 1590s there was a general vogue for Ovidian narrative, which waned thereafter. The partly decorative Ovidianism, with its frequently haunting and wistful music, which Shakespeare had inherited from Spenser and others, and himself relished so greatly, came to be felt as old-fashioned, and Shakespeare increasingly sought a greater tautness and concentration of style, to which leisurely mythological comparisons of a narrative type were less suited. Also significant is the question of the dominant character of a particular play, together with the essential matter of its decorum. If there are only five mythological allusions in *Julius Caesar*, that is because Shakespeare is creating a relatively unadorned style of dignified public utterance suited to Roman politicians (Cicero, as Shakespeare would presumably know, avoids mythology and excessive learning in his speeches). Significantly the most famous passage concerns Aeneas, a figure of moment in Roman history and politics (I.ii.111– 114). In the more romantic *Antony and Cleopatra* Shakespeare uses a much richer palette (thirty-nine allusions). When Root writes of the eight allusions in *Macbeth* that 'all but one are to the more terrible or destructive elements of ancient religion'[64] we may respond by asking what would one expect? The early more romantic mode of Ovidian allusion would obviously be out of place in this of all plays. By contrast the more artificial romance and masque modes of the last plays are naturally receptive of mythological embellishment and, in particular, representations of the classical deities.

Root's scheme depends too much on bare statistics to be a help when reading individual plays; he does not attempt a detailed discussion of the manner and style of particular allusions in particular local contexts. We therefore want to end by looking closely at a number of such passages, taken, fairly randomly, from different phases of Shakespeare's career. We claim no generally valid conclusions from what is obviously too small a sample. We would, however, maintain that such analysis is more useful than rather fruitless speculation to explain the varying statistics of different plays. Although *Measure for Measure* and *Troilus and Cressida* were probably written within a couple of years of each other, the first has two allusions, the second fifty-six.

## ORPHEUS: *TWO GENTLEMEN OF VERONA* (EARLY 1590s) II.ii.77–80

> For Orpheus' lute was strung with poets' sinews,
> Whose golden touch could soften steel and stones,
> Make tigers tame, and huge leviathans
> Forsake unsounded deeps to dance on sands.

Proteus is recommending to Thurio the persuasive powers of love poetry in a passage which mixes wit, romanticism and comic sublimity. It begins with a relatively brittle piece of quasi-metaphysical wit in what one might call an 'exegetical' mode ('what were the strings of Orpheus' lute but . . . ?'); perhaps there is an underlying suggestion of exquisite torment which could be related to the sufferings of devoted lovers, or, more obliquely, to Orpheus himself, and a nod at the Ovidian story of the flaying of Marsyas. There follow the standard details of the myth recording Orpheus' powers over nature, animate and inanimate, culminating in an unusual detail of far greater imaginative intensity, the slow, ponderous dance of the great sea monsters, so finely balanced between the comedy of ungainliness and something unfathomably noble and delightful. The heightened beauty of the passage within the speech is largely a matter of rhythmical dispositions, the final succession of monosyllables tautening the last line into a cadence which has not a little of the ring of Shakespeare's later style. This is distinguished writing in a play not much noted for it, and suggests how far Shakespeare's imagination at this stage was nourished by classical mythology of the gorgeous Ovidian type.

## HERCULES, *MERCHANT OF VENICE* (MID 1590s), III.ii.53–60

> Now he goes
> With no less presence, but with much more love
> Than young Alcides, when he did redeem
> The virgin tribute, paid by howling Troy
> To the sea-monster; I stand for sacrifice,
> The rest aloof are the Dardanian wives
> With bleared visages come forth to view
> The issue of the exploit: go Hercules!

Portia delivers a speech of 'conjuring', wishing Bassanio success in his choice of casket. She has referred to the music which she is preparing; music to accompany loss will give 'a swan-like end/Fading in music' (a fine mimetic cadence), while her tears will be his 'watery death-bed'; to accompany success it will be like the flourish when a 'new-crowned monarch' is saluted, or the sounds which summon the 'dreaming bridegroom' to marriage. These evocative comparisons are set out systematically, but, as they proceed, we slip almost inadvertently into seeing Bassanio as bridegroom and hero, which leads to the equally systematic but drier comparison with Alcides (a patronymic of Hercules). The simile, which derives from Ovid *Metamorphoses* XI.199ff., has something of a learned flavour. The story of Hesione's rescue is not among the best-known in the *Metamorphoses*, and the details are all slightly allusive. The simile gives Bassanio the heroic bearing of Hercules, and suggests that he is attempting a parallel rescue of a damsel in distress, who is a victim of forces beyond her control. There may be something droll in the discrepancy between tenor and vehicle, but the tone is difficult to gauge. The phrase 'with much more love' presumably refers to the fact that Hercules rescued the princess for a reward of horses, not out of love; and 'the virgin tribute', with its suppression of the girl's name, seems deliberately to tax our knowledge of mythology. Thus, despite its carefully explanatory nature, the comparison requires some additional knowledge for full appreciation. Although Shakespeare later wrote much more demanding poetry than this, there is a sense, abnormal with him, that he is parading his armoury of learning, rather in the manner of some of the Latin poets themselves (for example Propertius). The unusual nature of the allusion, appropriate perhaps for the clever Portia, is brought out if we compare some more characteristically opulent lines from earlier in the play, which employ a better-known story from Ovid. Bassanio is describing Portia, the lady whose rich inheritance precedes even the mention of her beauty and virtue. Portia is first compared to Cato's daughter – which perhaps hints at her more severe, judicious side – and then, with an easy shift characteristic of the Renaissance from Roman history to mythology, she is viewed romantically, as the cynosure of many suitors and a great treasure to win:

> For the four winds blow in from every coast
> Renowned suitors, and her sunny locks
> Hang on her temples like a golden fleece,
> Which makes her seat of Belmont Colchos' strand,
> And many Jasons come in quest of her.

(I.i.168–172)

Again the comparisons are systematic: Portia's hair is like the golden fleece, Belmont like Colchis, and the suitors like Jason. The passage moves with a grand motion to its ringing Marlovian close, and the glamour of the story is well established in the phrase 'Colchos' strand' (purloined in fact from Golding), the marine flavour suiting a play set in the island world of the Venetian lagoon and concerned with sea-voyaging in pursuit of wealth. Only the extravagant comparison of Portia's hair to the fleece (itself a term often used of the fortunes of merchants[65]), bizarre and far-fetched in a somewhat metaphysical vein, complicates the tone.

## ACTAEON, *TWELFTH NIGHT* (1601), I.i.19–23

> O, when mine eyes did see Olivia first,
> Methought she purged the air of pestilence.
> That instant was I turned into a hart,
> And my desires, like fell and cruel hounds,
> E'er since pursue me.

Orsino is clearly referring to the myth of Actaeon, recounted by Ovid in *Metamorphoses* III.138ff. One cannot know why Shakespeare did not include the name, for such a direct classical allusion would be perfectly decorous for the courtly Orsino (after all, the sea captain compares Sebastian with Arion, I.ii.15). The image is more elliptical and compressed than the others we have looked at; instead of narrative we have an intense expression of mood and psychology, which conveys the introspection of the love-sick Orsino. The psychologizing of the myth could be related back to medieval allegoresis, but the effect is far more conceited – there is the usual quibbling pun on hart/heart – and is concerned with the self-scrutiny of the lover rather than with moral evaluation. Barkan reminds us that the 'connection between passion and transformation' is a Renaissance recovery, in which Petrarch is the great originator;[66] in a poem like *Canzone* 23 art, sexuality, metamorphosis and self-consciousness are interwoven in complex Ovidian fashion, as the poet turns the spotlight on his own psyche. An earlier English example of the use of the myth in this way occurs in the fifth sonnet of Daniel's *Delia*, while Drayton's 'Epistle of Rosamond' from *England's Heroical Epistles* makes 'modern' psychological use of figures from the *Metamorphoses*, including Actaeon (139–146):

86

Here, in the garden, wrought by curious hands,
Naked Diana in the fountain stands,
With all her nymphs got round about to hide her,
As when Actaeon had by chance espied her.
This sacred image I no sooner viewed,
But, as that metamorphosed man pursued
By his own hounds, so by my thoughts am I,
Which chase me still which way so e'er I fly.

## THE UNDERWORLD, *TROILUS AND CRESSIDA* (1602), III.ii.7–12

I stalk about her door
Like a strange soul upon the Stygian banks
Staying for waftage. O be thou my Charon,
And give me swift transportance to those fields
Where I may wallow in the lily beds
Proposed for the deserver.

Troilus, awaiting admittance to Cressida, expresses his anticipation and anxiety, with a curious sense of unfulfilment typical of him. While his image culminates in a picture of the Elysian fields representing the achievement of his desire, there seems equal force in the initial picture of a lost soul; Troilus depicts his hoped-for success in terms of death, with more connotations than the merely sexual. The comparison, though it moves from simile to metaphor, is set out almost as systematically as in the passage from *The Merchant of Venice*: Troilus hovering about Cressida's door is the soul by the Styx, Pandarus is to play the role of Charon to take him on his way to the Elysian fields, which must correspond to Cressida's bed. Such comparisons, as it happens, are characteristic of Troilus' manner of speaking. The difference from the earlier passage lies in the far greater sophistication of diction and rhythm, with some of the cadences typical of Shakespeare's later phase. The heady mood may remind one of earlier Shakespearean lovers, but the phrase 'proposed for the deserver' is oddly prosaic for so romantic a context. Apart from the trisyllabic Latinate noun 'transportance' (first recorded instance in the *Oxford English Dictionary*) and the semi-technical nautical 'waftage' (commonly used in connection with Charon's skiff) the vocabulary eschews the recherché; the precise tone and feeling is difficult to assess. It was perhaps partly to simplify and clarify the mood, and remove the offensive 'wallow', that Dryden, in his rewriting of *Troilus and Cressida* (II.ii.78–82), while (unusually) retraining almost verbatim the first three lines, rewrote the remainder as 'And give me a swift transportance to Elysium,/And fly with me to Cressida'. The source of the image, if such commonplace material can be said to need a source, is the sixth book of the *Aeneid*. Virgil has no flowers in his Elysium, but the detail is common in the handbooks.[67] The erotic character is thus another example of the Ovidianizing of Virgilian material, but in this case the style itself does retain a Virgilian quality. Virgil's fondness for using ordinary words in unusual ways or contexts was stigmatized as a novel form of stylistic affectation (*nova cacozelia*) by a hostile critic (Donatus, *Life of Virgil*, 44), and there is something of the same timbre here. The oddity and measure of indeterminacy is characteristic of this play and of many of Troilus' other speeches. More than in our earlier examples the style is being used to delineate the speaker; even the relatively unobtrusive five-fold alliteration in the first sentence, not typical of late Shakespeare, may be designed to reflect the pointed rhetoric of the scholarly Troilus. Ovid is a major – and neglected – source for *Troilus*, and Shakespeare remains a pupil of Ovid (the heir of Euripides) in his scepticism, modernization of legend, and nuanced attitude to the heroic; but in general the style, or rather the styles, would not strike a Jacobean audience as Ovidian.

### PROSERPINA, *THE WINTER'S TALE* (1611), IV.iv.112–125

>         Now, my fairest friend,
> I would I had some flowers of the spring, that might
> Become your time of day; and yours, and yours,
> That wear upon your virgin branches yet
> Your maidenheads growing; o Proserpina,
> For the flowers now, that, frighted, thou let'st fall
> From Dis' waggon! Daffodils,
> That come before the swallow dares, and take
> The winds of March with beauty, violets dim
> But sweeter than the lids of Juno's eyes
> Or Cytherea's breath, pale primroses
> That die unmarried ere they can behold
> Bright Phoebus in his strength – a malady
> Most incident to maids...

Our final passage sees the full restoration of Shakespeare's earlier more lyrical manner, but at a much higher level of poetic sophistication. The story of Proserpina comes from Ovid (*Metamorphoses* V.385ff.; cf. *Fasti* IV.417ff.), although in this case we cannot tell whether Shakespeare was remembering the Latin or Golding's translation. The allusion is a particularly apt one, since this is a play controlled by the rhythm of death and rebirth ('thou met'st with things dying, I with things new-born'), and the story of Proserpina was frequently interpreted, in a 'physical' sense, as concerning the cycle of the year's changes.[68] In Ovid Proserpina's plucking of the flowers prepares for the loss of her virginity – as Milton, remembering this passage, puts it, 'herself a fairer flower by gloomy Dis/Was gathered' (*Paradise Lost*, IV.270f.).[69] Female sexuality is indeed something Perdita's language keeps touching on. Thus the opening lines fuse the virginity of her companions with natural growth in a somewhat surreal metaphor. Phoebus is not merely the sun, but a masculine deity representing all that fruition which the maids with their 'green sickness' will never experience. The pale primroses, which possess the precarious attraction of flowers which appear at the verge of winter, are personified as girls in that they die unmarried in early spring before the sun reaches its full potency. The sadness is focussed on the primroses, since the parenthesis about the girls and their green sickness seems touched with a gentle humour, but the pathos of early death and unfulfilled womanhood flickers through this whole section. The goddesses also carry some erotic charge: Venus, whose breath fuses with the scent of flowers, is the goddess of love, and the phrase 'the lids of Juno's eyes', while suggesting the nodding, face-like flower, shyly or coyly hidden, also gives a mildly erotic impression of the goddess' eyes. The 'violets dim' recall Virgil's *pallentes violas* (*Eclogue* II.47) – appropriately in this pastoral setting – where the ancient commentators saw a reference to the pallor of lovers.[70] The daffodils, with their temerity and attractiveness to the winds, are again presented as animated nature, and animated along the erotic lines of the love-sick winds and waves surrounding Cleopatra's barge. The world of flowers is thus intertwined with human emotions and a divine world of gods immanent in nature, where violets imply the heady attractiveness of classical goddesses and primroses inspire sad thoughts (flecked with wit) about those who fail to encounter the full force of the sun as a sort of cosmic bridegroom. Perdita is depicting such a world as is glimpsed sometimes in *Antony and Cleopatra*, one which links divine forces, natural energies and human beings, a world depicted with great power, but not without a touch of scepticism and irony.

The passage exhibits an exuberant, unpedantic classicism, where Dis has a sturdy English waggon,[71] and where the exotically euphonious and mellifluous 'Cytherea' (contrasted with the more normal Juno) can be conjoined with common English flowers; the classical names are like bright splashes of colour on a more restrained background. The diction is by turns solemnly artificial and tautly plain, and the passage displays a breathtakingly fluent mastery of blank verse technique, flexibly deployed. One may note the almost hectic redistribution of the pauses, not allowing the verse to rest in any set pattern of cadences, the bold elisions, the helter-skelter accumulation of syllables in 117 with 'frighted' placed, breathlessly, in mid course, contrasted with the slow, regular movement of the preceding exclamation. The verse is as accomplished as anything Shakespeare ever wrote, and the passage shows to what pitch Ovidian mythology could fire his imagination. Without Ovid, Shakespeare's plays (as English literature generally) would have been very different, and very greatly impoverished.

# 3

# SHAKESPEARE'S TROY

## SHAKESPEARE'S ILIAD?

In the view of Gilbert Highet, Shakespeare offered, in *Troilus and Cressida*, only 'a distant, ignorant, and unconvincing caricature of Greece'.[1] It is doubtless true that Shakespeare, even if he had wanted to, could not have given a historically convincing picture of the archaic or classical Greek world, still less of the Bronze Age (but then who could?), in the way that he did of the various stages in the history of Republican Rome in the three Plutarchan plays. Part of the reason for this, no doubt, is the overwhelming emphasis on Latin literature and Roman culture in the educational system. Shakespeare knew a great deal about Rome before his decisive encounter with Plutarch. A second factor is the stereotyped view of the Greeks widely held in Renaissance England, the subject of an influential article by T.J.B. Spencer.[2] Spencer argues that the use of 'merry greek' to mean a riotous liver illustrates the hostility to the character of Greeks and Greek culture typical of the period. There is some confirmation of this picture in *Troilus* itself, where there are two instances of this usage, both employed punningly with wry effect. In I.ii.110 Cressida calls the winsome Helen a 'merry Greek indeed', while, in IV.iv.55, she describes herself, with pretty pathos, as 'a woeful Cressid 'mongst the merry Greeks'. In IV.iv.84-87 Troilus presents himself as a plain man unlike the nimble Greeks:

> I cannot sing,
> Nor heel the high lavolt, nor sweeten talk,
> Nor play at subtle games; fair virtues all,
> To which the Grecians are most prompt and pregnant.

But this self-characterization, like that of the bluff Henry V of the

91

wooing scene, is hardly borne out by the play, and is rather, as Patricia Thomson observes, 'a highly sophisticated way of projecting sincerity'.[3] Spencer further points out that the Roman and later traditions were generally hostile to the Greeks, who were seen as immoral and dishonest; and he cites Erasmus' view, in *Adages* IV.1.64, that 'the Greek race is everywhere described as evil among the Latin poets, and likewise in Cicero, not only as being addicted to pleasures and rendered womanish by self-indulgence, but also as it were of slippery reliability'.[4] So Shakespeare's sordid Achilles is simply Horace's: *impiger, iracundus, inexorabilis, acer* ('indefatigable, angry, inexorable, fierce', *Ars Poetica* 121). Although there is truth in this picture, Spencer overstates his case. In treating Chapman's endorsement of Homeric heroism as eccentric, he fails to mention that Spondanus (Jean de Sponde), in the standard humanist edition of Homer (containing a Latin translation), expressed approval of the exemplary qualities of Achilles; or that his enthusiasm for Homer and the values he found in the Homeric poems was shared by Erasmus and by Thomas Elyot in *The Governor*, who wrote of 'noble Homer, from whom, as from a fountain, proceeded all eloquence and learning'.[5] Clearly the two views – merry greeks on the one hand and impressive Trojan and Greek champions on the other – could exist side by side, even in the same individual.

It would not be entirely satisfactory to attribute Shakespeare's comparative failure to depict Greece in a way that would satisfy a modern classical scholar merely to lack of knowledge. Dryden, who knew the *Iliad* intimately, and produced a fine vigorous translation of book I and the Hector/Andromache scene from book VI, and who was well-read in Greek literature generally, thought that Shakespeare, being 'untaught, unpractised, in a barbarous age' had written, in *Troilus*, a 'rough-drawn play', and set out to correct its 'faults'.[6] Yet, despite his familiarity with Homer, he produced a version even remoter from the *Iliad* than Shakespeare's. His Cressida is not false and commits suicide before her lover to prove her loyalty; his Hector is consistently noble, his Andromache the ever-dutiful wife who urges Hector to issue his challenge and condemns the lovers Paris and Helen; the fighting in the final act is heroized, and, in place of Shakespeare's sleazy epilogue, Ulysses draws a trite moral about the need for order. In other words, Dryden's characters are neo-classical ciphers, not sharply observed individuals with spiky characteristics, both good and bad, like Homer's.[7] The idea of dramatic decorum involved, and an impoverished conception of the heroic, here proved stultifying. By contrast Shakespeare's Hector, Agamemnon and Nestor at least are recognizable descendants of their Homeric prototypes.

The story of Troy, first set forth in Homer and subsequently the subject of innumerable reworkings, is perhaps the greatest secular story of the Western world. *Troilus and Cressida* is, we would argue, Shakespeare's *Iliad*, that is, his play on the matter of Troy, something which had interested him as early as *Lucrece*, and to which he had returned in the player scene in *Hamlet*. To that extent the play's title is misleading; all the world loves a lover, and it is easy to forget that, in terms of allotted space at least, the love plot is subsidiary. War, not love, is the theme announced in the prologue (31). The play's generic affiliations have of course proved controversial. The original prose preface calls it a comedy, and many have seen the satiric note as dominant,[8] though to treat the whole play as debunking is to privilege Thersites' blistering comments, some of which are obviously false (for example his claim, in V.iv, that there is no difference between Troilus and Diomedes); a case can also be made for calling *Troilus* a tragedy, at least in its treatment of Hector and Troilus himself. Of course this generic uncertainty is part of the point, but, when all is said and done, the Quarto's 'famous History' seems as good a description as any.

The prologue is essentially epical in style (although, as we shall see, in a peculiarly mannered and self-conscious way), and this epic discourse is certainly one of the competing discourses of the play, even if the speech initially proves something of a false start. There is an immediate contrast with the courtly banter and medieval ambience of the two scenes which follow, and it appears that after all love, not war, is going to be centre-stage, until we revert to the Homeric war-council. Likewise, in the best epic fashion, following the prescript of Horace, we are promised a Homeric epic structure 'beginning in the middle' (*in medias res*, *Ars Poetica*, 148); but in fact the beginning chosen is arbitrary, unlike the quarrel which inaugurates Achilles' wrath and determines the shape of the action in the *Iliad*. *Troilus* to some extent lacks a plot:[9] although it ends with Hector's death and with the fall of Troy imminent, the final act consists of a rapid sequence of perfunctory scenes treating the wrath motif. This arbitrariness of structure, along with other oddities, is ruthlessly excised by Dryden, who cuts the prologue, opens with the Greek council of war (thereby removing the ironic sequence of discrepant tones), 'improves' the randomness of the ending, reduces the intellectual content of the debates, and omits the sleazy Paris and Helen and the discussion about reputation between Achilles and Ulysses. Those who think that orthodox structures and generic propriety are necessarily virtues might ponder the result.

Shakespeare must have read a good deal on the subject of Troy before 1602 (when *Troilus* was probably completed) – he surely knew Chaucer's *Troilus and Criseyde*, an edition of which appeared in 1598[10] – but the nature of that reading cannot be determined, beyond all doubt, by the internal evidence of the play. It is a reminder that Shakespeare can be as imperious in his way as Milton when treating his 'sources'.[11] The only source whose use we can *prove* is Caxton's *Recueil of the Histories of Troy*, reprinted in 1596 (probably supplemented by Lydgate), although Shakespeare corrects the forms of names in Caxton – for example Andromache for Andromeda – in a properly Renaissance way. In the prologue the names of the Trojan gates come from Caxton, although the effect of their use in their new context is much more grandly epical. During the final battle (V.v.6ff.) we have two typical Iliadic routines in high epic style, first a list by Agamemnon of slayers and slain:

> The fierce Polydamas
> Hath beat down Menon; bastard Margarelon
> Hath Doreus prisoner,
> And stands Colossus-wise, waving his beam,
> Upon the pashed corpses of the kings
> Epistrophus and Cedius,

> (6–11)

and secondly an account by Nestor of Hector's *aristeia* (heroic feats), decorated with a couple of brief epic similes, the second with analogues in Homer (e.g. *Iliad*, XI.67ff.). The names of the warriors – and of Hector's horse (Galathe) – are taken from Caxton. The conclusion is, we believe, unavoidable. Shakespeare had Caxton closely to hand when he was writing *Troilus*, but not a version of Homer, whether Chapman's or another, even if, as we believe, he had read one earlier. Clearly he here wanted to evoke the world of Homeric warfare, and would surely have found his names in Homer had it been easy for him to do so.

All plays about historical events deal both with the past and with the present. Anachronism is thus, in one form or another, the necessary condition of their being. Not even the most learned historian could avoid it, because the past is only partly knowable, because we cannot wholly detach ourselves from our own time, and because any presentation of the past in contemporary language will involve accommodations. Nevertheless Shakespeare's Roman plays are given a reasonable unity of historical texture. By contrast, when, in the Trojan debate, Hector cites Aristotle's *Ethics*, we receive a shock of anachronism which is surely deliberate. It is inconceivable that Shakespeare thought that Aristotle lived before the Trojan War (even if unlearned, he was no Trimalchio or Bottom), and the effect of violent disjunction is quite different from that of a trivial anachronism, like the reference to Milo, a famous Greek athlete of the sixth century BC (mentioned by several classical writers, including Ovid) in II.ii.247; we are reminded that we are listening to a debate, conducted in 'modern' terms, but in a heroic setting (one could compare the Fool's fey remark in *Lear* III.ii.95: 'This prophecy Merlin shall make; for I live before his time'). Hector's unmotivated change of heart at the end of the debate, about which there has been so much discussion, could be said to dramatize the gap between Homeric/heroic and 'modern' virtues.

Chapman's translation of seven books from the *Iliad* (1–2; 7–11) appeared in 1598. In 1608 Chapman added the remainder of the first twelve books, and in 1611 the complete translation appeared with revision of the 1598 version. It was not in fact the first English rendering of Homer. Arthur Hall (?1539–1605) had already translated, from the French of Salel, *Iliad* I–X (1581).[12] On commonsense grounds it seems likely that Shakespeare, who knew Chapman, read the *Seven Books*; its publication must have been something of a literary event, it was dedicated to the Earl of Essex, and its appearance about four years before Shakespeare wrote his play looks significant. But, once again, we cannot prove it – none of the proposed parallels is decisive, and one of the more plausible is in fact to the fifth book, which Chapman did not publish until after *Troilus*. Indeed we cannot prove that Shakespeare read Homer in any form whatever, even if those who treat Shakespeare as a learned humanist think that he knew the whole *Iliad* in Latin or French. It is sometimes supposed that the presence of Thersites, who does not feature in the medieval Troy story, shows that Shakespeare read some version of the *Iliad*. However there is a lively Tudor interlude, *Thersites* ('In Homer of my acts ye have read, I trow', 5) expanded from a Latin work by Ravisius Textor, the author of a number of standard textbooks in use in Elizabethan schools.[13] Thersites is also vividly described by Leonard Cox in *The Art or Craft of Rhetoric* (1524), a description evidently based directly on Homer's. Anyway five minutes' conversation with a friend could have given Shakespeare all he needed to know, or he could have found the information in some note on Ovid *Metamorphoses* XIII.232f., where Thersites is mentioned. More significant is the fact that the 'Iliadic' episodes on which Shakespeare concentrates all occur in the *Seven Books*, and that there are larger parallels of a non-verbal type. Agamemnon's address to the troops (II.110ff.) is like his opening speech at the debate in *Troilus*; Nestor's speech in IX.96ff. has a long preamble to soften the blow to his leader's pride, which resembles his role in Shakespeare; Ulysses' speech on order elaborates his Homeric counterpart's assertion of the need to obey kings in II.200ff. But none of this even begins to constitute proof.

Nevertheless it is a reasonable hypothesis that Shakespeare read Chapman's *Seven Books*, that this was his only direct encounter with Homer, and that the experience was part of the genesis of *Troilus and Cressida*. For a classical scholar it requires an effort of the imagination to reconstruct the effect of Homer encountered solely through this distorting medium. But two centuries later Keats repeated the experience, and seems to have believed that Chapman had provided him with a gateway to the original:

> Oft of one wide expanse had I been told
>    That deep-browed Homer ruled as his demesne;
>    Yet did I never breathe its pure serene
> Till I heard Chapman speak out loud and bold.

Shakespeare might well have been surprised, and even disconcerted, by what he encountered. Aristotle had praised the artistic structure of the Homeric poems, but a reader of Chapman's particular selection would have found a work, full indeed of powerful moments, but apparently random and even incoherent in organization (compare *Troilus* itself). Chapman in his preface offered Essex 'the true image of all virtues and human government', yet the hero is seen quarrelling over a girl, allowing his friends to die, and refusing their overtures even as he admits the justice of their case. Many modern readers of Homer prefer Hector to Achilles; C.S. Lewis famously thought the latter 'little more than a passionate boy',[14] and Horace, in another unheroic age, found, in the *Iliad*, a picture of the effects of the vices of leaders on the welfare of their followers (*Epistles* I.2 6–16).

In some ways Chapman's 1598 version, despite additions, contractions and misunderstandings, is closer to Homer's 'sense' than most of its successors, including Pope's. Indeed its literalism can be grotesque when Chapman tries to reproduce exactly the Homeric compound epithets to create such monstrous births as 'famous both-foot-halter' and 'heavenly-wild fire-god' (I.592f. of Hephaistos and Zeus = *Iliad* I.607–609).[15] But in terms of style the results are remote from the smooth-running, leisurely and relaxed Homeric manner. Chapman substitutes Latin names for Greek (e.g. Saturnides = son of Chronos, I.539 = *Iliad* I.552), and employs a large number of Latinate words, partly under the influence of the parallel Latin translation by Andreas Divus in Spondanus' text of Homer: for example 'opprobrious breath' (I.509; *Iliad* I.519); 'to give this excitation act' (II.82; *Iliad* II.83); Ulysses 'the razer of repugnant towns' (II.269, *Iliad* II.278); 'orbicular targe' (Bullough p.128). To avoid metrical monotony, he sometimes uses, in his handling of the problematic fourteener, enjambment and mid-line pauses to create an effect rugged, difficult and unmusical. The result is both denser and more bombastic than Homer, in a way which can recall *Troilus and Cressida*. When he revised the *Seven Books* for his later complete version, and in particular rewrote books I and II, Chapman removed many clumsy touches, and in some ways approached closer to the 'spirit' of Homer, but he also, if anything, increased the overall grandeur and knottiness. Thus 'the general' (II.84) becomes 'the people's rector' (70; *Iliad* II.85 'shepherd of the people'); new phrases include 'revoluble orb' (II.257; *Iliad* II.295) and 'redemptory hire' (I.94; *Iliad* I.95); and the detail of the bees simile (*Iliad* II.87ff.)

> as when black swarms of bees
> Break ceaseless from a crannied rock, and none the
> exhausture sees
> Of their sweet vault

(87–89)

is rendered still more 'artificially':

> as when of frequent bees
> Swarms rise out of a hollow rock, repairing the degrees
> Of their egression endlessly with ever rising new
> From forth their sweet nest.

(71–74)

The manner can approximate closely to that of *Troilus*, as when, before the catalogue of ships, Chapman prays for 'a voice/Infract and trump-like' to recount 'so inenarrable troops' (II.418–21; *Iliad* II.488–90). In short this is what Chapman believed a proper Homeric and heroic style ought to be like. And why should Shakespeare have thought any differently? There are many ways of looking at *Troilus and Cressida*; one that is too seldom tried is to examine it against the background of the *Iliad* as mediated by Chapman.[16] When this is done, we find a range of common themes, even if differently treated: war, debate, value, fame, time. These Iliadic materials, which Shakespeare covered with a medieval-chivalric wash, will be the subject of the next section of this chapter.

## HOMERIC TRACES IN *TROILUS AND CRESSIDA*

### War

War is obviously central to both works, yet the sense of it is strikingly different. Ancient commentators pointed to the tragic texture of the *Iliad*, whose announced theme is nothing like 'hair-breadth scapes in the imminent deadly breach', but 'Achilles' baneful wrath' which 'did worlds of woes disperse' (Chapman's 1598 version of *Iliad* I.1-2).[17] The poem emphasizes the pity of war as well as its glory; indeed the two are fused – glory is precious because of the price which it entails. By contrast there is little pathos in Shakespeare's *Troilus*, and its atmosphere is overwhelmingly harsh and bleak. The debunking element is strong, though not so much as to make the play merely a deconstruction of Homeric warfare and of Chaucerian love.[18] Homer's gentle Patroclus becomes a catamite, in Thersites' phrase a 'male varlet' (V.i.14), following a tradition which is Greek but post-Homeric. *Troilus* V.iii contains a briefer and less moving treatment of Andromache's pleas to Hector not to fight than *Iliad* VI (not in the *Seven Books*). Hector, having spared Achilles in single combat, is treacherously killed by Achilles' Myrmidons in a short but powerfully atmospheric and anti-heroic scene (V.viii). In consequence *Troilus* is often seen as a play of disillusionment. But it should not be treated as a straightforward key to its author's views at this or any other period of his life; like all his other plays it is an exercise in dramatic and moral possibilities, partly reflecting the taste of the time and the expected interests of the public, here particularly in relation to the fashion for satiric drama. There is a danger too of over-simplification. For example we are presented with a genuinely heroic image of a merciful Hector, however flawed. His 'ruth' is confirmed by friend and foe alike (V.iii.37ff.; IV.v.184ff.); Cressida's man, Alexander, testifies to his 'patience' 'as of a virtue fixed' (I.ii.4f.).

When Thersites encounters him in battle and denigrates himself, Hector responds, with ostentatious if exaggerated nobility, 'I do believe thee: live' (V.iv.30) – ironically on this code only the worst will survive. Certainly he is not faultless, and he shows some of the inconsistency and discontinuity typical of the play's characters, but something of constancy shines through. We have seen that many readers of the *Iliad* have found Hector a more sympathetic figure than his opponent, and even (wrongly) treated him as the poem's hero.[19] The post-Homeric tradition is generally favourable, and this Shakespeare follows. Yet he never gives Hector the full glamour of (say) Hal in *1 Henry IV* (IV.i.97ff.):

> All furnished, all in arms,
> All plumed like estridges that wing the wind,
> Baited like eagles having lately bathed,
> Glittering in golden coats, like images,
> As full of spirit as the month of May,
> And gorgeous as the sun at midsummer,
> Wanton as youthful goats, wild as young
>                     bulls;
> I saw young Harry with his beaver on,
> His cushes on his thighs, gallantly armed,
> Rise from the ground like feathered Mercury.

Similarly Shakespeare's Achilles is not as purely black as he is often painted. Rather he displays an interesting mixture of oafishness, arrogance, cruelty, philosophical intelligence and turbulent strangeness of mind (this last a feature of the Homeric Achilles also): 'My mind is troubled, like a fountain stirred,/And I myself see not the bottom of it' (III.ii.306f.). Winifred Nowottny has noticed of his experience, as of the whole play, that it 'turns upon a tragic view of life: the view that the "unbodied figure of the thought", whatever it may be, can never be realized in action'.[20] Many modern Homerists have written in similar terms of Achilles' anguish of mind revealed in his turbulent answer, in *Iliad* IX, to the proffered gifts, in which he wheels inconclusively around his resentments and uncertainties.[21] But in the end he will play the role which his society expects of him.

## Debate

Homer's characters are great talkers, most notoriously the garrulous (but respected) Nestor. Little that happens in the *Iliad* happens in silence. Formal discussions are frequent. The two debates in *Troilus* belong to the Homeric, not the Chaucerian tradition, even if they contain some medieval features, like the chivalric character of Hector's challenge, 'a sportful combat' (I.iii.335). There is however a constant tension between the heroic setting and such unheroic notions as that the planning of a war is more important than individual deeds (I.iii.197ff.).

The debate in the Greek camp (I.iii) is concerned with the reasons for the poor progress of the war and the measures to be taken to counteract this. The centre-piece is Ulysses' speech on degree, which used often to be taken as representing the play's philosophical and moral keynote. The manner of the opening three speeches is public and political – words predominate over ideas – and even Ulysses here offers only elaborate compliments and no eager thought. Many argue that the intended effect is parodic (Graham Bradshaw supposes that usually in this play 'Latinisms signal pretentiousness').[22] Agamemnon uses words like 'protractive' and 'persistive' (20f.), and Nestor's speech (31ff.) is written partly in a hyperbolic epicized style:

> But let the ruffian Boreas once enrage
> The gentle Thetis, and anon behold
> The strong-ribbed bark through liquid mountains cut.
>
> (37–39)

Certainly Patroclus, as reported – perhaps maliciously – by Ulysses, mocks, for the amusement of Achilles, the pomposity of Agamemnon and his 'terms unsquared' (159). But the disaffected Achilles is hardly an objective judge, and Paris, while adopting so different a style with Helen (III.i.42ff.), talks like the Greek leaders in the debate in Troy, employing the words 'propension' and 'propugnation' (II.ii.134 and 137). In this of all plays discourse is king, and different contexts can be more important than the character of the speakers.

Bradshaw is also less intellectually nimble than usual over Ulysses' degree speech, which he sees as wholly 'orthodox', even if at odds with Aeneas' subsequent failure to identify Agamemnon correctly.[23] There is at this point a strong sense of disjunction and disparity of purpose: Agamemnon and Nestor (unashamedly verbose and echoing his leader) wish to boost morale, Ulysses to administer a warning about lack of respect for rank. He establishes his ground, at length, by lecturing the meeting on the nature and importance of hierarchy in the universe, in nature and in human communities. Where Agamemnon had differentiated categories of human beings good and bad,

Ulysses has no interest in the value of individuals, even for rhetorical amplification. When he talks about 'the unworthiest' masquerading as his superior, he does not attempt to explain, even briefly, what such unworthiness might entail. The matter is treated simply as transparent, so that degree, readily visible, should not be 'vizarded'. Despite the authoritative manner – perhaps partly because of it, since Ulysses is defter in private conversation – the argument is uncomfortably circular at certain key points. When Ulysses claims that the heavenly bodies observe degree,

> And therefore is the glorious planet Sol
> In noble eminence enthroned and sphered
> Amidst the other,
>
> (89–91)

the 'therefore' is logically suspect. Sol's eminence, it is true, is partly a 'medicinable' one, but partly Sol is eminent because it is placed in eminence. Similarly in the description of human affairs:

> How could communities,
> Degrees in schools and brotherhoods in cities,
> Peaceful commerce from dividable shores,
> The primogenity and due of birth,
> Prerogative of age, crowns, sceptres, laurels,
> But by degree stand in authentic place?
>
> (103–108)

the 'authentic place' seems, in many ways, rather identical with degree than the result of it. Ulysses sounds as if he is in intelligent control of his surroundings and arguments, and his coolness and scepticism cut through the circuitousness of Agamemnon but, on careful probing, his assessments, like those of others, weaken and crumble.[24] The argument is pursued too single-mindedly; degree is valued for degree's sake, without any interest in what differences of degree might signify in a specific human context. In Ulysses' depersonalized universe, degree, emptied of any differentiation of human value, is the object of veneration. It is a chilling picture, as an abstract system becomes sole bulwark against chaos. Agamemnon's response: 'The nature of the sickness found, Ulysses,/What is the remedy?' can, and perhaps should, be read as sardonic. Dryden may have sensed some of the problems. He evidently thought the speech too long and elaborate, and he cut the section about the cosmos, shortening and clarifying the argument. Kings and generals must be obeyed, or faction destroys the common weal (this is closer to the simpler picture in Homer, where Odysseus berates the ordinary soldiers on the need for obedience to kings). Dryden also cut Agamemnon's dry rejoinder. Instead of suggesting a plan of action, Shakespeare's Ulysses, in response, merely illustrates his previous point by describing the disruptive behaviour of Achilles, Patroclus and Thersites. At this juncture Aeneas' interruption with Hector's challenge effects an abrupt change into a different mode, and the debate dematerializes. All the lengthy talk has come to nothing. It is a pattern, perhaps in part suggested by *Iliad* IX, which will be repeated.

## Value

In the Homeric world values are things comparatively uncontroversial.[25] It can of course be argued that Homer's values may not always be those of his characters, but the *broad* impression remains of a world of agreed *mores* and settled procedure (illustrated by the frequency of phrases like 'as is fitting'). The hero as an *agathos* displays *arete*, which involves military prowess, coupled with high social standing, and usually other marks of competitive excellence, including skill in debate. He seeks to avoid defeat in war as shameful; heroic death in battle can, however, be admired, and the death of the gallant Hector, although it will entail the destruction of his people, is presented as a tragic event, evoking the sympathy of the auditors. 'Quiet' virtues are openly appreciated in the case of women, and at least insinuated in the case of men. Hector's kindness is mourned by Helen, while his gentle treatment of his mother, wife and child is part of his attractiveness. It likewise calls forth admiration when Achilles returns Hector's body to Priam, and the two men establish a relationship of mutual respect in these most unpropitious of circumstances; Agamemnon's jibe at Achilles during the quarrel that only 'contention and stern fight/To thee are unity and peace' (Chapman I.184f. = *Iliad* I.177) thus proves false.

In such a world is value something intrinsic or extrinsic? The Homeric hero inhabits what anthropologists call 'a shame culture'; that is, he avoids actions which will make him feel shame before his peers, and embraces those which he thinks will arouse their respect. In a shame culture much clearly depends on what others think of you. On the other hand there is a strong sense in the Homeric poems, conveyed in part by the fixed epithets, that the hero's essential qualities and characteristics are stable entities. So, while Adkins may be right in theory to claim that in Homer 'facts are of much less importance than appearances', and that 'the Homeric hero cannot fall back upon his own opinion of himself', it is also true that there is in general little sense of a gap between appearance and reality in individuals or communities. There is thus a potential clash about the source of value (whether it resides in the prized individual or is bestowed upon him by others), which becomes increasingly problematic in the post-Homeric classical world. For example the Stoic conception of virtue remains essentially one of competitive excellence, but now paradoxically internalized and deprived of its audience; hence an unHomeric fear of instability and a constant reaffirmation of personal authenticity in a writer like Seneca. There is also some disagreement about what is valuable in *Iliad* IX, but Achilles' disillusionment, which brings him insights both unfamiliar and clear-eyed, is nonetheless eccentric in the world of the poem. By contrast, in *Troilus*, the fissures are exposed to general view, and subjected to intense and constant scrutiny.

Value is a continual preoccupation in *Troilus*.[26] A simple iconic treatment occurs in the scene in which the worthless man in golden armour, who embodies the gap between being and seeming, is pursued and killed by Hector for his 'hide' (V.vi.27–31; viii.1–4). The question of value is particularly focussed on the issue of Helen's return, the subject of the Trojan debate in II.ii (in Renaissance schools the matter was a stock topic for argument). Hector maintains that Helen should be returned, since she is not worth the continuing price; Troilus that the choice has been made and must be adhered to. In the *Iliad* Helen, the cause of the war, is a surprisingly attractive figure. Her beauty is such that even the old men of Troy can understand why she has aroused such strife, although they wish that she would go home; but she herself regrets the wrong she has done, dislikes bedding with Paris and is treated with affection by Priam and Hector – yet it is also true, as Richmond Lattimore has observed, that 'in neither epic can she make a speech without talking about herself'.[27] It is a less subtle, more Euripidean Helen we encounter in *Troilus*. In IV.i.55ff. Diomedes denounces her, bluntly and with increasing power:

> For every false drop in her bawdy veins
> A Grecian's life hath sunk; for every scruple

Of her contaminated carrion weight
A Trojan hath been slain.

(70–73)

To the reductive Thersites 'All the argument is a whore and a cuck-
old' (II.iii.74f.). When we eventually see Helen in III.i, she is
something of a vamp, a shallow coquette, whom Paris calls 'my Nell'
(133) and who engages in silly, camp court-conversation. On the
other hand, the discontinuous nature of the characters in the play
makes any definitive valuation problematical. As Stephen Medcalf
puts it, the play sometimes suggests that 'there are no selves, only
sequences of volitions'.[28] Certainly Cressida's behaviour – the same
Cressida who in III.ii.113f. had given so movingly direct expression
of her love: 'Prince Troilus, I have loved you night and day/For many
weary months –' seems in the later part of the play moulded by the
opinion which the Greeks hold of her. There is an insight here about
the behaviour of women in a man's world.

In the debate the comparative worthlessness of Helen has the
measured support of the worthy Hector (who cannot be accused, like
Diomedes, of any lack of gallantry), and the prophetic judgement of
Cassandra. Even Priam, who to an extent occupies the position of
neutral chairman, in his opening résumé sets Helen against a collec-
tion of concerns so weighty – 'honour, loss of time, travail, expense,/Wounds, friends and what else dear' – that it seems her worth
must buckle. However the case for keeping her has an unexpected
champion both ardent and intelligent in Troilus, who is, as we know
already and as the play continues to allow us to believe, a man of some
integrity. Even if, in the event, his convictions fall on stony ground,
his case retains power and interest. The common assumption that
Hector's position is the obviously correct one ignores Troilus' considerable argumentative skill, which makes his opponents look both
dull and conventional.

The focal point of the debate is stated baldly in 51–53:

> *Hector:* Brother,
> She is not worth what she doth cost the keeping.
> *Troilus:* What's aught but as 'tis valued?

Troilus has already impetuously rebutted Hector's point that too
many lives have been lost 'as dear as Helen', with the implication that
Hector's worries for the common good betray a sort of vulgar
tradesman's attitude; with aristocratic and Homeric disdain he rejects Hector's language of measurement and calculation – Priam's

'worth and honour' should not be weighed 'in a scale of common ounces'. Both here and in his angry exchange with Helenus, Troilus points us towards the acknowledgement that reason and heroism sit uneasily together. But the argument about value moves the discussion on to a more abstract, technical and philosophical plane. Hector asserts the 'orthodox' position that there are objective values for things in the universe, and not merely personal assessments (54ff.). The examples move away from war and the immediate issue to other areas, especially those of personal relationships (thereby indirectly helping to bridge the war plot and the love plot). Hector suggests that the 'idolatry' of some love affairs where the lover sees more in the beloved than the reality justifies is a kind of madness (57–61). Troilus does not attempt a direct answer, but builds up to his view of Helen with a series of parallel but different examples. He starts with the one closest to his heart – though in its present form carefully distanced – about choosing a wife. The choice would be influenced by 'will', which in turn would be 'enkindled by mine eyes and ears' in a way not necessarily rational, but, the choice once made, even if the will revolts and alters, there can be no reneging on the decision. After further analogous instances he reminds the Trojans, with dazzling shifts of tone by turn satiric, flamboyant, flippant and romantic (79f.: 'a Grecian queen, whose youth and freshness/Wrinkles Apollo's, and makes stale the morning') that they gladly and unanimously welcomed Helen's coming. Troilus' strenuous, radical opposition to Hector is linked with his belief that, once chosen, a course of action must be maintained. There is an obvious personal dimension to this position, as also to Hector's. Both Hector and Troilus are honourable men, heroic and decent; but, whereas Hector is in the personal sphere calm and at peace with himself, and thus fits comfortably with the view of a settled and ordered universe where values are fixed, Troilus is full of anguished tension, craving some means of stability which he thinks achievable by fixity in decisions and affections. As later he is overwhelmed by Cressida's alteration, so here he is wounded by the Trojans' changed attitude towards Helen, almost as if it were undermining his grasp of the world. His concern with fidelity to the point of nervous obsession later makes it difficult for him to fix upon the disloyal Cressida as the same individual as the one he has loved. In other words he can be likened to a certain sort of existentialist, combining a scepticism about values in the universe with a strong moral instinct to forge his own values, in his case with an intense and perilously unfixed idealism. As a result there is some crossing over of expected patterns of argument in the debate. Hector takes a pragmatic view of the war which he thinks should be ended, but at the same time he espouses a traditional view of objective value, whereas the true pragmatist might prefer compromise with current circumstances to adherence to general principle. Troilus is philosophically a sceptic, but is passionately devoted to an heroic assessment of the war, which could sit more comfortably with a world-view that admitted objectivity.

In a movement highly characteristic of the play – and one which Euripides would surely have relished[29] – the interruption of Cassandra prophesying doom breaks off this discussion. There is a change of gear from modern philosophizing to old-fashioned heightened drama with keening apostrophes and prominent alliteration. Hector tries to use her prophecy to support his case, but Troilus – who, like many sceptics, can be curiously intolerant of others – simply dismisses her as 'mad'. Eventually Hector starts to bring the debate to its end with the tones of a philosophy tutor who has listened patiently to his pupils' attempt at argument. Patronizingly he remarks that Paris and Troilus have spoken well but 'superficially' – 'not much/Unlike young men, whom Aristotle thought/Unfit to hear moral philosophy' (166–168). Whereas they are moved by 'pleasure and revenge', he will reach a mature, balanced decision. He then starts a wholly new point about right of possession in families and nations, which requires Helen's return. In thus admitting that the Trojans have done wrong and that persistence in this wrong only worsens the situation, he has reached a view completely opposite to Troilus'. But then he suddenly crumbles with a brief, awkward distinction between 'truth' (perhaps an absolute standard which can be argued for) and some other opposing factor:

> Hector's opinion
> Is this in way of truth; yet ne'ertheless,
> My spritely brethren, I propend to you
> In resolution to keep Helen still,
> For 'tis a cause that hath no mean dependence
> Upon our joint and several dignities.

(189–194)

He even reveals that, to stir events, he has already (as we know) sent 'a roisting challenge' to the Greeks. All the careful and intense discussion has led nowhere. Hector, after reiterating his position nearly to the bitter end, suddenly and breathtakingly switches, without further pressure, with hardly any explanation and for no good reason. (Dryden, a careful if conventional reader of the play, makes Hector issue the challenge only *after* the conclusion of the debate.) The long build-up and brief fizzling-out has the curious futility of much of the play's action; Shakespeare seems also to project something of the special psychology of group discussions, of meetings.

## Fame

*Troilus* displays a preoccupation with fame which parallels Homer's. In the world of the *Iliad* a man performs high heroic deeds, and in return receives *timē* (honour, worth) in this life and a lasting reputation (*kleos*) after his death. The poem itself is thus an act of memory, of remembering the mighty dead. It also to an extent scrutinizes the notions involved, for there is some truth in Adam Parry's observation that the *Iliad* is a 'poem dealing critically with the heroic conception of life'.[30] Characters in *Troilus* sometimes echo these relatively straightforward heroic concepts: in I.iii.333ff. Nestor refers to the 'honour' and 'opinion' which a victory over Hector would bring the Greek champion; in II.ii.199ff. Troilus argues that fighting for Helen will make 'fame in time to come canonize us' (203). But in general the play subjects conceptions of fame, honour and heroism to quasi-philosophical scrutiny.

In *Iliad* XII (again not in the *Seven Books*) the Trojan Sarpedon serenely enunciates an heroic code. He and his peers receive concrete benefits, and in return have the obligation to lead their people into battle. From this idea of *noblesse oblige* he moves to one more metaphysical:

> O friend, if keeping back
> Would keep back age from us, and death, and that we might
>     not wrack
> In this life's human sea at all, but that deferring now
> We shunned death ever – nor would I half this vain valour
>     show,
> Nor glorify a folly so, to wish thee to advance;
> But, since we must go though not here, and that, besides the
>     chance
> Proposed now, there are infinite fates of other sort in death
> Which (neither to be fled nor 'scaped) a man must sink
>     beneath –

Come, try we if this sort be ours, and either render thus
Glory to others or make them resign the like to us.
                    (Chapman XII, 323–332 = *Iliad* XII.322–328)

Heroism is seen as a rational response to our mortality. Death comes
in a thousand forms, and fame is the only lasting prize for men who
are mortal. A rough equation of a similar kind is also implicit in the
choice of Achilles, whereby he can have a full-length life of obscurity
or a brief one with honour (*Iliad* IX.410–416). His quarrel with
Agamemnon and his ensuing mental turmoil lead Achilles to question his previous mode of proceeding. In his answer to Odysseus he
inverts the argument of Sarpedon with jerky forcefulness.[31] If coward
and hero alike are to die unhonoured, heroic values are futile:

Even share hath he that keeps his tent and he to field doth go.
With equal honour cowards die and men most valiant;
The much-performer and the man that can of nothing vaunt.
                    (Bullough, p.135 = *Iliad* IX.318-320)

Life, he subsequently avers, is too precious to be thrown aside; it is
worth more than any gifts. Achilles' extremism, here as elsewhere,
marks him out from his fellows and confirms his heroic superiority to
them (the point is frequently reduced to pale moralizing about his
overstepping of the mark).

In *Troilus* too the discussion of the nature of fame, honour, heroism focusses on Achilles, whose withdrawal raises problems which
continue the interrogation of these traditional ideas, and draws forth
complex philosophical ruminations. Ulysses' plan that the Greek
leaders should try to humble Achilles into returning to the war is set
in motion, and in II.iii Agamemnon crossly observes to Patroclus:

Much attribute he hath and much the reason
Why we ascribe it to him; yet all his virtues,
Not virtuously on his own part beheld,
Do in our eyes begin to lose their gloss,
Yea, like fair fruit in an unwholesome dish,
Are like to rot untasted.

                                                        (118–123)

'Attribute' seems most naturally to mean 'reputation', but the word
hovers uneasily between the reputation ascribed and the quality on
which the reputation is based, which is precisely the central problem.
Likewise 'virtue' slithers between the vaguer sense 'good qualities'
and, in this heroic context, the older meaning of courage and martial

prowess. Agamemnon, like others in the play, manages to talk about military and heroic matters in a style characteristic of more modern societies, a partly philosophical style in which direct mention of war is evaded. Agamemnon's central point is a traditional one; but, partly because of his exasperation, there is something unstable in the picture. While the argument suggests that attribute is related to intrinsic worth (there is 'reason' for it), the emphasis falls rather on the unreliable nature of reputation. Achilles' virtues are losing their gloss, as if only their surface is really valued anyway – now that the gloss is fading, the rest may fall into oblivion. Agamemnon thus partly pre-echoes the chilling vision of Ulysses in III.iii where all value crumbles under the pressure of time. Later in the scene the dialogue jestingly incorporates riddles, which also suggest profound thoughts on value:

| Ajax: | What is he [Achilles] more than another? |
|---|---|
| Agamemnon: | No more than what he thinks he is. |
| Ajax: | Is he so much? Do you not think he thinks himself a better man than I am. |
| Agamemnon: | No question. |

(144–148)

As part of his manipulation of Ajax, Agamemnon claims that pride is an emptiness in which there is no image and no story, because these can only be provided by the judgement of others: 'He that is proud eats up himself; pride is his own glass, his own trumpet, his own chronicle' (156–158). For there to be even a mirror-image of pride there has to be a mirror; the point drifts us towards some objectivity, but without a thorough-going scale of values in objects and persons and qualities. Similarly Ulysses describes Achilles' condition as an extreme state of egocentricity in which his mind circles round itself and his world is peopled only by his own thoughts and utterances (164–167; 171–179; 186–189). Achilles' obsession with 'imagined worth' (parallel to Troilus' obsession with the deceptive worth of another) takes him further and further from human society and affects his grasp of 'reality'. All this can reasonably be regarded as a development of Homer's Achilles.

In III.iii, after organizing the Greek leaders to pass 'strangely' by, Ulysses gives Achilles a lesson on the slipperiness of reputation which unsettles him. The plot in the end comes to nothing, since Achilles reneges on his decision to fight on receipt of another letter from Polyxena, and only finally goes into battle, as history dictates, because of Patroclus' death. But it is not just in the longer term that Ulysses' clever scheming amounts to so little. As the episode progresses, we seem to leave the world of cynical, manipulative plotting, for one of grim and private meditation on the bleakness of a universe without lasting values. As a result it comes as something of a shock when Ulysses starts to put the screws on Achilles in relation to Polyxena. But perhaps this is only to say that Shakespeare gives a brilliant portrayal of a suave secret policeman with all the cool misdirections, delaying tactics and general but relevant reflections of the master tactician. Do we foreground the action, or the atmosphere, or the ideas? Ulysses introduces his programme with a comment on pride and the image of mirrors, so recurrent in this play (47–48: 'pride hath no other glass/To show itself but pride'). We cannot know whether Ulysses sees an educative role for his scheme – to bring Achilles to an awareness of his vices – or simply wishes to goad him into action by playing on his jealousy of Ajax. Achilles' subsequent musings combine intelligent, dispassionate comment with superb impercipience in his failure to relate his observations to himself (74–92). He sees, with an eye that could be Ulysses', that the honour given to men depends on the gifts of fortune, on extrinsic circumstance, and that such honour is no longer accorded when fortune frowns; yet he remains puzzled by what he has seen (74–90). The mirthless witticism about honour(s)

> And not a man for being simply man,
> Hath any honour, but honour for those honours
> That are without him
>
> (80–82)

nevertheless opens a gap between reputation, its external and accidental sources, and, by implication, true value in an individual, so that Achilles seems partly to accept that there is an objective value beyond the estimation of others. As part of his contrivance, but also in a pointedly contemplative stance, Ulysses is 'discovered' reading a book by a philosopher, whom he calls, not to sound over-enthusiastic, a 'strange' fellow whose views he doubts. The author of the book, while apparently accepting that an individual can have good qualities, denies that he is able to judge such qualities except when they extend to others and are reflected back. The argument may have a moral basis but, as formulated, it has lost any moralizing shape (95–102). Ulysses' ploy of fictive scepticism draws Achilles into the argument in a way which suggests that, despite his accidie, Achilles enjoys flexing his intellectual muscles. He defends the writer's viewpoint by developing an analogy with the nature of sight and of the eyeball which cannot see itself; again the image of reflection draws together much of the thought on the relativity of value and fame.

Ulysses presses ahead with a fine philosophical distinction: the Arden editor glosses 'position' as 'opinion or tenet advanced' and 'drift' as 'general line of argument', but so defined there seems insufficient difference.[32] We would suggest that Ulysses is attempting to nudge the discussion from the world of abstract philosophical debate to the situation of Achilles; the problem is how to apply the familiar ideas to present realities. When giving the 'drift' (114–123) Ulysses seems merely to be going over old ground, with the recurrent images of reflection and reverberation, but the language is moving us, stealthily, to apply the philosophy to the present situation:

> in his circumstance expressly proves
> That no man is the lord of anything,
> Though in and of him there be much consisting,
> Till he communicate his parts to others;
> Nor doth he of himself know them for aught
> Till he behold them formed in the applause
> Where they are extended; who, like an arch, reverberate
> The voice again, or like a gate of steel
> Fronting the sun, receives and renders back
> His figure and his heat.

The author's 'circumstance', that is his provision of detail, suggests that he does not merely tinker with abstractions. A man's 'parts' have to be formed in the applause of others, and applause is something close to Achilles' heart. Ulysses is now ready to address the present situation and the promotion of Ajax. Hereupon, with a tone which wavers between humour and bitterness, he presents an unstable world where all things of value crumble away, and in which men hectically pursue new fashions and enthusiasms. Honour becomes a social commodity which has to be perpetually polished to prevent its decay, and descent into the 'monumental mockery' which awaits the trophies of yesteryear. A haunting image then gives a nightmarish vision of a continual movement in a narrow passage, where there appears to be no goal to reach, no stopping places except those which take one out of the race; the sons of emulation have no standard to follow. The image does not measure achievement, but presents a terrifying picture where success is simply the negative business of avoiding failure:

> Take the instant way;
> For honour travels in a strait so narrow
> Where one but goes abreast. Keep then the path;
> For emulation hath a thousand sons
> That one by one pursue; if you give way,
> Or hedge aside from the direct forthright,
> Like to an entered tide they all rush by
> And leave you hindmost.

(153–160)

So, with a certain virtuosity, Ulysses is able to reach his directly stated conclusion that everything which men value – and the examples build up wearily through 171–173, social factors, external advantages, ethical criteria – 'are subjects all/To envious and calumniating Time.' With this grim conclusion Ulysses and Shakespeare seem to bid farewell to Homer's world, but, as we shall see, there are also faint glimmers of more optimistic possibilities for living.

## Time

Two points are often made about time in Homer. One is that Homeric time is simply a continuum, cyclic insofar as its patterns constantly reappear and disappear, meaningless in that it contains no purpose or end; by contrast time in Virgil is teleological and linear. (This distinction is powerfully made by Auden in his poem 'Memorial for the City'.) Troy is a great city but others, equally significant, will replace it; whereas Virgil's Rome is a type of all earthly cities and – in the Christianized version of Virgil which stretches from Augustine to T.S. Eliot – a type too of the heavenly city, the goal of our pilgrimage. Secondly, as we have already seen, the one victory over time available in Homer's world is through song, which keeps alive the deeds of men. In that sense the *Iliad* itself is the fulfilment of the promise which it predicts for its heroes, and the Homeric hero needs the poet as much as the poet needs the hero.

In respect of time the world of *Troilus* is both like and unlike that of the *Iliad*, like in that it offers no ultimate meaning or goal, unlike in that it foregrounds this lack of meaning (so creating a sense of disappointment) and fails to give any secure fame as a foil. As Medcalf well says, 'it is haunted by a sense of time as only a succession of presentational immediacies, offering no meaning but oblivion'.[33] We have observed how Ulysses, in his conversation with Achilles, suggests that time renders all human values worthless; what unites mankind is the frenzied pursuit of the new. This is the 'one touch of nature' that 'makes the whole world kin', so often misunderstood (sentimentally) out of its context. As an argument to persuade Achilles to fight, it is bizarre; there is no encouragement in it for a jaded or depressed or confused soldier, nothing of the heroic consolation that great deeds will be recalled, lovingly, in song, to compensate for the sacrifice of life. Ulysses suggests a world where nothing is remembered, and where effort and great deeds will achieve only the most fleeting recognition. Achilles might as well sit in his tent for all this offers him. As with the speech on degree, so here Ulysses' arguments are pushed to an extreme where they become counter-productive.

Such, however, is not the only stance of *Troilus* on time. In III.ii love is seen in its perspective. In some beautiful lines Cressida guarantees her profession of constant love for Troilus, and thereby pronounces judgement on herself (182–189):

> If I be false, or swerve a hair from truth,
> When time is old and hath forgot itself,
> When water-drops have worn the stones of Troy,
> And blind oblivion swallowed cities up,
> And mighty states characterless are grated
> To dusty nothing – yet let memory,
> From false to false, among false maids in love,
> Upbraid my falsehood.

The subordinate clauses carry more poetic weight than the ostensibly more important but more conventional phrases of the vow itself. Cressida's vision of the future, while sad and empty, brings gentleness and peace. She reflects on the loss of identity of all we know and value, the inevitable loss that the passing of time must bring – oblivion is blind and mighty states will be nothing – but she presents the process as one gradual and quiet. Even Troy is not seen in terms of the speedy destruction of war; the stones could be those of a ruined or of a complete city – no matter which – while the age-long erosion by water-drops differs hugely from the brutal clamours of much of the play. In part Cressida's vision could be seen as Homeric; ironically she will be remembered in story precisely as a false lover –

Troilus and Pandarus too have their recorded roles in history which poets keep alive. But with the 'water-drops' we move to an Ovidian rather than a Homeric sense of time, to the world of flux depicted in the fifteenth book of the *Metamorphoses* which made such an impression on Shakespeare. Dryden, faced with the gentle discordances of this Ovidian moment, predictably cut it (III.ii.73ff.: in a better vein, in the *Fables*, he relished Ovid's account of the transience of all things, and translated it wonderfully).

In IV.v, after the drawn contest between Hector and Ajax, Agamemnon has to find words to greet a valued enemy. He begins, ham-fistedly, by trying to be pithy and bluffly honest, realizes his failure to strike the right note and begins afresh. On his second attempt he is able to free himself from the restrictions of the present and to see events in larger perspective; as a result he can focus on what is genuinely heart-warming in the present moment:

> Worthy all arms! as welcome as to one
> That would be rid of such an enemy –
> But that's no welcome. Understand more clear:
> What's past and what's to come is strewed with husks
> And formless ruin of oblivion;
> But in this extant moment, faith and troth,
> Strained purely from all hollow bias-drawing,
> Bids thee with most divine integrity
> From heart of very heart, great Hector, welcome.
>
> (162–170)

Again the lines on time carry the main emotional weight, and they also have a way, typical of Shakespeare, of spilling out beyond their immediate context. It is not the least of this play's startling effects to see the stiff, perhaps absurd, certainly unglamorous and insensitive Agamemnon pour forth, if ever so briefly, such delicate, ravishing words; 'husks' is excellent in its combination of the concrete and mundane with a sense of lightness, the melancholy of autumn leaves, while the 'of' in line 166 keeps the words floating somewhat impressionistically. The lines cancel out the initial gruesome *bêtise* and mould this moment into one of positive harmony; only this moment, of course, but a play which seems so often to deny all value provides this and a few others which are not wholly nullified by their temporariness. In terms of ideas the two speeches we have discussed correspond to the views of Ulysses: nothing, no matter how strong and admired, has lasting power. But the tone, lyrical wistful elegiac, is wholly other, and Agamemnon, in particular, achieves, by acknowledging time's power, a temporary but important victory over it.

*Troilus* is one of the most strenuously intellectual of Shakespeare's plays. For this reason we have been obliged to explore the dense arguments in a number of key scenes in some detail. We hope that we have thereby demonstrated the play's involvement in several of the principal concerns of the *Iliad*. Of course the treatment differs radically from Homer's, sometimes, but by no means always, to the extent of constituting a deconstruction of those concerns. It cannot be proved that the impulse for all this came from Shakespeare's reading of Chapman's Homer, but this is, at the very least, a plausible hypothesis. The result was Shakespeare's *Iliad*, a modern re-handling of ancient epic themes.

## SHAKESPEARE'S TROJAN STYLE

There are obvious similarities between the style of some parts of *Troilus* and that of the player's narration of scenes from the sack of Troy in *Hamlet* (II.ii.430-516), written not long before. For Dryden such 'pompous' writing was 'the delight of that audience which loves poetry, but understands it not', and came close to 'the blown puffy style', though Shakespeare had the excuse of writing in a less refined age.[34] In both we find a diction which combines the bombastic and Latinate and neologistic with contrasting blunt monosyllables. Moderns tend to suspect an intention of parody, of deliberately contrived 'figures pedantical' (*Love's Labour's Lost* V.ii.408). We would rather argue that this is Shakespeare's 'Trojan style', a style deemed appropriate to epic, as the age understood epic, part of a tradition which stretches from Marlowe, in particular *Dido, Queen of Carthage* and the translation of Lucan's first book, via Chapman's *Iliad* to the war in heaven in Milton's *Paradise Lost* (the style of which has also worried twentieth-century critics). Although in *Dido* the matter comes from the *Aeneid*, the style does not strike a modern reader at least as convincingly Virgilian, but English Renaissance writers seem often to have assimilated Virgil to later Latin poets, so that their work in this mode comes to resemble Lucan or the messenger-speeches in Seneca's tragedies.[35] Thus Marlowe's description of the treatment of Hecuba by Pyrrhus and his soldiers lacks all Virgilian 'restraint':

> the frantic queen leapt on his face,
> And, in his eyelids hanging by the nails,

A little while prolonged her husband's life.
At last the soldiers pulled her by the heels
And swung her howling in the empty air.

(II.i.244–248)

The player's 'passionate speech' (428) is certainly admired by
Hamlet and those he regards as still better judges, however much it
proved 'caviare to the general' (433). It is not easy to know how to
interpret Hamlet's taste. His observation that the play was 'well
digested in the scenes, set down with as much modesty as cunning'
(435–437) is almost bland enough to please Polonius, a conventional
but uninformative humanist critical position. What follows

> I remember one said there were no sallets in the lines to make
> the matter savoury, nor no matter in the phrase that might
> indict the audience of affection [i.e. affectation], but called it an
> honest method, as wholesome as sweet, and by very much more
> handsome than fine,
>
> (437–441)

suggests the authority of a plain style which avoids excessive wit and
polish. However the speech itself sits rather uneasily with this description, since, while craggy rather than slick or witty, it contains a
number of bizarre phrases and strained hyperboles. Hamlet specifies
that it comes from 'Aeneas' tale to Dido' (442f.), and, were we not
told of its provenance in a play, we might assume that, as a narrative
piece, it is a rendering of part of the *Aeneid* itself. It is thus reasonable
to argue that Shakespeare is attempting an epic style, grand, slow-
moving, with strange and archaic words, numerous tropes, adjectival
doublets and half-lines, a distinctively Virgilian feature.[36] Those who
think the speech parodic have failed to establish the object of the
parody. There is the odd touch which recalls Aeneas' 'woeful tale' to
Dido in Marlowe's play (II.i.114ff.), but Shakespeare could hit off the
Marlovian manner with complete accuracy when he wanted, and he
does not do so here. While there is a general stylistic similarity with
Marlowe (since both poets are working in a highly-wrought epic
style), there is nothing specific enough to suggest parody. Prosod-
ically the player's speech is rather more old-fashioned and more
stiffly artificial than anything in *Troilus*, but that is presumably
because Shakespeare wants to mark it off decisively from the style of
the rest of the play.[37] Apparently, particularly in view of his later
instructions to the players, Hamlet thinks the performance 'realistic'

as well as moving, possibly a reminder, by the sophisticated play-wright, of the clichéd character of much literary response and of the relative nature of realism.[38] It is worth remarking that there are some distinctly grand and epic features of style in the main action of *Hamlet* too, for example in Horatio's description of Old Hamlet in his heroic ethos (I.i.65f.: 'So frowned he once, when in an angry parle/He smote the sledded Polacks on the ice'). Horatio's account of subsequent events employs a distinctly leisurely form of the high-style; there are numerous phrases with inversions, repetitions and 'windy' and abstract language which would almost certainly have been described as fustian if they had occurred in *Troilus*: 'in the gross and scope of my opinion'; 'pricked on by a most emulate pride'; 'a moiety competent'; 'the same covenant/And carriage of the article designed'; 'terms compulsatory'; 'into our climatures and country-men' (70ff.).

The player's speech begins with a description of Pyrrhus covered in blood:

> The rugged Pyrrhus, he whose sable arms,
> Black as his purpose, did the night resemble,
> When he lay couched in the ominous horse,
> Hath now this dread and black complexion smeared
> With heraldry more dismal – head to foot
> Now is he total gules, horridly tricked
> With blood of fathers, mothers, daughters, sons,
> Baked and impasted with the parching streets
> That lend a tyrannous and a damned light
> To their lord's murder. Roasted in wrath and fire,
> And thus o'ersized with coagulate gore,
> With eyes like carbuncles, the hellish Pyrrhus
> Old grandsire Priam seeks.
>
> (448–460)

'Rugged', which, as the Arden editor observes,[39] is 'apt ... for both the landscape and the beasts of Hyrcania' – an image which comes from Virgil and which Hamlet uses of Pyrrhus in his first, mistaken opening – corresponds to Virgil's *horrens*, and means 'terrifyingly wild in appearance'. The black armour – in Virgil it is rather 'shimmering' (*coruscus*, *Aeneid* II.470) – resembles the darkness in the horse, so that Shakespeare does not merely draw together the physical and the moral, but gives a sense of black on black (such preoccupation with fine shadings of colour is typical of Renaissance poetry);

Pyrrhus' 'complexion' is his general colouring, but also suggests, more vaguely, his whole body and being. Black then gives way to red. The notion of heraldry, in grim ironic understatement, is continued in the phrases 'total gules' and 'horridly tricked with blood'. Pyrrhus, paradoxically as well as zeugmatically, is 'roasted in wrath and fire', and has become both literally and metaphorically monstrous in size with his outer coating of blood – a hyperbole worthy of Lucan. Equally extreme and paradoxical is the picture of Priam falling through the mere 'whiff and wind' of the blow of Pyrrhus' sword, which overgoes a similar conceit in Marlowe's *Dido* (II.i.253f.): 'Which he [Pyrrhus], disdaining, whisked his sword about,/And with the wind thereof the king fell down'. The death of Priam is described in slow motion. The moment of stillness, and the subsequent descent of the blow, is related with the help of an epic simile depicting the lull before the storm and its onset, and there is a stately build-up of clauses towards the climactic verb, in a Latinate, epical and indeed Virgilian manner:

> And never did the Cyclops' hammer fall
> On Mars's armour, forged for proof eterne,
> With less remorse than Pyrrhus' bleeding sword
> Now falls on Priam.
>
> (485–488)

The light pause after 'sword' followed by the two heavy monosyllables is finely mimetic. This is, in its peculiar way, distinguished writing, whose effect, in a sympathetic listener, is clearly the arousal of fear and, above all, pity. So, in *Dido, Queen of Carthage*, a comparable narrative manner prompts the queen to the response: 'I die with melting ruth' (II.i.289).

Hamlet's fondness for a play which was only acted once suggests an elitist and academic taste appropriate to the university-educated prince. But, while we would want to call the speech a pastiche, it should not be treated as parody. *Troilus* is a more complex case, for the epicizing manner is employed with a distinct self-consciousness and may sometimes be pitched at the edge of absurdity, while never, in our view, quite toppling over into it; in that sense the style can be closer to the excesses of Milton's war in heaven than to the more straightforward manner of Marlowe or Chapman.[40] This is partly the effect of the play's competing discourses already discussed, partly of its overall indeterminacy. But the point should not be coarsened. Critics who see in the play's grand style nothing but 'cant and rant' are not only yielding to the vision of Thersites, but ultimately depriving its epic moments of any real interest. Bradshaw talks of the prologue's 'signalled inflation', its 'stylistic dissonances', its 'flawed grand style', although he does allow 'a momentary, curiously Miltonic, grandeur' to lines 11–15:[41]

> To Tenedos they come,
> And the deep-drawing barks do there disgorge
> Their warlike fraughtage. Now on Dardan plains
> The fresh and yet unbruised Greeks do pitch
> Their brave pavilions.

Certainly the prologue has its own anti-heroism incorporated within it; after the grand opening we learn, flatly, of the cause of the war: 'The ravished Helen, Menelaus' queen, / With wanton Paris sleeps – and that's the quarrel'(9f.), and the ending, dismissive and cynical, is likewise unheroic. But the effect of these sardonic touches is spoiled if we do not concede to the rest some authentic grandeur achieved in part by inversions, archaisms ('orgulous', perhaps from Caxton, 'fraughtage', the rare Germanic word 'sperr', if that is the correct reading in 19) and Latinisms (e.g. 'immures'). The description of the shutting of the gates – 'with massy staples/And co-responsive and fulfilling bolts' (17f.) – juxtaposes, in a positively Miltonic way, long rolling words which are also learned etymological Latinisms with the calculated brutality of the monosyllabic 'bolts' placed in an emphatic position at the end of the line. One can compare the Miltonic sinewy pedantry of Agamemnon's 'Tortive and errant from his course of growth' (I.iii.9).

When Ajax (not the most subtle of heroes) addresses his trumpeter thus:

> Now crack thy lungs, and split thy brazen pipe;
> Blow, villain, till thy sphered bias cheek
> Outswell the colic of puffed Aquilon,
>
> (IV.v.7–9)

we may suspect bombast, but in the event Hector's visit in the rest of the scene proves uplifting enough, even if powerfully darkened by Achilles' dire threats, which the other Greek leaders find inappropriate. Yet some of the diction is particularly lofty ('multipotent', 'impressure', 'mirable', 'prenominate', 'convive'; 128, 130, 141, 249, 271). To T. McAlindon such things are 'verbosity', 'mere wind', 'strain and unnaturalness' – his conclusion about *Troilus* as a whole, that 'its subject ... is its own indecorum', is fashionably reflexive.[42] But, in the play's most gripping scene (V.ii), it is difficult to believe that Troilus' use of words like 'recordation', 'deceptious' or 'calumniate' (114ff.), or his subsequent violent language against Diomedes (170ff.), convicts him of mere bombast. There is an important point of principle here. It is easy for both Renaissance and modern critics to define 'decorum' in a general way, or to list stylistic vices like *macrologia* (excessive length) or *cacozelia* (frigid affectation of novelty) – both criticized by George Puttenham in his *Art of English Poetry* – but there can be no objectivity about their application to specific instances. If we take *macrologia*, we have to ask 'how long?' and 'for whom?', and Puttenham cannot tell us, because there is no answer. The objection applies to those modern critics who argue that Ulysses' degree speech displays this fault.[43] The central problem of rhetorical analysis is how to apply it. There is far too much hyperbole in Shakespeare for all of it to be considered rant, and some of the speeches of Lear or Othello are quite as extreme, in their different ways, as anything in *Troilus*. The use of adjectival doublets by Othello does not convict him of pomposity, but rather establishes his heroic status. In practice it is our knowledge of the characters, and our sense of the whole timbre of the language, not just the question of vocabulary or rhetorical style, which enables us to say that Don Armado's 'posteriors of this day' (*Love's Labour's Lost*, V.i.81) is ridiculous, whereas the presence of a similar and, in some ways, even more indecorous metaphor in Henry IV's lines:

> O Westmoreland, thou art a summer's bird,
> Which ever in the haunch of winter sings
> The lifting up of day,
>                                       (*2 Henry IV*, IV.iv.91–93)

does not detract from their exquisite effect of lyrical melancholy. If we want to show that Shakespeare's Trojan style has no genuine power – and the play is actually much more interesting if it has – we shall need to do better than scan the pages of the rhetoricians. We might instead develop a taste for heroic verse, which would enable us to enjoy a greater variety of English Renaissance texts.

# 4

# SHAKESPEARE'S ROME

## THE USES OF ANACHRONISM

Anglo-Saxon pragmatism tends to jib at the suggestion, sometimes made by serious-minded foreigners, that Shakespeare's historical 'mistakes', like the notorious 'sweaty night-caps' and striking clock in *Julius Caesar* (I.ii.242; II.i.192), are a blemish in his plays. Ben Jonson, of course, would have agreed with the criticism; he himself demanded 'truth of argument', that is factual accuracy, as a feature of responsible historical drama.[1] It would be wrong to dismiss his attitude as mere pedantry without further thought. Presumably the historical poet has *some* responsibility towards the past that he treats. It should not be implied that artists operate on too high a plane for 'facts' to matter, or that history (like politics) is of lesser importance than other more 'universal' topics. And it is not self-evident that Shakespeare's plays would not be improved if some of the minor errors and anachronisms had been removed.[2] Editors sometimes attempted the task for him. So Pope, 'with more zeal than judgement' in Dr. Johnson's phrase, argued that such errors were due to 'the many blunders and illiteracies of the first publishers of his works';[3] for example he emended Coriolanus' 'hat' (II.iii.98 and 165) to 'cap', and others followed his lead, including, in this instance, Johnson himself.

Shakespeare's practice, however, can be defended without too much difficulty. One possible line of defence would be to argue that Shakespeare is not interested in the history of Rome as such, but only in personality and politics in some wider sense. Dr. Johnson, in his robust way, claimed that Shakespeare 'had no regard to distinction of time or place, but gives to one age or nation, without scruple, the customs, institutions, and opinions of another, at the expense not only of likelihood but of possibility'. This did not matter because Shakespeare also transcended his age by 'his adherence to general nature': 'Shakespeare always makes nature predominate over accident; and, if he preserves the essential character, is not very careful of distinctions superinduced and adventitious. His story requires Romans or kings, but he thinks only on men'.[4] This appeal to 'Nature' is unlikely to satisfy a modern;[5] such 'essentialism' is now regarded as an ideological construct, and what to Johnson were 'adventitious distinctions' are seen as the products of crucially significant determinative factors. It is perhaps not altogether clear which side Shakespeare would himself have taken in this dispute, since it is at least plausible to argue that his ability to appeal beyond his age is partly due to his sense, not shared to the same degree by other writers of the period, of the way that individual personality interacts with social and political factors, a major concern of the history plays. At all events Johnson exaggerates Shakespeare's indifference to changes in social *mores*. One has only to recall Horatio's comment (*Hamlet* V.ii.345) that he is 'more an antique Roman than a Dane', or contrast Macbeth's reference to 'the English *epicures*' (V.iii.8) with Cassius' words to Messala (*Julius Caesar* V.i.77f.) 'You know that I held Epicurus strong,/And his opinion', where Shakespeare not only makes Cassius an Epicurean in the technical sense, but shows some knowledge of the doctrines of the sect. Shakespeare does in fact differentiate, stylistically and in other ways, between his Roman and his 'modern' characters, drawing his knowledge of Roman practices not only from Plutarch, his main source, but also from other ancient and Renaissance writings (Erasmus' popular *Adages* was a storehouse of such material).

Another approach would be to recall the statements of Renaissance theorists.[6] In discussing the question of the 'truth' of poetry, most (following Aristotle) agreed that it consisted not in minute factual accuracy but in verisimilitude. Anachronisms could be justified as a means of bringing the past to life and making the representation convincing to the audience. (This has always been the norm in religious paintings, providing a means whereby the Biblical story is made to live anew.) Anachronism was also sanctioned by the practice of Roman poets like Virgil, who included in the *Aeneid* customs and objects which clearly did not belong to the heroic world of primitive Italy that he was describing. We have already argued that all plays about the past must be to some extent anachronistic; all the more so one like Christopher Fry's *The Lady's Not For Burning*, in which a partly pseudo-Elizabethan language is used for the expression of some distinctly modern thoughts. The danger about too much 'authenticity' of background is that a gap opens between the setting and other elements which undermines a convincing sense of the past (as with so many modern historical novels).

The point can be illustrated by comparing two representations of ancient Rome in art. Andrea Mantegna's series of paintings of the 'Triumphs of Caesar', produced for the Gonzaga family of Mantua (who had pretensions as patrons of scholarship) and now housed in the Orangery at Hampton Court, reflects the artist's serious interest in classical archaeology and his knowledge of antique costumes derived from Roman coins, medals, gems, reliefs and monuments. Mantegna must have done considerable research in the Gonzaga library, and probably consulted Flavio Biondo's standard work *Roma Triumphans*. 'The total effect', writes the leading British authority on these paintings, 'is such as instantly to make one feel that one is in the presence of the Age of the Caesars'.[7] But in fact, despite some attempt to represent movement, the depiction – presumably by design – is like a sculptured frieze, in part because the figures are 'in sculptural isolation'.[8] There is also an inconsistency which opens a gap between ancient and modern: the archaeological detail conflicts with our sense that the paintings are, in some ways, typical of Renaissance decorative *trionfi*; and the result is a two-dimensional representation, a pageant or show, not a construction of 'reality'. One may contrast this sequence with the frescoes of the life of Antony and Cleopatra which Giambattista Tiepolo painted in the Palazzo Labia in Venice in the 1740s within illusionist settings by Mengozzi Colonna. The two main scenes show a meeting of the lovers at a port, which inevitably reminds us of Enobarbus' barge speech, and the famous banquet at which Cleopatra dissolved a pearl in vinegar. Tiepolo lacked Mantegna's detailed knowledge of antiquity, and it is far from certain if, for example, he had any idea who the Roman noble Plancus was, since, in the banquet scene, he dresses him like an Eastern monarch. The costumes are baroque-Roman, that is pseudo-antique, derived from those of Veronese. But the result is a consistently imagined world, which we can enter and whose totality we can accept – as Michael Levey puts it, 'All is illusion in the room ... making the visitor lose – like Antony – any awareness of reality beyond'.[9] As we shall see, a similar contrast can be drawn between the Rome of Jonson and the Rome of Shakespeare.

Shakespeare's anachronisms are in fact of different kinds, and it is not easy to determine which are simple errors due to lack of knowledge alone. For example Shakespeare may well not have known what sort of dress the historical Cleopatra wore (how many of us do?); but when he makes his Cleopatra say 'cut my lace' (*Antony and Cleopatra* I.iii.71) this has no bearing on the question, since (as a professional man of the theatre) Shakespeare would have been thinking of his boy actor's costume. We have a drawing, apparently made by one Henry Peacham, showing characters from *Titus Andronicus* (though their arrangement does not quite conform to any scene in the play as we have it). Titus himself, holding a ceremonial spear, wears Roman armour and a laurel crown, but the soldiers behind him carry halberds and are in Elizabethan dress, while the queen, who, wearing a pointed crown, kneels at Titus' feet, is in the dress of no particular period.[10] The mixture of costumes is probably typical of the age, though doubtless Jonson would have insisted on something more authentic for his Roman plays. Similarly, when, in *Julius Caesar*, Brutus keeps a book in his pocket and turns down a page (IV.iii.251f., 272), this does not necessarily prove Shakespeare's ignorance, but may only point to his awareness of performance needs; he had presumably met reference to papyrus rolls in his reading from Latin literature. Modern references must sometimes be deliberate: when Portia complains to Brutus that he treats her like a mistress, not a wife, 'in the suburbs/Of your good pleasure', there is obviously no reason to suppose Shakespeare assumed an identity of custom between ancient Rome and modern England, where prostitutes lived in the suburbs of Elizabethan London, any more than that he imagined that the language of Roman marriages resembled that of the Anglican Prayer Book (II.i.285f., cf. 272f.). Such anachronisms are clearly designed to bring the past to life, and to evoke an appropriate response in the audience. Another example is the description of Coriolanus' triumphal progress (II.i.260ff.) with its Biblical and chivalric resonances:

> I have seen the dumb men throng to see him, and
> The blind to hear him speak. Matrons flung gloves,
> Ladies and maids their scarfs and handkerchiefs,
> Upon him as he passed.

Other instances are more problematical. Obviously Shakespeare did not think that members of the Roman proletariat were called Hob and Dick (*Coriolanus*, II.iii.115) – the names are as it were translated as well as the speech – but he could have supposed that they carried the bats and clubs (I.i.55) used by London apprentices. In II.i.116 Menenius refers to Galen, a Greek doctor of the second century AD. Shakespeare perhaps could not have put a date to Galen (we suspect that the same would be true of most students reading Classics at university today), and been influenced by a vague feeling that Greece came before Rome; on the other hand he may have deliberately ignored the chronology because he wanted the name of the best-known medical writer of antiquity. In I.iv.57 there is an anachronistic reference to the elder Cato ('Thou wast a soldier/Even to Cato's wish'); here Shakespeare is simply following a comment of Plutarch: 'For he was even such another as Cato would have a soldier and a captain to be'.[11] Plutarch of course is at liberty to refer forward in history in his own voice; but, in giving Plutarch's sentiment to Titus Lartius, Shakespeare introduces an anachronism. The passage certainly suggests that Shakespeare did not think very carefully about matters of chronology, something which need hardly surprise us.

## SHAKESPEARE'S AND OTHER ROMES

Why does Shakespeare's Rome appear to many so much more convincing than the Rome of other English Renaissance dramatists? A cynic might reply that this is simply a matter of Shakespeare's cultural authority; Englishmen form their view of Rome partly from Shakespeare's plays, and then congratulate him on the veracity of his portrait. But the cynical argument will not quite serve. Lear and Macbeth have equivalent, or greater, cultural status, but no one bases his view of ancient Britain or early medieval Scotland on these works. Moreover it is not all Shakespeare's plays with Roman settings which impress us in this way, only the three from Plutarch.

A number of possible answers can be suggested. First, the Roman plays give us if not 'true' pictures of the ancient world – and in an age of meta-history the question of historical truth is anyway somewhat problematical – at any rate a sense of a possible past culture with its own imaginative consistency, achieved in part by numerous details discreetly deployed. As we have suggested, there is a danger in devoting too much attention to 'correctness' of background, the danger of 'costume drama'. In Sejanus V.178ff. Jonson describes a scene of ritual in which a flamen (a type of Roman priest) attempts to propitiate the goddess Fortune, which includes the following carefully composed stage direction:

While they (tubicines, tibicines) sound again, the flamen takes of the honey with his finger and tastes, then ministers to all the rest; so of the milk in an earthen vessel he deals about. Which done, he sprinkleth upon the altar milk; then imposeth the honey and kindleth his gums, and after censing about the altar placeth his censor thereon, into which they put several branches of poppy, and, the music ceasing, proceed.

We may feel that at such moments Jonson is trying too hard. There is just a hint here of the way Rome is represented in Henryk Sienkiewicz's novel *Quo Vadis?* (1896), a farrago of nonsense full of carefully researched local colour, in which typical sentences read 'he was about to be removed to the tepidarium when, raising a curtain, the nomenclator announced the presence of Marcus Vinicius' or 'he quoted Seneca's *mot* on women: "Animal impudens, etc.;" after which he laid his arm upon the young man's shoulder and conducted him to the triclinium'. The aggressively Roman detail of the ritual conflicts with the presentation of Sejanus as a religious sceptic who overturns the statue and altar with blasphemous words, an action with no basis in the historical record and one which assimilates Sejanus rather too readily to a type of familiar Renaissance villain. Shakespeare has a lighter touch with his Roman details. For example the description of Coriolanus' triumphal return to Rome is packed with vivid particulars, but only the mention of the 'seld-shown flamens' (deftly reinforced by the Latinisms 'popular' and 'vulgar') locates the scene specifically in Rome:

> Your prattling nurse
> Into a rapture lets her baby cry
> While she chats him ...
>        Stalls, bulks, windows
> Are smothered up, leads filled, and ridges horsed
> With variable complexions, all agreeing
> In earnestness to see him. Seld-shown flamens
> Do press among the popular throngs, and puff
> To win a vulgar station.
>
>                     (II.i.204ff.)

By means of what is in effect sleight-of-hand – a limited but skilfully used Roman colouring in a description which in other respects could as well belong to different periods – Shakespeare is able to convince us of the reality of the scene, without any sense of jarring anachronism. Above all, as such a passage illustrates, it is as an artist in

126

language that Shakespeare outstrips his rivals; in each of the Roman plays he devises a different solution to the problem of finding a style appropriate to his Roman context; no one else managed so successfully to solve this essential problem of decorum.

Rome in Shakespeare's Roman plays is neither blackened unduly nor unduly idealized. When Cleopatra uses the phrase 'a Roman thought' (*Antony and Cleopatra* I.ii.80), she means one that is 'soldierly, severe, self-controlled, disciplined'.[12] Such was the ideal, but the reality was often different. Cleopatra's irony not only hints at this, but also refuses obeisance before Roman conceptions of virtue. Shakespeare too can imply criticism of qualities often seen as admirable,[13] for example the moral rectitude exhibited by Brutus. The result is an impression of impartiality, which convinces us that characters and events could indeed have been thus. The point can be illustrated by Shakespeare's handling of the suicides of defeated Roman generals.[14] There is nothing especially remarkable about his understanding that, among the Romans, suicide could be seen as a noble act; *Romanitas* is regularly so characterized in Renaissance drama. Indeed pagan values could appear in plays with modern settings. Cassio's comment on Othello's suicide ('This did I fear, but thought he had no weapon,/For he was great of heart', *Othello* V.ii.361f.) reflects a classical and heroic, not a Christian perspective, although one's response is complicated by Othello's own language of damnation. What differentiates Shakespeare's treatment from the norm is not so much a superior intellectual understanding of ancient conceptions, but a more complex dramatic technique in exhibiting them. His suicides are oddly time-consuming or messy or both: Cassius acts recklessly in ignorance of the true situation; Brutus is forced to beg his comrades one by one to hold the sword for him, and only succeeds on the third attempt; Antony, deceived about Cleopatra's intentions, has to despatch himself when Eros prefers suicide to killing his master, and he bungles it badly. And yet all these deaths are moving, in no way satiric or even heavily moralized; we do not have to withhold our admiration. Once again the result is an increased plausibility We are reminded that Montaigne, who shared Shakespeare's sceptical humanity, pointed to limitations in the Stoic *apatheia* (freedom from perturbation) of his admired Cato the Younger.[15] Both writers share a sense that the complexities of experience rarely harmonize with human aspirations. 'The typical Roman suicide', writes Rowland Wymer, 'was an act of deliberate, self-conscious nobility which ... carried strong suggestions of theatricality'.[16] As we shall see, only Cleopatra's death wholly fulfils this ideal.

Shakespeare's historical imagination (as we have defined it) can also be linked with the unusually wide range of human feelings displayed in his plays. He can imagine what it might feel like to be a Jew in a Christian society, or a Moor serving the Venetian Republic, and persuade us of the validity of his imagining. Not surprisingly Cleopatra's eunuchs aroused the disgust of Roman writers (e.g. Horace *Epode* IX, *Odes* I.37), but in *Antony and Cleopatra* Mardian is sympathetically presented, and, in one witty, wry little exchange with undertones of pathos, we are given an insight into his experience of sexual deprivation (I.v.12-18):

| | |
|---|---|
| *Cleopatra:* | Hast thou affections? |
| *Mardian:* | Yes, gracious madam. |
| *Cleopatra:* | Indeed? |
| *Mardian:* | Not in deed, madam; for I can do nothing, |
| | But what indeed is honest to be done. |
| | Yet have I fierce affections, and think |
| | What Venus did with Mars. |

(One may compare this delicate exchange with the grotesque sequence in Jonson's *Volpone* (I.ii) in which the eunuch Castrone, together with a dwarf and a hermaphrodite, makes sport for his master and, as we later discover, putative father.) A sense of the past and a sense of cultural relativity naturally go together, and allow for an enlargement of human possibilities.

There can be no doubt that Shakespeare's reading of Plutarch provided the essential catalyst. T.J.B. Spencer exaggerates when he claims that Shakespeare's interest in the *Lives* was unusual for the period, even if it is true that the *Moralia* were better known.[17] For example Sir Francis Walsingham, Elizabeth's Secretary of State, recommended the *Lives* to his nephew, since 'knowledge of histories is a very profitable study for a gentleman',[18] while in Jonson's *The Devil is an Ass* (1616) III.ii.21–25 a character says:

> That year, sir,
> That I begot him, I bought Plutarch's *Lives*,
> And fell so in love with the book as I called my son
> By his name, in hope he should be like him,
> And write the lives of our great men.

It is true that, in the 1590s, among avant-garde circles, there was a sudden upsurge of interest in Tacitus, with his bleak and cynical vision of the loss of liberty and the hypocrisy of life under the emperors. The neo-Stoic writer Lipsius valued him for showing the way men fawn and inform when living under a tyranny, 'evils not unknown to this age', *sub tyrannide adulationes, delationes, non ignota huic saeculo mala*.[19] But Shakespeare rightly saw that Plutarch was uniquely suitable as a source for his sort of drama at least, since he offered, in G.K. Hunter's words, 'a concentration on the inexplicable individuality of personal lives, seen together with the tortuousness of the process by which subjective traits become objective and politically significant facts'.[20] Montaigne's interest in odd quirks of human behaviour had also led him to an enthusiasm for Plutarch, who, in the well-known words from the *Life of Alexander*, claimed that 'The noblest deeds do not always show men's virtues and vices, but oftentimes a light occasion, a word, or some sport, makes men's natural dispositions and manners appear more plain than the famous battles won wherein are slain ten thousand men'.[21] By keeping close to one source of high quality – closer than he generally does with Holinshed, for example – Shakespeare was able to offer a remarkably coherent picture of Rome (for *Sejanus* and *Catiline* Jonson used a variety of ancient sources, but sometimes had trouble in harmonizing them). This fidelity to a single source is unusual for Shakespeare, and should, we think, be seen as a deliberate artistic choice – the facts of Roman history were not to be manipulated with the freedom which could be applied to other, less authoritative, traditions. This is not to say that Shakespeare approached the matter in any spirit of scholarship; he was quite content to follow North's translation of the French of Amyot, and to reproduce any errors it contained.[22] By keeping close to North's words he also achieved some of his finest local effects. In Plutarch, when the guards find the dead Cleopatra, one of them says to the dying Charmion: '"Is that well done, Charmion?" "Very well", said she again, "and meet for a princess descended from the race of so many noble kings"'.[23] In Daniel's *The Tragedy of Cleopatra* this becomes the tangled '"Charmion, is this well done?" said one of them./"Yea, well", said she, "and her that from the race/Of so great kings descends, doth best become"' (1655–1657). Dryden, whose changes are in the direction of greater grandeur and explicit pathos, gives: 'Yes 'tis well done, and like a queen, the last/Of her great race. I follow her' (V.503–504). Shakespeare effects most by altering least, but each alteration is an improvement, especially the enigmatic, understated ending, diminuendo:

> Is this well done?
> It is well done, and fitting for a princess
> Descended of so many royal kings.
> Ah, soldier!
>
> (V.ii.304–307)[24]

Thirty-nine plays with Roman subjects survive out of more than fifty recorded for the period 1566–1635.[25] A brief examination of some of these plays may be of assistance in defining Shakespeare's individuality. We may start with what is in effect the first surviving 'Roman play', Thomas Lodge's *The Wounds of Civil War* (published 1594, written c.1589), which is largely based on the historian Appian, and whose theme is the horrors of the civil war between Marius and Sulla.[26] Given its early date and experimental character the piece is not to be despised; it shows some overall dramatic structure and some effective construction of scenes. There is, initially, a sense of the nature of Republican Rome to which the power-hungry Sulla, a 'private man' (I.i.98) – that is one not elected to the appropriate public office – is a threat. But the coherence of the constitutional arrangements soon starts to falter. When Sulla abolishes the tribunate, there is little feeling for the party conflicts involved; later Marius is declared consul by Lepidus and Cinna, then to act and speak like a monarch appointing his son commander of the army (IV.i.160ff.). The famous and powerful episode at Minturnae, in which a Gaul sent to murder Marius fled in panic when he saw flames emanating from the great man's eyes and heard a terrible warning voice in the darkness, is reduced to farce (III.ii). The end of the play (V.v) also descends into bathos. Sulla, made dictator for life, hearing of young Marius' suicide, thinks of fortune's fickle power and resigns. He is then bearded by two citizens with 'the very Roman names', as MacCallum drily puts it, 'of Curtall and Poppy'.[27] Genius enters to prophesy Sulla's death in feeble Latin elegiacs, and Sulla responds in similar fashion. Beside such absurdities, minor mistakes like the fact that Sulla's wife and daughter, Caecilia and Fausta, are misnamed Cornelia and Fulvia, are of little significance. The characters are not easily divided into heroes and villains, and one critic even diagnoses an effective 'realignment of sympathies' between Marius and Sulla;[28] but the overall effect is rather of moral incoherence, not least because of a failure of decorum and a lack of stylistic continuity.

In the opening scene Lodge finds a reasonably dignified public mode of utterance for the Senate's debate in the Capitol, typified by these words of Marius:

> Sage and imperial senators of Rome,
> Not without good advisement have you seen
> Old Marius silent during your discourse;
> Yet not for that he feared to plead his cause,
> Or raise his honour trodden down by age,
> But that his words should not allure his friends
> To stand on stricter terms for his behoof.

(I.i.113–119)

By contrast, when Sulla with his troops interrupts the meeting, he talks in the glittering language of the over-reacher Tamburlaine:

> I'll make streets that peer into the clouds,
> Burnished with gold and ivory pillars fair,
> Shining with jasper, jet and ebony,
> All like the palace of the morning sun,
> To swim within a sea of purple blood,
> Before I lose the name of general.

(I.i.218–223)

Later in the play Marius too falls into this Marlovian mode (e.g. IV.i.393–400). The comic Frenchman, Pedro, who does duty for the Gaul, belongs to a wholly different linguistic world: 'Mes messiers, de fault avoir argent, me no point de argent, no point kill Marius' (III.ii.75). Equally unintegrated into any overall decorum is the Elizabethan lyrical patterned rhetoric of the peace-loving orator Antonius (IV.ii.87ff.), or the language of young Marius in the echo scene in the wild, reminiscent of *Titus Andronicus*: 'Within my breast care, danger, sorrow dwells;/Hope and revenge sit hammering in my heart' (III.iv.62f.) These stylistic fluctuations run out of control, and are the ultimate cause of the play's failure to project a convincing image of Rome.

An altogether less lively piece but one marked by greater stylistic assurance and a greater grasp of Roman constitutional issues is Kyd's *Cornelia* (published 1594), translated from the French of Robert Garnier. This belongs to a small group of Senecan plays, which includes Mary Herbert's *Antony*, also translated from Garnier, and Samuel Daniel's *Cleopatra*. Like them *Cornelia* is constructed out of long speeches, stichomythia and lyric choruses, and there is little

131

sense of either society or setting. The play involves a constant meditation on the opposition between tyranny and freedom:

> And let another Brutus rise,
>     Bravely to fight in Rome's defence,
> To free our town from tyranny
> And tyrannous proud insolence.

(II.405–408)

Kyd understands the Roman meaning of liberty – the absence of the
unchecked rule of a single individual, guaranteed by the republican
constitution with its two key principles that all offices should be held
for a limited period and that all those in office, from the consuls
downward, should have at least one colleague with equal powers.
Caesar, who speaks like Tamburlaine and, in the rhetorical high style,
refers to himself in the third person, aims at a quasi-monarchical
position outside the constitution. Shakespeare may have read this not
uneloquent play, and even taken the odd hint from the scene between
Brutus and Cassius, but there was a limit to what could be learned, by
a writer for the popular stage, from such an academic production.
Similarly little of a historical setting is found in Chapman's *Caesar
and Pompey* (between 1604 and 1613); instead there is endless ethical
discussion, conducted in difficult, tortured verse, around the theme
of the epigraph 'only a just man is a free man'. The characters,
influenced by Lucan, are quite carefully drawn, but not the society
which produced them and against which their struggles were played
out. And, although Chapman was a scholarly writer, the play includes one scene of an absurdity to which the unlearned Shakespeare
would never have stooped: the comic encounter between the cow-
ardly Fronto and the evil serpent-god Ophioneus (I.ii).

In the address 'to the readers' prefixed to *Sejanus* (1603) Jonson
listed the four 'offices of a tragic writer' as 'truth of argument, dignity
of persons, gravity and height of elocution, fulness and frequency of
sentence'.[29] The last three (characters of high standing, a grand style,
constant ethical generalization) need cause no surprise when advanced by an admirer of the ancients. But in the case of the first,
Jonson went beyond most of the theorists to demand not merely
verisimilitude but factual truth which could be verified from original
sources (in the 1605 Quarto of *Sejanus* he cited his classical authorities in marginalia). His insistence is perhaps in part to be explained
as a response to the puritan charge that the theatre was concerned

132

only with lies. The demand, which if followed, would considerably reduce the dramatist's freedom, was obviously controversial, and in the preface to *Sophonisba* (1606) Marston, clearly with Jonson in mind, attacked those who 'transcribe authors, quote authorities and translate Latin prose orations into English blank verse'. His own aim was not 'to tie myself to relate anything as an historian, but to enlarge everything as a poet'. But it was not mere pedantry that moved Jonson; he held history in the highest regard as a means for understanding human life. In *Epigram* 95 he praises Sir Henry Savile, the translator of Tacitus' *Histories*, with these words:

> We need a man can speak of the intents,
>     The counsels, actions, orders and events
> Of state, and censure them; we need his pen
>     Can write the things, the causes, and the men.
> But most we need his faith – and all have you –
>     That dares nor write things false, nor hide things true.
>
> (31–36)

Naturally Jonson was careful to avoid the anachronisms he so despised in less learned writings (although there is a reference to a watch in *Sejanus* I.36). For example in IV.438 he changed the oath to 'By Hercules' on discovering that only women swore by Castor, a striking example of his passionate pedantry. Nevertheless the contrast between Jonson and Shakespeare cannot be made simply in terms of the contrast between pedantic antiquarianism and living drama. There may well be some contemporary allusions in *Coriolanus* (James I in 1605 had, when opening Parliament, referred to 'some tribunes of the people' in remarks on the royal prerogative),[30] but in general *Sejanus* is far more clearly directed at the contemporary political scene and actually caused Jonson trouble with the authorities in consequence; it was perhaps Jonson's attack on favourites and on informers and the spy system employed by tyrannous rulers which, *inter alia*, worried the Privy Council. Indeed the more time-bound character of Jonson's Roman plays may in part derive from a too obvious desire to make the events depicted exemplary to his own age. Jonson is forever finger-wagging, insisting on the relevance of Roman history, in a way Shakespeare never does; hence Cremutius Cordus, though speaking words derived from Tacitus, becomes a direct spokesman for Jonson's own views about the integrity of the writer (III.407ff.).

*Sejanus* has many merits. The deviousness of Tiberius is well conveyed (for example over the famous letter to the Senate which destroys Sejanus), and we are given, with some brittle but effective satire, a convincing picture of how a tyranny – but any tyranny – operates. But, despite the austerity of language and the careful use of sources, the play is, in certain respects, cruder than *Julius Caesar*. Sejanus himself is a combination of Senecan villain and Machiavel, and the play's action shows a debt to the medieval *De Casibus* tradition. The blackness of the villains is matched by the spotless purity of their opponents. Thus Silius' noble suicide in the Senate (III.325ff.) is an example of Stoicism more two-dimensional than anything in Shakespeare, or in Tacitus for that matter. In short, Jonson follows sources carefully, but on his own initiative does not really have a powerful historical and political vision nor a historical imagination as we have defined it – that is not to say the ability to recreate past events truthfully (anyway impossible), but the ability, on the basis of transmitted 'facts', to imagine a believable past society which has its own coherence. There is also the problem of style; the excessive decorousness inhibits a deeper decorum. Just as Jonson lacks Tacitus' cynicism (which makes the historian suspicious of the victims as well as of the perpetrators of evil), so his style is less interesting, less highly flavoured. Taut, monochrome, spare (and without much distinction of persons), the style of *Sejanus* evinces an austerity beyond its Roman models. For example Jonson's account of the fall of Sejanus is based on Juvenal, but lacks Juvenal's ferocious brilliance. Juvenal's lines describing the melting-down of a statue of Sejanus, which fairly crackle with life

> iam strident ignes, iam follibus atque caminis
> ardet adoratum populo caput et crepat ingens
> Sejanus, deinde ex facie toto orbe secunda
> fiunt urceoli, pelves, sartago, matellae.

> (*Satire* X.61–64)

> *(Now the fires hiss, and bellows and furnace bring a glow to the head worshipped by the whole people and huge Sejanus crackles; then from the face second in all the world are made pitchers, basins, saucepans and – chamber pots)*

are drained of energy and particularity to become the relatively colourless:

> Now
> The furnace and the bellows shall to work,

The great Sejanus crack, and piece by piece
Drop in the founder's pit.

(V.773–776)

As H.A. Mason puts it, Jonson's rendering 'represents only the *surface* of Juvenal. It is an abstraction from the text. What is absent from Jonson is Juvenal's *wit*'.[31] And, one might add, his descriptive vividness achieved in part by the inclusion of 'low' words, which would have been inadmissible in a tragedy. Dryden's freer rendering, from his Juvenal translations of 1692, shows us what is missing:

> The smith prepares his hammer for the stroke,
> While the lunged bellows hissing fire provoke;
> Sejanus, almost first of Roman names,
> The great Sejanus crackles in the flames;
> Formed in the forge, the pliant brass is laid
> On anvils, and of head and limbs are made
> Pans, cans and pisspots, a whole kitchen trade.

(91–97)

Perhaps only once, in the icon of Sejanus' mother Apicata mourning and demanding vengeance, does Jonson's language rise to a level which can call forth the pity and fear that Aristotle thought proper to tragedy:

> After a world of fury on herself,
> Tearing her hair, defacing of her face,
> Beating her breasts and womb, kneeling amazed,
> Crying to heaven.

(861–864)

Latinisms are also used to give a Roman colour. One result is a number of phrases which, as it were, demand to be translated back into Latin before they can be understood, or which at any rate can hardly be appreciated by the non-Latinate, for example: 'popular studies' (courting of the people = *popularia studia*, II.359); 'masculine odours' (the adjective *masculus* was used of certain larger plant varieties and the noun *odor* concretely of perfumes, V.91); 'favour your tongues' (= *favete linguis*, a call for silence at a religious ceremony, V.177). In III.496 the curious 'with so good vultures' works the other way; the English 'vulture' is substituted for the familiar Latin word *auspices*, which refers to observing the omens of birds. Such touches, while they can afford a curious pleasure, may be

135

felt to be caviare to the general. Shakespeare, at any rate, used Latinisms rather differently.

*Sejanus* is arguably the finest Roman play of its period, Shakespeare's apart. Jonson was not satisfied with its reception, but, never a man for compromise, when in 1611 he wrote a successor, *Catiline*, he repeated the classicizing features of *Sejanus*, even adding choruses in lyric metres on the classical model.[32] In a *tour de force* of imitation, which tired the patience of his first audience, he adapted into blank verse large parts of Cicero's *First Speech against Catiline*. Like its predecessor, *Catiline* is in some ways satiric rather than tragic, and in the second act, perhaps the most successful in the play, we find in the conversations of the immoral Fulvia and Sempronia, with their scintillating sexual innuendos, a hard-edged satiric mode reminiscent of Jonson's modern comedies. Jonson has not corrected what we have argued are the major weaknesses of *Sejanus*. Again his picture of Roman history is crude in comparison with Shakespeare's, as the first act shows. The opening speech of Sulla's ghost which contains some of the play's sharpest writing – 'Dost thou not feel me, Rome? Not yet? Is night/So heavy on thee and my weight so light?' (1f.), the supernatural darkness of the meeting of the conspirators as at Thyestes' cannibal feast (310ff.), their drinking of the blood of a slave as a sacrament (482ff.): all these things are, theatrically, not ineffective, but hardly the stuff of responsible history. Significantly Sallust, Jonson's source for the story of the blood sacrament, does not commit himself to its truthfulness (*Catiline* XXII), merely recording it as a belief held by some at the time but doubted by others. This technique of mentioning discreditable stories which are yet not endorsed by the sober judgement of the historian later became a favourite of Tacitus. Jonson shows no critical sense, at least as a modern historian would understand the matter, in his evaluation of his sources; he simply accepts what they record. Catiline is presented as a monster and over-reacher, as is his follower Cethegus, who is compared, in a memorably hyperbolic image, to one of the giants who defied the gods:

> he would
> Go on upon the gods, kiss lightning, wrest
> The engine from the Cyclops, and give fire
> At face of a full cloud.

(142–145)

As in this passage the writing can be of a remarkable, jagged brilliance, but the best moments do not particularly evoke the world of Rome, or mirror a Latin style:

> Come, we all sleep and are mere dormice, flies
> A little less than dead; more dullness hangs
> On us than on the moon. We are spirit-bound
> In ribs of ice, our whole bloods are one stone,
> And honour cannot thaw us, nor our wants,
> Though they burn hot as fevers to our states.
>
> (I.211–216)

By contrast, when imitating passages in his Roman authorities, Jonson tends to blunt the force of the original. Cicero's *First Catilinarian* may not be one of his richest speeches, but it has élan, pace, variety, which Jonson's close imitation fails to match (IV.ii.116ff.). Jonson gives a translation of the famous opening sentence *Quo usque tandem abutere, Catilina, patientia nostra?* ('How long then, Catiline, will you abuse our patience?') which is metaphrastic to the point of absurdity: 'Whither at length wilt thou abuse our patience?' (In fact, as Jonson must have known perfectly well, *tandem* in questions means 'then' or 'I ask', not 'at length'). Perhaps the aim was to make the listener recall the exact form of the Latin, but the result reminds one uncannily of the efforts of a schoolboy who does not fully understand what he is reading of the kind which so enraged Mr King in Kipling's story 'Regulus' ('*Tendens*, sir? Oh! Stretching away in the direction of, sir'). Perhaps a smile is the appropriate response. Again 'the consul/Bids thee, an enemy, to depart the city' (251f.) misses the packed forcefulness of Cicero's *exire ex urbe iubet consul hostem* (13), where subject and object are strikingly juxtaposed, and where *hostis* ('public enemy') has a special pointedness – Catiline was Cicero's antagonist, but had not yet been formally declared an outlaw by the Senate. There is frequently a lack of clarity in the organization of the syntax. Cicero's *hos ego video consul et de re publica sententiam rogo et quos ferro trucidari oportebat eos nondum voce vulnero* ('these men I the consul see and ask their opinion about the state and I do not yet wound with my voice those who should have been butchered with the sword': (9)) is both lucid and elegant: the sentence is organized into three clauses of increasing length (*tricolon crescendo/ ascendens*) and its effectiveness is heightened by *homoioteleuton* (*video ... rogo ... vulnero*), antithesis (*ferro/voce*), balanced clauses (*quos ... eos*), and alliteration (*voce vulnero*). By contrast Jonson, who tries to reproduce the way the relative clause precedes its antecedent (but without the clarifying *eos*), produces only tangled syntax and obscure sense:

> These I behold, being consul; nay, I ask
> Their counsels of the state, as from good patriots,
> Whom it were fit the axe should hew in pieces,
> I not so much as wound yet with my voice.
>
> (220–223)

Even when it is clear the writing lacks Cicero's rhetorical power. For example in 119ff.:

> Do all the nightly guards kept on the palace,
> The city's watches, with the people's fears,
> The concourse of all good men, this so strong
> And fortified seat here of the Senate,
> The present looks upon thee, strike thee nothing?

Jonson's rendering, close as it is, ignores two key features of the Latin, the hammer-blow of the six-times-repeated *nihil*, which also articulates the structure; and the suspense achieved by the early introduction of the object (*te*) and the long subsequent wait for the heavy climactic verb *moverunt*: *Nihilne te nocturnum praesidium Palati, nihil urbis vigiliae, nihil timor populi, nihil concursus bonorum omnium, nihil hic munitissimus habendi senatus locus, nihil horum ora vultusque moverunt?* (1) Jonson weakens the gradual build-up of six subjects by turning one of them into a prepositional phrase ('with the people's fears'), while 'the present looks upon thee' lacks the immediacy of the climactic and deictic 'the faces and looks of these men'. Rhythmically too Jonson's verse is inferior to Cicero's prose. Of course no translation can capture all the details of an original, but Cicero without the proper rhetorical punch is not really Cicero.

By contrast, in *Julius Caesar*, Shakespeare devises a superb blank verse equivalent for a Roman oratorical manner in the speech of Marullus to the people (I.i.32ff.):

> 32  Wherefore rejoice? What conquest brings he home?
>     What tributaries follow him to Rome
> 34  To grace in captive bonds his chariot wheels?
> 35  You blocks, you stones, you worse than senseless things!
>     O you hard hearts, you cruel men of Rome,
>     Knew ye not Pompey? Many a time and oft
>     Have you climbed up to walls and battlements,
>     To towers and windows, yea to chimney pots,

Your infants in your arms, and there have sat
The livelong day, with patient expectation,
To see great Pompey pass the streets of Rome;
And when you saw his chariot but appear,
Have you not made an universal shout,
That Tiber trembled underneath her banks
To hear the replication of your sounds
Made in her concave shores?
48 And do you now put on your best attire?
And do you now cull out a holiday?
And do you now strew flowers in his way
That comes in triumph over Pompey's blood?
Be gone!
53 Run to your houses, fall upon your knees,
Pray to the gods to intermit the plague
55 That needs must light on this ingratitude.

Here we have the syntactical and rhetorical control, the fire and variety of movement, which we find in Cicero's speeches. Shakespeare obviously noticed for himself, or had pointed out to him at school, the fondness of Latin prose-writers, including Cicero, for the *tricolon crescendo*: 'You blocks, you stones, you worse than senseless things' (cf. the three questions in 32–34 and again in 48–50, the latter with anaphora of 'And do you now', and the three clauses with imperatives in 53–55, the first two carefully balanced structurally). There are rhetorical questions, apostrophes and exclamations (in 36 with anaphora of 'you' and balance between 'hard hearts' and 'cruel men'), personification (Tiber trembling) and a careful variation in the length and impact of sentences. In 37ff. there is a relentless rhetorical build-up from 'walls' to 'chimney pots', and on several occasions a special emphasis falls on the last word in the sentence, for example 'Pompey's blood' (which contradicts the sense of triumph) or 'ingratitude', a climactic point which ends the speech. The language, like Cicero's, generally employs common words, here seasoned by three elegant Latinisms ('replication', 'concave', 'intermit') in contrast to the overall simplicity of diction. Shakespeare may not have read much Latin, but he learned from what he read. This, we may feel, is how a Roman orator might speak if he spoke in English. No wonder *Julius Caesar* caused Jonson such irritation.

Finally, we may look forward to the changed fashions of Restoration England and to a later Roman play, Dryden's *All For Love*

(1677). In some ways this is the most effective of the non-Shakespearean works we have examined, since the stylistic problems are skilfully managed and much of the verse is both accomplished and attractive, like the speech of Antony when, as he thinks, Cleopatra has betrayed him:

> My whole life
> Has been a golden dream of love and friendship;
> But now I wake; I'm like a merchant roused
> From soft repose to see his vessel sinking
> And all his wealth cast o'er. Ingrateful woman!
> Who followed me but as the swallow summer,
> Hatching her young ones in my kindly beams,
> Singing her flatteries to my morning wake.
> But now my winter comes, she spreads her wings
> And seeks the spring of Caesar.
>
> (V.204–213)

In such verse, Dryden is, as he claimed, imitating Shakespeare, not least in the finely judged cadences, but the language is clearer and simpler, more 'correct', with a more coherent and lucid use of simile and metaphor (though the two figures become interestingly blurred in 209ff.). Shakespeare, on the other hand, uses a more extravagant and, to certain tastes, a more bombastic poetic mode, but one which allows for a larger psychological range and more poetic and theatrical power.

In fact, in *All For Love*, Cleopatra surprisingly does not attempt to pack cards with Caesar. Dryden, like other writers of his period, favours clear motive and, unlike Shakespeare, idealizes his Roman world. This play, despite the smooth charm of its language and its almost domestic intimacy, is in that sense more heroic than *Antony and Cleopatra*. This is neo-classical drama in which the unities are observed and in which we meet noble and exemplary characters like Ventidius, the ideal Roman and faithful friend (I.105f.: 'the plainness, fierceness, rugged virtue/Of an old true-stamped Roman lives in him'), and the heroic conflicts between love and friendship, duty and love (III.316f.: 'For I can ne'er be conquered but by love,/And you do all for duty'). There is little sense of an alien world and less of the political bustle of Rome; indeed Dryden's play is not really political at all in the narrower sense of the word. Interestingly, in order to explore the whole gamut of set-piece emotions, Dryden is prepared to engineer a meeting in Alexandria between Cleopatra and Octavia, mistress and wife; an anticipation, in its bold departure from history, of the meeting of Elizabeth I and the Queen of Scots in Schiller's *Mary Stuart*. It is the far less learned Shakespeare who keeps closer to the records. On the stage Dryden's play easily surpassed Shakespeare's in popularity until the end of the eighteenth century and beyond; the point is a timely reminder of the relativity of taste.[33] Less artificial than Dryden's rhymed heroic plays and both freer from rant and richer in imagery than they are, *All for Love* nonetheless illustrates the diminished classicism of Augustan drama, and lacks the capacity to appeal widely beyond the cultural environment in which it was created. Shakespeare's play is superficially more vulgar than Dryden's, and perhaps for that very reason is a more persuasive vision of its subject, at least for a democratic age.

This survey of Roman plays confirms the view that Shakespeare is unusual in the degree to which he can convincingly project a Roman ethos, and it is to his vision of Rome that we must now return.

## MORE AN ANTIQUE ROMAN

Shakespeare's Roman plays are history plays, and Shakespeare, we have been suggesting, shares something of our sense of history, in a manner and to an extent that other writers of such plays do not.[34] We put the point in that way because recent theoretical discussion makes it problematic to determine how exactly a sense of history *tout court* could be defined. Theorists like Hayden White have cast doubts on the triumphalist claims of 'objective' history, have blurred the formerly clear distinction between history and fiction (since historians are necessarily implicated in the rhetoric and tropes of narrative like other storytellers), and have reminded us that modern historical methodologies constitute culturally determined discourses; there is no way in which we can escape the contingency of our own historical moment. This makes it more difficult to adopt a patronizing attitude towards earlier historical writings, or to congratulate certain authors merely because their approach in some way prefigures our own. We have long recognized the presence of shaping conventions, rhetorical invention and other constraints on the facticity of the works of ancient historians – less palatable to some is the reflection that the same lesson applies to the history written in our own times. Historical narratives must partly be seen as one way in which societies make sense of their past and thus of their present, as part of a continuous traffic between present and past. The sacred history of the Old Testament, or the demonstration of the operation of reciprocity (giving and receiving back, action and recoil) which lies at the heart of Herodotus' account of the Persian Wars, may not be the way we understand the past, but they have their own legitimacy and rigour in terms of the societies which produced them. Much Elizabethan history is strongly providentialist, or demonstrates the dangers of faction and the merits of monarchy. By contrast Shakespeare in his Roman plays seems closer to modern historical thinking in three main respects: first, because he has a strong sense that past cultures were different from present ones, together with the ability to embody that perception in the texture of his plays; secondly, because his picture of Roman history is so unidealized and so coolly secular, and involves an awareness that ethics and politics are very different pursuits; and, finally, because, as G.K. Hunter puts it, he used Plutarch to 'escape from the pressure of teleology',[35] that is to examine historical events which had not directly determined the present lives of his audience and which did not have to be shaped into any kind of sacred history or aetiology. There may be no such thing as a 'true' picture of Rome; but at any rate Shakespeare gives us one which is of extraordinary imaginative and intellectual power, beyond the grasp of any of his fellow dramatists.

It is sometimes suggested that the group of 'Roman plays' should be enlarged to include *Titus Andronicus* and *Cymbeline*.[36] But the three Plutarchan plays, with the alert political intelligence and 'dialectical imagination' revealed in them,[37] are the natural successors of *Henry IV*, and not of *Titus* with its strong if incoherent sense of ultimate good and evil. It is true that *Titus* was listed in the Stationer's Register as 'a noble Roman history'. It is also true, as we have seen, that Shakespeare uses Latinate words to give the play a superficial Roman gloss. For example in I.i.182 the 'palliament of white and spotless hue' which Titus is to wear as *'candidatus'* is borrowed from Peele's *Order of the Garter*, although its meaning is apparently mistaken (the word properly refers to a red robe). As H.T. Price puts it, 'We see ... with what consummate impudence he borrowed Roman-sounding words from his contemporaries in order to create a Roman atmosphere in his play'.[38] Spencer goes so far as to argue that, to an Elizabethan audience, the confusions of *Titus* would seem a convincing picture of the character of Roman history as it was then understood: 'One could say almost without paradox that ... *Titus Andronicus* is a more typical Roman play, a more characteristic piece of Roman history, than the three great plays of Shakespeare which are generally grouped under that name'.[39] This is clearly an exaggeration (even in Lodge we found a superior sense of historical period). But conceivably at this date Shakespeare would have thought that *Titus* gave an adequate image of Rome. If so, it was reading Plutarch that opened his eyes to larger possibilities. Certainly it was only in the 1590s that a full account of Roman history was made available to English readers with the first translations of the complete works of Tacitus and Livy (Sir Henry Savile's *Histories* was published in 1591, Richard Greneway's *Annals* in 1598, and Philemon Holland's Livy in 1600); previously they had to make do with translated excerpts, which could more easily be given a traditional monarchical slant. However Shakespeare may well have read some Roman history at school, so that the character of *Titus* need not be put down to ignorance alone; rather the play reflects a different kind of dramatic interest – an interest not so much in political manoeuvre in a precise historical context as in sensational violence, and the extremes of suffering and revenge, on the model of Kyd's *Spanish Tragedy*. Significantly the classical authors chiefly evoked are not the historians but, as we saw in chapter 2, the poets, especially Ovid and Seneca, together with mythic patterns derived from their works. Shakespeare makes no effort to give the play a precisely identifiable historical setting. G.K. Hunter argues that he created a generalized Roman ambience by deliberately combining two contradictory features of the Roman ethos as traditionally defined (in a way that is itself largely a Roman myth): the decadence of the Empire and harsh Republican virtue, the latter derived from his reading of Livy's account of early Rome, which he also utilized for *Lucrece*.[40] (Spencer puts the point wittily: 'the author seems anxious, not to get it all right, but to get it all in'.)[41] Thus perhaps *Titus* should be regarded, not so much as a crude precursor of the Roman plays, but as a work of an altogether different type; in some ways its most obvious links are with *Lear*.

If the 'Roman plays' do not descend from *Titus*, still less do they look forward to *Cymbeline*, that mannerist/baroque extravaganza, which can rather be assigned to a sub-genre of Romano-British plays which includes Fletcher's *Bonduca* and *Prophetess*. *Cymbeline* differs in almost every respect from the three Plutarchan Roman plays: in it we find a romance structure with providentialist Christian overtones; an artful mingling of ancient Romans and Britons with modern Italians (the wager plot probably comes from Boccaccio); a queen who (with her box of poisons) is like the wicked witch in a fairytale and her booby son; a heroine who disguises herself as a boy; a masque-like sequence with the descent of Jupiter; and a comic climax with multiple disclosures and recognitions. The play is no more designed to present an historical picture of Rome than *The Winter's Tale* is of the Greek world. Significantly in III.iv.77–79 Imogen rejects suicide with the words:

> Against self-slaughter
> There is a prohibition so divine
> That cravens my weak hand,

thereby confirming the play's unRoman orientation. If the final triumphant Romano-British peace has any Latin associations, it is rather with the Messianic, imperialist fantasies of Virgil's fourth *Eclogue*, or the extravagant celebration of the Augustan peace as a restored Golden Age in the *Aeneid*.[42]

The three Roman plays are best seen as developments of the English histories. By switching his attention to Rome, Shakespeare was able to achieve both a greater detachment and a rather greater freedom of manoeuvre. One recalls that a proclamation of 1559 had forbidden plays 'wherein either matters of religion or of the governance of estate of the common weal shall be handled',[43] and there were constant troubles with the censor throughout the period. Even so the danger was that analogies, real or imaginary, would be perceived between ancient Rome and modern England, as happened with *Sejanus*. The fact that Shakespeare did not apparently run into such difficulties might confirm our contention that he was more interested in creating the sense of an alien world, and exploring political activities in a specific historical environment, than in commenting on his own time. The detachment, together with the lack of inwardness in the presentation of historical figures, creates a greater distance between audience and characters than in tragedy as defined by Aristotle. We do not so much find the characters 'like us' and feel pity for them as watch them from outside as it were, if with a rapt and fascinated attention.[44] Many have said, with Hazlitt, 'it is *we* who are Hamlet',[45] fewer 'it is we who are Coriolanus or Antony'. The sense of distance is reinforced by a certain measure of irony which seldom if ever turns to sarcasm, or implies any general disenchantment with antiquity. In all these ways Roman society is seen as 'other', an object of contemplation rather than of direct involvement. The references, in *Julius Caesar* and *Antony and Cleopatra*, to theatrical performances are not reflexive comments on the plays themselves, proclaiming their artificiality and fictionality, rather they deepen the sense of historical reality. In *Julius Caesar* an exultant Cassius and Brutus look forward to the time when the successful assassination of Caesar will be made the subject of plays, which will keep alive the memory of the great deeds in which they have participated:

*Cassius:*　　　　　　　How many ages hence
　　　　　　Shall this our lofty scene be acted over,
　　　　　　In states unborn, and accents yet unknown!
*Brutus:*　　　　How many times shall Caesar bleed in sport,
　　　　　　That now on Pompey's basis lies along,
　　　　　　No worthier than the dust!
*Cassius:*　　　　　　　　　So oft as that shall be,
　　　　So often shall the knot of us be called
　　　　The men that gave their country liberty.
　　　　　　　　　　　　　　　　(III.i.111–118)

The final irony – liberty will not in fact be restored but expunged – reminds us that the meaning of historical events can never be clear to the participants. It is only we who – with Shakespeare's help – can see those events *sub specie historiae*. Still more breathtaking is Cleopatra's reference to the squeaking boy who would act her part at Octavian's triumph:

　　　　　　　　The quick comedians
　　　Extemporally will stage us, and present
　　　Our Alexandrian revels. Antony
　　　Shall be brought drunken forth, and I shall see
　　　Some squeaking Cleopatra boy my greatness
　　　In the posture of a whore.
　　　　　　　　　　　　　　(V.ii.215–220)

Shakespeare must have been sure indeed of his boy actor and of his audience to take such a risk at such a moment. In MacCallum's words, 'We experience a kind of vertigo, in which we cannot distinguish the real and the illusory and yet are conscious of both in their highest potence'.[46] The play is one which dwells on the relationship between art and imagination and reality, and Cleopatra herself displays an extraordinary ability to turn life into performance which reaches its climax in her artistically staged suicide, which ensures her triumph over time. A play so concerned with time and change shows that historical events can be fixed in art. As Robert Ornstein puts it, 'And because Shakespeare has written, she will die many times again and be staged over and over to the show – so long as men can breathe or eyes can see, Cleopatra is again for Cydnus'.[47] It is thus not the paradox it might seem that a play so concerned with art, and thus apparently with self-reference, is also one of Shakespeare's supreme achievements in verisimilitude, a sustained mimesis of actions and persons.

A failure to recognize the secular and detached character of Shakespeare's historical vision has led to much reductive or one-sided criticism. For example, it is frequently argued that contemporary accounts of Antony and Cleopatra, which were generally providentialist and condemned the lovers as vicious,[48] should guide our response to the play. Some critics also maintain that apparent echoes of the Bible, for example Antony's 'Then must thou needs find out new heaven, new earth' (I.i.17; cf. Revelation 21:1) mean that the events of the play must ultimately be judged from a Christian perspective.[49] Such Biblical resonances also appear, as we have noted, in the description of Coriolanus' triumph (II.i.260f.), where it would be absurd to suggest that Coriolanus is being in any way compared to Christ, just as Portia's words 'that great vow/Which did incorporate and make us one' (*Julius Caesar* II.i.272f.) suggests the language of Christian marriage. Such writing can be explained as a local means of emotional intensification, of appealing – possibly below the level of explicit consciousness – to the deepest reserves of feeling in the audience. We may say, if we like, that Antony's love for Cleopatra is a sort of idolatry; we need not conclude that we are required to see it from the higher perspective of Christian truth and Christian history. There are perfectly good Roman objections to Antony's behaviour, which it is the job of Philo and Demetrius and others to articulate. Furthermore, as always, generic considerations must be taken into account. It is true that political theorists and historians generally expressed hostility to the lovers, but there were rival poetic traditions which showed events in a very different light. To the gentle Gower, and to Chaucer, Cleopatra is one of love's martyrs (in *The Legend of Good Women* I, she dies for her 'husband' by entering a snake-pit naked); and the lovers are generally treated sympathetically too by dramatists in the Senecan tradition – indeed many of the Cleopatras in these plays are *less* devious and enigmatic than Shakespeare's.[50] Moral attitudes are frequently specific to particular discourses in just this way. The co-existence of these rival traditions means that historical context alone cannot determine our proper response to *Antony and Cleopatra*; as always texts are more real than contexts, and contexts when fully known are usually too complex to allow any determination of the way in which the individual work is to be interpreted. *Antony and Cleopatra* allows the audience to see the strengths and weaknesses of the lovers as well as those of their opponents. As Emrys Jones says, 'We are induced to assume a contemplative posture: unsparingly observant but sympathetic, and finally acquiescent. We have the means of passing judgement, but we refrain from doing so. This is the vision of the historical poet, as Shakespeare conceived it in this play'.[51] Modern moralizing readings of the play, like those of L.C. Knights and Derek Traversi, could be felt to be working against the grain of the text. Renaissance moralizations were at least based on clear and agreed conceptions of the nature of vice and virtue and were sufficiently generalized to leave free most of the details of a work of literature. By contrast 'moral maturity', 'life' and other similar irrelevances replace the Renaissance's ethical clarity in the relentlessly moralistic twentieth-century Anglo-Saxon world, and a censoriousness, masquerading as discrimination, is applied to speech after speech. What can it mean, for example, to say that Shakespeare ultimately 'discards' (Knights's word)[52] his lovers? History gave the events, and, by contrast with Antony and Cleopatra, Octavian is cold and ruthless; as Hunter drily puts it, 'the coming efficiency of the world will not be reduced by the fact that its directors have not invested a great deal of personal nobility in the system'.[53] Shakespeare's vision is both richer and tougher than Knights allows. Octavian is not victorious because he is a more virtuous man than Antony; rather, a glamorous past gives way to a new order at once more practical and less colourful. The pattern is a common one in Shakespeare's plays – it seems to constitute one of his most deeply felt intuitions about the nature of historical change.[54] Thus, while clearly some of the characters are more attractively presented than others, we need not rush to take sides.

It is the same with *Julius Caesar*. It was a matter of long debate whether the murder of Caesar was justified or not. The matter was clearly complex; even the resolutely Republican Milton was forced to concede 'the error of the noble Brutus and Cassius, who felt themselves of spirit to free a nation, but considered not that the nation was not fit to be free'.[55] Humanist education, we should remember, encouraged pupils to argue on both sides of a question. The epilogue to *Caesar Interfectus*, a Latin play performed at Oxford, reflects, in its structure of arguments for and against, school exercises of a common type:

Caesar triumphed forcibly over the Republic; Brutus over Caesar ... neither of them was more at fault than the other. There is something for me to praise in both; there is something in both for me to regard as vicious. It was evil that Caesar seized the Republic; good that he seized it without slaughter or bloodshed. Brutus acted rightly when he restored its liberty; but wickedly when he thought to restore it by killing Caesar.[56]

It is always wrong to talk of the Renaissance view of Rome. There were many different views, some hostile, some admiring, and the arguments – as such arguments usually do – played their part in the contest for current meanings as well.

Shakespeare not only distinguishes Rome from England, he characterizes differently different phases in Roman history. Such at any rate was the view of Alexander Pope: 'In *Coriolanus* and *Julius Caesar* not only the spirit, but manners, of the Romans are exactly drawn, and still a nicer distinction is shown between the manners of the Romans in the time of the former and of the latter' (by 'manners' Pope means, of course, *mores*, behaviour patterns).[57] MacCallum disagreed; in his view *Antony and Cleopatra* came closest to being an accurate picture of antiquity, but that was only the fortunate accident of the character of the story: 'he [Shakespeare] knew about soldiers of fortune like Enobarbus and pirate-adventurers like Menas; a ruler like Henry VII had in him a touch of Octavius, there were not a few notabilities in Europe who carried a suggestion of Mark Antony, the orgies of Cleopatra's court in Egypt were analogous to those of many an Italian or French court at the Renaissance'.[58] A consideration of *Coriolanus* (c.1608), however, will confirm Pope's view: 'To write *Coriolanus*', observes Spencer, 'was one of the great feats of the historical imagination in Renaissance Europe'.[59] It was a subject rarely chosen for dramatic treatment, and while the story was popular with political theorists, it was normally used merely to demonstrate the evils of democracy or mob rule. Shakespeare was evidently on his mettle, and he used hints in Plutarch to construct an image of a primitive Roman society; indeed he gives a stronger flavour of ancientry than his source. Shakespeare read in Plutarch that 'in those days valiantness was honoured in Rome above all other virtues, which they called *virtus*, by the name of virtue itself, as including in that general name all other special virtues besides'.[60] Not only does Shakespeare echo this in Cominius' account of Coriolanus' deeds of prowess (II.ii.83–85: 'It is held/That valour is the chiefest virtue and/Most dignifies the haver'), but he tries to imagine the character of a society built on such values. In a scene of his own invention (I.iii) he draws an austere picture of the home-life of Coriolanus' household. Young Marcus is proving a true son of his father, as Valeria reports approvingly:

> I'll swear 'tis a very pretty boy . . . I saw him run after a gilded butterfly, and when he caught it, he let it go again, and after it again, and over and over he comes and up again, catched it again . . . O, I warrant, how he mammocked it!
>
> Volumnia: One on's father's moods
> Valeria: Indeed, la, 'tis a noble child.
>
> (57ff.)

(In IV.vi.95 Cominius compares the Volscian warriors who follow Coriolanus to 'boys pursing summer butterflies'.) Earlier Volumnia rebuked her daughter-in-law's squeamish fears for her husband's safety:

> His bloody brow? O Jupiter, no blood!
> – Away, you fool! It more becomes a man
> Than gilt his trophy. The breasts of Hecuba,
> When she did suckle Hector, looked not lovelier
> Than Hector's forehead when it spit forth blood
> At Grecian swords contemning.
>
> (39ff.)

Shakespeare has not only been careful to give Volumnia an appropriate literary allusion to the grim heroic world of the *Iliad*, but also shows how the values of a warrior culture pervade every aspect of Coriolanus' world. Obliquely the scene tells us a great deal about why he is as he is. Clearly this is not a society much devoted to the gentler virtues. It is also, despite Volumnia's influence over her son (so that she can truly say in V.iii.63f. 'Thou art my warrior;/I holp to frame thee'), a society in which male values are more than usually dominant. In the gentle Virgilia Shakespeare gives his portrayal of a traditional type of Roman womanhood, her existence wholly bound up in that of her man – 'my gracious silence', Coriolanus later calls her (II.i.174), and that silence is eloquent and soothing in this play of clamours. But all erotic imagery is displaced on to warfare (I.vi.29–32; IV.v.114ff.). The scene with the women alone would rebut the claim that Shakespeare could not construct a society radically different from his own.

*Coriolanus* also displays some understanding of class struggle in the youthful Republic. Shakespeare made some accommodations to contemporary interests. For example, the initial cause of conflict in Plutarch is the effect of a harsh debt law; Shakespeare substitutes a shortage of corn from a later episode as something more familiar to his audience (there were food riots in Shakespeare's Warwickshire and other counties in 1607). Coriolanus denounces the fickleness of the plebeians (I.i.180: 'With every minute you do change a mind'), a judgement to some extent confirmed by subsequent events and shared by the tribunes, who are contemptuous of those they are elected to represent, whom they think easily manipulable. But equally the plebeians have good grounds for complaint, and the first citizen, in particular, is capable of considerable shrewdness; in I.i.36ff. he says of Coriolanus, 'Though soft-conscienced men can be content to say it was for his country, he did it to please his mother and to be partly proud, which he is, even to the altitude of his virtue'. This may not be the last word about Coriolanus, but it is as much of the truth as any other character possesses, and nothing in the play directly falsifies it.

In this first scene Menenius attempts to win over the citizens with the familiar parable of the body and the members (which Shakespeare knew from a number of sources as well as from Plutarch).[61] His verse is set off against their prose, and thus stands out as having more organization, authority and grandeur, but also less colloquial flexibility. It is a comparatively dry verse mode, which enjambment and word-order are continually pushing towards prosiness:

> The Roman state, whose course will on
> The way it takes, cracking ten thousand curbs
> Of more strong link asunder than can ever
> Appear in your impediment,

> (68–71)

and which in some respects is less lively than the citizens' prose. The tale itself is plain and uncomplicated, as might be expected of a speech designed to instruct and pacify the 'ignorant' mob, enlivened by one or two phrases which are quirkily colourful (99: 'cupboarding the viand'), or well-adapted to the recipients (in 143 the belly makes its audit up). In some of the speech one might see pomposity, or simply the efficiency of a fluent public speaker. The liveliest moments reside not in the tale itself, nor in its application (which Menenius reels off very pat), but in Menenius' interaction with the citizens, always quick with their answers. In particular the sceptical presence of the first citizen prompts Menenius into a witty extension of the parable, in which he names his interlocutor 'the great toe of this assembly' (154). While Coleridge's talk of 'the wonderful philosophic impartiality in Shakespeare's politics' may be overdone,[62] in such a scene it is not easy to be sure which side scores best, and whether it is true that Shakespeare's ultimate sympathies lie with the authorities, as is so often alleged. Throughout the play we feel the somewhat claustrophobic atmosphere of a small city state, which, despite all the internal rancours, will unite whenever threatened from outside. Into this small world of cynical political junketings and shabby compromises, Coriolanus' bracingly intransigent, heroic integrity cannot easily be accommodated. Aristotle said that someone who lives outside the *polis* must be a beast or a god; Coriolanus, 'a lonely dragon' (IV.i.30) is something of both.[63]

Shakespeare was fascinated by the way in which power operates, but he – or his audience – was less interested in the constitutional forms which it takes. Perhaps indeed his somewhat ironical or cynical attitude towards politics meant that he regarded such forms as of no great significance. This is most of a defect in *Julius Caesar*, where the issue is the transition from one set of constitutional arrangements to another, the change from Republic to Empire. The play marks a turning-point in Shakespeare's development; it has always been a success in the theatre, and its moulding into a single action of three of Plutarch's *Lives* is something of a *tour de force* in the creative use of a source, but in some respects it is a less supple work than its two successors (and indeed a number of the plays which came before it), with at times even a certain creakiness. That Caesar should break into Latin for his famous last words *et tu, Brute* is perhaps a trifle naive, meriting the censure of Jonson.[64] Caesar's thrasonical mode of speech – including his 'illeism', his way of referring to himself in the third person – teeters on the brink of exaggeration. This manner of self-reference is a feature of the high tragic style which was perhaps felt as Senecan. Velz and others who suppose that Shakespeare was thinking of the prose *Commentaries* in which Caesar, in a cool classical style and with seeming detachment, describes in the third person the events in which he was himself involved, quite miss the point.[65] These narratives create a (spurious) sense of objectivity; Shakespeare's Caesar engages in conscious self-dramatization as the great man. The ironic juxtaposition of his bombastic rhetoric and his physical weakness is, by Shakespeare's highest standards, a little crude. The puzzling references to Cicero have something of the feeling of a schoolboy joke:

> Did Cicero say anything?
> Ay, he spoke Greek.
> To what effect?
> Nay, and I tell you that, I'll never look you in the face again. But those that understood him smiled at one another, and shook their heads; but for mine own part, it was Greek to me.
>
> (I.ii.275ff.)

Moreover, it may be felt, Shakespeare does not present the constitutional issue clearly enough, misunderstanding or deliberately blurring it. In 1599 Thomas Platter, a Swiss doctor, saw what was almost certainly Shakespeare's play and described it as 'the tragedy of the first Emperor Julius Caesar'.[66] Platter presumably did not realize that Caesar was murdered precisely to prevent him from overturning the Republican constitution. But his mistake is not wholly unreasonable. Shakespeare makes a great deal of the portents surrounding Caesar's death, using not only the material in Plutarch but additional details from *Georgics* I, *Metamorphoses* XV, and perhaps too from the first book of the *Pharsalia*, where Lucan, probably with polemical intent, transfers them to the outbreak of civil war following Caesar's crossing of the Rubicon. In Shakespeare these materials introduce, even if briefly, a different timbre – something more like the brooding evil and cosmic disturbance of *Macbeth* – which to some extent is naturally associated with an imperial outlook (as Calphurnia puts it in II.ii.31, 'the heavens themselves blaze forth the death of princes'). They are readily adaptable to later European notions of the sanctity of monarchy, but less suitable for the conflicts of Republicanism. Of course the portents were a well-attested part of the historical tradition, and some of the characters in the play express scepticism about attributing any significance to them, but in an Elizabethan context they would encourage any tendency to see Caesar as a divinely appointed monarch. Initially the play includes authentically Republican sentiments; Cassius in particular expresses a willingness to die rather than be enslaved by Caesar, and reminds Brutus that his ancestor drove the kings out of Rome (I.iii.89ff.; I.ii.156–159; cf. 1.ii.96ff. and the tribunes in I.i, especially 72ff.). But Brutus' garden soliloquy (II.i.10ff.) not only takes us into a different verse mode – one which looks forward to *Hamlet* or even *Macbeth*, and which is used to mirror the obscurer movements of the mind – but seems to present the political issue in a new way. Brutus is worried that if Caesar becomes king, his nature may change for the worse; to forestall this possibility, he must be killed. Coleridge expressed a puzzled disgust:

> This is singular ... nothing can seem more discordant with our historical preconceptions of Brutus, or more *lowering* to the intellect of this Stoico-Platonic tyrannicide, than the tenets here attributed to him, to *him*, the stern Roman republican; viz. that he would have no objection to a king, or to Caesar a monarch in Rome, would Caesar be as good a monarch as he now seems disposed to be. How too could Brutus say he finds no personal cause; i.e. none in Caesar's past conduct as a man? Had he not passed the Rubicon? Entered Rome as a conqueror?
>
> *(Coleridge on Shakespeare*, p. 268)[67]

Whitaker argues that the issue in the play is the difference between tyranny and good monarchy, not the difference between Republicanism and autocracy, and he quotes with approval Sir Mark Hunter's remark that '"Liberty" as an end in itself had no meaning for Shakespeare'.[68] This is to put the point too strongly, but certainly Brutus' speech is very different from the equivalent monologue in Muretus' Latin play, *Julius Caesar* (1544), which reveals an exact sense of the issues as a Republican politician might have seen them:

> Does the virtue of your ancestors not move you and the name of Brutus? Does not the hard lot of your groaning fatherland oppressed by the tyrant and asking for your help? ... Is the objection that he is not king but *dictator* [a Republican office conferring unlimited power for a period of crisis]? So long as the thing is the same, what difference does another name make? Is another objection that he has shunned the name of king and the crown offered him? This is mere pretence and mockery. If so why did he remove the tribunes?[69]

Shakespeare's concern is rather with the tortuous and self-deceiving ways in which men reach decisions, and, following Plutarch, he shows Brutus as a decent man who, by his actions, harms his political cause.[70] For all his good qualities, he is weak, patronizing, and of poor judgement (thus, with egregious prudishness, he argues that Antony, because of his loose living, is not a man to be feared;

II.i.185ff.). His enemies triumph in part because they are more ruthless than he is, less concerned to live up to their own self-image. The cruelty and cynicism of the proscription scene (IV.i) projects a picture of Roman politics as bleak as anything in Tacitus. Plutarch criticizes the actions of the triumvirs at some length,[71] but it is Shakespeare who makes us feel the full horror of their actions, starting the scene baldly *in medias res*:

*Antony:* These many then shall die; their names are pricked.
*Octavian:* Your brother too must die; consent you, Lepidus?
*Lepidus:* I do consent –
*Octavian:*                    Prick him down, Antony –
*Lepidus:* Upon condition Publius shall not live,
            Who is your sister's son, Mark Antony.
*Antony*: He shall not live. Look, with a spot I damn him.

(1–6)

In the previous scene, one of the blackest comedy, the mob has torn to pieces Cinna the poet. To such straits has Brutus' failure to seize the political initiative brought Rome.

# IN SEARCH OF A ROMAN STYLE

## *Julius Caesar*

Dr. Johnson found a comparative coolness about the writing in *Julius Caesar*:

> I have never been strongly agitated in perusing it and think it somewhat cold and unaffecting compared with some other of Shakespeare's plays; his adherence to the real story and to Roman manners seems to have impeded the natural vigour of his language.[72]

Whatever is thought of the overall judgement, Johnson alerts us to an important characteristic of the play.[73] The style is not based on North's Plutarch, but is generally plain, oratorical, public, even at more emotional moments, suited to the *gravitas* of Rome's political leaders. The vocabulary is comparatively restricted, flamboyant imagery is largely avoided, such similes as there are are clear and decorous like Cassius' reference to Aeneas, founder of the Roman people:

> I, as Aeneas, our great ancestor
> Did from the flames of Troy upon his shoulder

154

The old Anchises bear, so from the waves of Tiber
Did I the tired Caesar.

(I.ii.112–115)

The lucidity, the exactness of correspondence, the straightforward-
ness of vocabulary, in particular the adjectives ('great', 'old', 'tired'),
in this familiar image of *pietas*, establish a dignified Roman tone.
(Perhaps, in view of the Virgilian nature of the material, the strikingly
hypermetric third line is designed to represent the Virgilian
hexameter.)

Shakespeare's feeling for the character of Roman rhetoric is clearly
shown in the contrasted speeches of Brutus and Antony to the people
after the assassination (III.ii). Plutarch describes, in *oratio obliqua*,
the main points made by the two speakers, but he does not attempt to
distinguish them stylistically. Shakespeare's Brutus, as Zanvoort has
observed,[74] uses rhetorical schemes (that is, stylistic patterns), in
particular *isocolon* (phrases of the same length), *parison* (correspondence of word to word) and *paromoion* (similarity in the sound of
words), whereas Antony prefers tropes ('figures of thought', like
metaphor). Zanvoort rightly attaches importance to the fact that
Brutus speaks in prose, Antony in verse. But his explanation, that
Brutus' is 'a style for the *intellect*', Antony's for the emotions, does
not accord with any of the more widespread distinctions between
verse and prose as Shakespeare uses them, and is rather too pat.
Antony's addresses to the crowd cohere, stylistically, with the process of the drama at this stage, and are fully integrated into the scene
as a whole. There is moreover less sense that they allude to a particular style of Roman oratory (though Plutarch attributes to Antony a
taste for the florid, orotund 'Asiatic' mode). By contrast, Brutus'
prose oration is marked off, as it were, in quotation marks, like prose
letters elsewhere in Shakespeare or spoken letters in classical opera. It
is often argued that some letters quoted by Plutarch provided Shakespeare with a model for Brutus' patterned rhetoric:

for the Greek tongue, they do note in some of his epistles that
he counterfeited that brief compendious manner of speech of
the Lacedaemonians. As when the war was begun he wrote
unto the Pargamenians in this sort: I understand you have given
Dolabella money; if you have done it willingly, you confess
you have offended me, if against your wills, show it then by
giving me willingly.[75]

However these letters are specifically said to be in Greek. So Bullough suggests that Shakespeare may rather have been influenced by Cicero's criticisms of the jejune style of Stoic oratory[76] (but it is uncertain whether Shakespeare presents Brutus as a Stoic). It is more probable that he is here, *inter alia*, recreating the so-called Attic style; he will presumably have learned at school about the controversy between the Atticists, who aimed at a controlled classical style, and their opponents the Asianists, who, as we have just observed, spoke more fully and flamboyantly. If so, the results, according to a leading student of Ciceronian oratory, are fully convincing: 'Some of Cicero's contemporaries and juniors claimed to imitate the simplicity and purity of the best Attic orators. Caesar was one of these stylists ... Brutus was another, and when Shakespeare makes him address the crowd in dry prose, the touch is authentic'.[77]

Brutus begins his oration with the words 'Romans, countrymen and lovers', putting shared citizenship first and personal acquaintance or admiration last (Antony reverses the emphasis with his 'Friends, Romans, countrymen'). 'Lovers' is not a word which suggests intimacy, but in this context means something like political supporters; Brutus' tone is less man-to-man than Antony's. He assumes that his audience will share his own Republican feelings, his own liberal and aristocratic viewpoint ('Who is here so base that would be a bondman?'), but, in his misguided sincerity, he shows no real knowledge or understanding of the people. The point emerges with brilliant irony when, at the end of his address, they shout their approval in terms like 'Let him be Caesar'. They have no appreciation of his views, and at this moment are both vulnerably leaderless and emotionally volatile. Stylistically, the speech is restrained for so critical a juncture. Brutus deploys his clauses and sentences with balance and symmetry, achieving emphasis through repetition, building cumulatively towards vital points:

> hear me for my cause, and be silent that you may hear. Believe me for mine honour, and have respect to mine honour, that you may believe. Censure me in your wisdom, and awake your senses, that you may the better judge.

Apparent paradoxes are carefully explained, and, after one seemingly rhetorical question, Brutus inserts, rather pompously, 'I pause for a reply'. There is no place for hesitations or disruptions in the structure of rhythm or argument, nothing to bring a shiver to the spine. Even the crucial turns become rather predictable:

As Caesar loved me, I weep for him; as he was fortunate, I
rejoice at it; as he was valiant, I honour him; but, as he was
ambitious, I slew him. There is tears for his love, joy for his
fortune, honour for his valour, and death for his ambition.

If this were not the noble Brutus and the situation so evidently
serious, might there not be something comic in such calculated
balance, something which could appear in the misguided efforts of
Malvolio or Don Armado, or, more impertinently, in the verbal
games of Falstaff? It is with careful decorum that Shakespeare assigns
such stiff rhetoric to the particular tactics and general character of
Brutus, so fatally unwilling to compromise his principles, or to
indulge in emotionalism even to save himself and his friends.

Brutus apparently awes the crowd into silence. Antony prefers to
use its violent energies, even during its initial hostility. His persuasive
arguments are taken from the three Plutarchan *Lives*, probably supplemented by Appian, but there are striking changes in the ordering
of various points. Plutarch places the reading of Caesar's will first,
Shakespeare last, after numerous tantalizing references to it and shifts
in topic – only when the crowd is already leaving does Antony call it
back, almost as an afterthought, to hear the contents. All this has a
characteristic Shakespearean improvisatory, haphazard quality, very
different from the smoother accounts in the sources; Antony thus
seems, with much greater immediacy, both the careful calculator and
the desperate, energetic opportunist. His verbal style is relatively
plain (and thus not noticeably 'Asiatic'), although he uses rhetorical
devices like irony and emphatic repetition to play upon the crowd's
emotions. From a quiet opening he orchestrates his irony about the
conspirators as 'honourable men' until the word itself is twisted into
the sharpest of denunciations. Similarly, while constantly deferring
to Brutus' opinions, he slips in his own with the lightest of demurs –
'if it were so' (81) – continues with the little grumble 'And grievously
hath Caesar answered it', finally blossoming, more fully, if briefly,
with 'He was my friend, faithful and just to me'. Even when he
employs balanced clauses like 'When that the poor hath cried, Caesar
hath wept' (93), he does so less stiffly than Brutus, with results which
seem less apparently calculated. He reserves his first apostrophe, 'O
judgement, thou art fled to brutish beasts!' (106), to the climax of this
section, and then immediately seems to break down, apologizing for
the strength of his emotions.

Antony, after a pause, switches to a different tactic, the arousal of pity for Caesar, veering abruptly from point to point, before focussing on the will. Instead of reading it, he builds up a strong circumstantial report of the assassination. When he points, with lachrymose sentimentality, to Caesar's mantle and refers to his great victory over the Nervii (at which Antony was not present) we cannot tell whether the historical 'error' is Shakespeare's or (deliberately) Antony's. Certainly Antony is concerned rather to develop emotive details than to report sober truth. He attributes 'rents' to specific conspirators, in what must be construed as fictitious amplification and *enargeia* (making the events vivid to the listeners' imaginations), and draws a picture of Caesar's death which he has not witnessed. (The producer will have to decide whether or not to corroborate any of Antony's details.) The reference to the statue of Pompey 'which all the while ran blood' (191) may be either a hint of further portents or just an emotive way of depicting the blood splashed over it – it hovers between the two and Antony does not explain. Grand apostrophes – 'Judge, o you gods, how dearly Caesar loved him!' (184), and 'O what a fall was there, my countrymen!' (192) – are marks of the high style, proper for the arousal of emotion. Antony also envelops his listeners in the disaster he has depicted: 'Then I, and you, and all of us fell down' (193). With rich irony he contrasts his skill as an orator with Brutus': 'I am no orator, as Brutus is,/But, as you know me all, a plain blunt man/That love my friend' (219–222), claiming that only because of his lack of skill has he been allowed to speak. It is possible that Brutus indeed despises Antony as a comparatively uneducated orator; certainly he fatally underestimates him. Like Othello Antony revels in being a plain blunt man whilst speaking with consummate skill. The irony is deepened because there is a sense in which Antony is telling the truth – his rhetoric is very different from that of the scholarly, tasteful Brutus, and he is genuinely driven by violent personal emotion. Finally, Antony calls the crowd back when on the point of departure, and after rattling off the details of the will, he ends with a resounding shout 'Here was a Caesar! When comes such another?' (254) and releases it to go about its anarchic business. Cicero, most fluent and varied of Roman orators, might have been proud to have delivered such a speech as is here given to his arch-enemy Antony.

## Antony and Cleopatra and Coriolanus

Ben Jonson, as we have seen, employed a similar style for his two Roman plays. By contrast, Shakespeare, always experimental in his use of language, devised fresh solutions for each of his three essays in the mode, in which a suggestion of *Romanitas* is only part of the picture. The open-textured oratorical manner of *Julius Caesar* suits its concern with the public aspects of politics and debate in a still partly Republican state. The politics of *Antony and Cleopatra* revolve rather around private negotiations and manoeuvre between great men on a world stage. While it has a less successful stage history than its predecessor, *Antony and Cleopatra* might be thought Shakespeare's greatest poem. Its poetry, and its prose, of a quality which is almost excessive for a play, are used for a largely externalized presentation of behaviour, of a delicacy and suppleness which has never been surpassed. The rich and flexible language is in a sense superficial, that is to say of an extraordinary fineness of surface – like that of *The Rape of the Lock* in its different way – which does not call us to much plumbing of the depths. John Bayley talks of 'a felicitous bravura', of poetry 'full of humour and agility, Tiepoloesque gorgeousness and nervous strength',[78] Coleridge of its 'happy valiancy of style'.[79] Like many other of the masterpieces of literature the play establishes a special linguistic world unique to itself; the achievement of this in a work which spans Egypt and Rome, politics and love, and contains a kaleidoscope of scenes and persons, is a *tour de force*.

Alongside the exuberant hyperboles and the gorgeousness there are passages of the utmost simplicity: 'Tonight we'll wander through the streets, and note/The qualities of people' (I.i.53f), and of melting delicacy: 'the swan's down feather/That stands upon the swell at the full of tide/And neither way inclines' (III.ii.48–50). With this image of flux and balance Antony takes the role of a disinterested connoisseur, more characteristic of others in the play, as he observes Octavia saying goodbye to her brother. The impact is partly caused by the introduction of the image after the plainer description of Octavia's speechless predicament. Structurally it operates as a simile with the introductory comparative word omitted, which makes it especially free-floating; and there is a fine pattern of sound with 'swell' and 'full', and a very characteristic late-Shakespearean cadence in the concluding half-line. There are other passages of a similar romantic and pictorial character, in which the poetry is like a fine pot which we can turn over in our hands. Of the ambassador's unexpectedly lyrical

> Such as I am, I come from Antony.
> I was of late as petty to his ends,
> As is the morn-dew on the myrtle leaf
> To his grand sea,
>
> (III.xii.7–10)

Emrys Jones observes, 'The dignified utterance is not unsuitable to the speaker, but its stylistic grace distances the moment, turning it into an object for our detached, almost aesthetic, scrutiny'.[80] There are frequent conjunctions of the colloquial and the Latinate. The sentimental remember Antony only as a lover, but he can talk the language of a politician with complete assurance. Shortly after dismissing kingdoms as clay, he decides to return to Rome (I.ii.174ff.):

> Let our officers
> Have notice what we purpose. I shall break
> The cause of our expedience to the queen.

Bringing an abrupt end to his bantering conversation with Enobarbus ('no more light answers'), Antony switches to verse and to thoroughly Roman and public matters in the brisk accents proper to a *princeps civitatis*. The Roman thought affects his whole diction, as he gives expression to a series of blunt comments and decisively-voiced intentions, using the plural 'we' as an expression of his dignity and public standing, and avoiding sentiment and personal emotion:

> For not alone
> The death of Fulvia, with more urgent touches,
> Do strongly speak to us.
>
> (177–179)

The 'strongly' conveys political pressure, not personal involvement, and the subject matter ('our contriving friends' etc.) revolves around the Roman political scene. Even the fickleness of the mob ('our slippery people') is mentioned without passion as a fact of political life of which the dutiful Roman commander must take note when the occasion calls. When Antony tells Cleopatra of his departure, he employs similar arguments in a similar style (I.iii.41ff.); looking coldly at the turmoil of the age, Antony speaks like his rival Octavian, showing the lost sparks of the tough *Romanitas* of his past, which certain puritanical Romans hanker after, but which elsewhere we seldom see. A similar diction (with Latinisms, dignified or pompous) is used by Octavian, outraged by his sister's return without a proper train ('raised by your populous troops'; 'you ... have prevented/The ostentation of our love'; 'supplying every stage/With an augmented greeting': III.vi.42ff.). In *Antony and Cleopatra*, as much as in *Troilus*, inwardness of character gives room to a play of contrasted discourses, which control men as much as they are controlled by them.

Certainly a lyric note predominates, anticipating the late romances, and for this reason Emrys Jones argues that the style is modelled on that of the Roman lyric poet Horace.[81] He rightly points out that Horace was admired for his bold positioning of words one against another (Quintilian X.i.96: Petronius 118). The ancient critics were probably thinking of such clever collocations as *divites insulae* (*Epode* XVI.42) for the islands of the blest, where *divites* replaces the expected *beatae* which means 'rich' as well as 'happy'.[82] It is true that there are examples of such *callidae iuncturae* (Horace, *Ars Poetica*, 48) in *Antony and Cleopatra*, as elsewhere in Shakespeare (e.g. 'lass unparalleled', V.ii.315), but in general the 'surprising rightness' of which Jones talks is surely the mark of many great poets. Horace in fact is a rather unlyrical lyric poet: each word clicks into place with precision to form what Nietzsche called a 'mosaic of words, in which every word by sound, by position and by meaning, diffuses its influence to right and left and over the whole; the minimum in compass and number of symbols, the maximum achieved in the effectiveness of those symbols'.[83] The result of this condensation is quite unlike the elusive delicacy of the more lyrical poetry of *Antony and Cleopatra*, with its images of flux, of ebb and flow, of clouds dislimning. The American poet Elinor Wylie (1885–1929) has some verses entitled 'Bronze Trumpets and Sea-Water: On Turning Latin into English', which may not contain the whole truth about the difference between the two languages, but which well encapsulate the contrast between Horace and Shakespeare:

> Alembics turn to stranger things
> Strange things, but never, while we live,
> Shall magic turn this bronze that sings
> To singing water in a sieve.
>
> The trumpeters of Caesar's guard
> Salute his rigorous bastions
> With ordered bruit; the bronze is hard,
> Though there is silver in the bronze.

> Our mutable speech is like the sea,
> Curled wave and shattering thunder-fit;
> Dangle in strings of sand shall he
> Who smooths the ripples out of it.[84]

For *Coriolanus* Shakespeare reverted to a more austere style, which has sometimes been compared with that of *Julius Caesar*. Any similarity is only superficial; for where the language of *Julius Caesar* is uncomplicated and often not unmusical, that of *Coriolanus* is dense, taut, and jagged, suited to a play so full of violent noise. Occasionally it flowers into a moment of weird intensity like Coriolanus' 'In the city of kites and crows' (IV.v.44), and there is a single passage of lyrical compliment, which anticipates the style of the romances:

> The moon of Rome, chaste as the icicle
> That's curdied by the frost from purest snow
> And hangs on Dian's temple – dear Valeria.
>
> (V.iii.65–67)

It is curious to find this from Coriolanus about Valeria, of the trio of women visitors the one of least concern to him. The drift of the lines, where the moon is an emblem of chastity, not of fleeting time, is to emphasize her standing as a chaste wife in the community, but this play, with its emphasis on military prowess, is not one where compliments in any shape or form come easily, let alone one couched in so romantic a verse. The Arden editor suggests that, as in *Othello* (V.ii.4–5), Shakespeare is using 'an image of cool and exquisite purity to lend poignancy to incipient violence',[85] but this hardly accounts for what Coriolanus says, since purity of that sort is not a burning issue in this play. Perhaps, as in the words which accompany the kiss he gives Virgilia, we see the briefest glimpse of a whole side of life which military and political Rome seems to have turned its back on. But such poetic superfluity – not to be pressed into any organicist notion of unity – is characteristic of Shakespeare, and one of the reasons for his greatness. The language concentrates on an intensifying, a crystallizing of purity, as the icicle is seen to be formed from snow by frost. The lines have a very similar movement to those in *Antony and Cleopatra* about 'the swan's-down feather' – there is a floating, half-realized pause at the end of the one unbroken line before we slip into the final cadence with 'and' – though, in keeping with the different timbre of the play, these lack the warmth of the earlier passage, they are, nonetheless, gentle and contemplative.

But in general the language of *Coriolanus* is marked by a relentless toughness appropriate to its early Roman setting. An example is Cominius' account of Coriolanus' deeds of valour (II.ii.82ff.). The style of the speech is heightened, as befits a public oration, but at the same time relatively dry and plain in language, not flamboyant, ornate, or 'poetic'. Even in this comparatively leisurely narrative there is a linguistic compression and difficulty characteristic of later Shakespeare (e.g. 'His pupil age/Man – entered thus', 98f.). Many of the clauses are brief to the point of bluntness:

> he bestrid
> An o'erpressed Roman, and in the consul's view
> Slew three opposers; Tarquin's self he met
> And struck him on his knee.
>
> (92–95)

Enjambment and median pauses break up the lines, and in this speech there is no sense of melancholy in the formations – in fact a similar blunt cadence falls mainly on the sixth syllable, repetitively (83, 85, 87, 89, 92, 94f., 98, 103, 105, 107f., 110, 114, 120, 122) – and the sentence and verse structures create a prosaic effect. There is more than a hint of an epic manner, appropriately so for a play so dominated by its heroic protagonist.[86] We find a certain grandeur of diction ('When with his Amazonian chin he drove/The bristled lips before him': 91f.), combined with a palpable plainness, which does, at times, characterize the vocabulary of the *Aeneid*, if not its mien (cf. the messenger's narration of the duel in *Bussy D'Ambois*, II.i.25ff.). There are also brief but grand similes:

> as weeds before
> A vessel under sail, so men obeyed
> And fell below his stem,
>
> (105–107)

and 'struck Corioles like a planet' (113f.). The speech is also a piece of calculated *Romanitas*. 'Dictator' (89) is used in its technical Roman sense without any fuss or explanation, while 'Whom with all praise I point at' (90) appears to approximate to a phrase of Latin oratory (editors suggest the Ciceronian *quem honoris causa nomino*), and has a somewhat Jonsonian quality, hard-edged and not entirely lucid or idiomatic. 'Fatigate' (117) also has Latin connections. The compounds 'brow-bound' and 'man-entered' (98f.) contribute to the compact effect, the first using plain words but producing a heightened tone, the second heavy and unevocative, and there is a preponderance of monosyllabic terms:

> his sword, death's stamp,
> Where it did mark, it took; from face to foot
> He was a thing of blood.
>
> (107–109)

There is a clearing-away of slack, easy-going extra words in this writing. The result is charmless, but a remarkable feat, the total effect somewhat 'foreign', like Milton's style in *Samson Agonistes*, another work dealing with a grimly heroic past.

The style of *Coriolanus* is also capable of the utmost expressive power. For example in V.vi.112–116:

> Boy! False hound!
> If you have writ your annals true, 'tis there
> That, like an eagle in a dove-cote, I
> Fluttered your Volscians in Corioles –
> Alone I did it. Boy!

Coriolanus, in language of the most explosive energy, reminds the Volscians of his former triumphs over them, as if he were asking for death. Rhythmically the most remarkable point occurs at the end of 114; there is a tricky pause before the last syllable creating a sort of hiatus before the word 'fluttered' which, when it comes, comes as a gigantic blow cutting against the lighter if scornful suggestion of the word's meaning. 'Alone I did it' triumphantly celebrates his extreme heroic success, and trumpets his characteristic solitude to the world, before the final furious grumble. Shakespeare's third essay at a Roman style, influenced perhaps by Jonson, makes fewer concessions to the audience than its predecessors – and for this reason will perhaps always be a minority taste – but, in its bleak way, it is no less a triumph of decorum and of the imagination.

# 5

# SHAKESPEARE'S STOICISM

At grammar school Shakespeare would have been instructed in the rudiments of moral philosophy,[1] illustrated in part from ancient texts, and he would have encountered some of the principal philosophical systems of antiquity, including Stoicism. Gilles Monsarrat, in *Light From the Porch*, argues that the influence of Stoicism on English Renaissance drama has been exaggerated.[2] His examination of the evidence leads him to conclude that it was largely confined to a few aphorisms and the presentation of tragic villains, an unimpressive harvest indeed. But that examination is marred by certain questionable assumptions and arguments. Monsarrat is constantly searching for Stoic characters in the plays, and (not surprisingly) finds few; he observes that the term Stoic is employed without precision by many modern students of the drama; he argues that much that is described as Stoic is simply Roman; and he points out that Seneca's plays should not be assimilated to his philosophical prose, since their authorship was regarded as uncertain by Renaissance scholars (for example Giles Farnaby, in a standard edition of the period, allowed only four to be the work of the philosopher).

None of these arguments is impregnable. The absence of Stoic heroes (of the sort we find in Chapman) proves nothing about the dramatists' interest in Stoic ideas; Shakespeare in particular – but not he alone – would have been alert to the gap between ideology and personality. Any modern lack of precision about terminology is, in a sense, true to a similar Renaissance imprecision; part of the attraction of Stoicism was the way it could be blended with other traditions. (Thus Stoic *patientia* and Christian patience could easily fuse, however much religious writers insisted on the gulf between them.) Similarly the conflation of Stoic and Roman accurately reflects the situation in Rome itself; Stoicism eventually became the most influential Greek philosophical system precisely because it harmonized with aspects of the Roman character and tradition. Cato the Younger was both a Roman and Stoic hero, as at once the defender of the old order and the Republican constitution and the fullest embodiment of the Stoic *sapiens* (wise-man). The question of the authorship of the tragedies is unduly pedantic. While there was a long tradition (based on a misunderstanding) of differentiating Seneca *philosophus* from Seneca *tragicus*, many thought that the philosopher and the tragedian were one;[3] and we can be sure that Shakespeare would not have worried much about the matter.

Shakespeare's familiarity with some of the principal tenets of Stoicism cannot be in doubt. In *The Taming of the Shrew* I.i. Lucentio's devotion to 'sweet philosophy'

> for the time I study
> Virtue, and that part of philosophy
> Will I apply that treats of happiness
> By virtue specially to be achieved,

(17–20)

and Tranio's punning response:

> Only, good master, while we do admire
> This virtue and this moral discipline,
> Let's be no stoics nor no stocks, I pray,

(29–31)

show that Shakespeare understood, and expected his audience to understand, the Stoic identification of *virtus* and happiness. In *Hamlet* III.ii.65–72

> for thou hast been
> As one, in suffering all, that suffers nothing,
> A man that fortune's buffets and rewards
> Hast ta'en with equal thanks; and blest are those
> Whose blood and judgement are so well commeddled
> That they are not a pipe for Fortune's finger
> To sound what stop she please. Give me that man
> That is not passion's slave,

Horatio is clearly being presented as a Stoic foil to the prince, even if some of his later actions are unstoical in practice (in V.ii.346 Roman and Stoic fuse in the notion of a noble suicide). As we have already suggested, Monsarrat may be right to argue that Shakespeare's Brutus is not clearly a Stoic, as so many interpreters have simply assumed. It was in fact only under the Empire that Stoicism became widely popular in Rome. Plutarch states that Brutus, an eclectic in philosophy, was in particular a follower of the Old Academy (that is, in many respects a Platonist), and, while Shakespeare may not have had a clear idea what Academics believed, he will have known that they adhered to a separate system.[4] In V.i.10–18, following Plutarch, he makes his Brutus record an earlier disagreement with Cato about suicide. Plato had rejected suicide as a form of moral cowardice, whereas many Stoics believed it justified in certain circumstances and if conducted in the proper spirit. Brutus then concedes that present experience has forced him to rethink the matter. Our view is that Shakespeare deliberately blurs the issue, so that elsewhere in the play (e.g. IV.iii.189–194) it is not unreasonable to regard Brutus as a not wholly successful aspirant after Stoic self-control. However, in view of Plutarch's explicit testimony, he leaves the matter of the identity of Brutus' 'philosophy' unclear and ambiguous. The blurring of the philosophical issue – like the blurring of the nature of the political struggle – we regard as a weakness in a play so concerned with moral and political ideas.

The view is gaining ground that Shakespeare is ideologically hostile to Stoicism.[5] This we would reject. Shakespeare rather uses commonplace ancient ideas, as he uses other sorts of ancient material, as a means of creating and illuminating scenes and characters and controlling the audience's response to them, in just that spirit of creative opportunism which differentiates him from dramatists like Jonson and Chapman, and which is a principal source of his greatness. Out of certain uninteresting commonplaces of Stoic provenance, he provides a series of great dramatic moments. There is no more point in asking whether he endorsed or rejected these commonplaces than in asking whether he endorsed or rejected classical mythology. They constituted raw material to be refashioned in the making of immortal plays. In the remainder of this chapter we will examine Shakespeare's use of one Stoic commonplace – that the good man is the constant man – to try to demonstrate the dramatic power which Shakespeare draws from his 'ideas'.

## CONSTANCY IN THE RENAISSANCE

The ideal of constancy was part of a general tradition of moralizing thought and writing, but it was also recognized by many in the

Renaissance as a characteristic virtue of the Stoic philosophy, deriving from antiquity, studied especially through the works of Seneca, but also those of Cicero, Marcus Aurelius, Diogenes Laertius, Boethius and others, and recreated by numerous writers from the fifteenth to the seventeenth century. In particular the treatise *De Constantia* by Justus Lipsius (1547–1606) was a major influence from the date of its publication in 1584.[6] The cultivation of detachment, of freedom from passion, led to an admiration for people whose personalities were unwavering in viewpoint, attitude or mood, who despised the vicissitudes of Fortune, showed equanimity in the face of death, disregarded the changing fashions of the world and possessed an unshakeable inner serenity. This ideal of personality – repellent to many today – could be presented as something moving or thrilling. The *De Constantia* concedes the way in which Stoic wisdom might appear unattractive, and attempts to mitigate this impression: 'Even so all wisdom seemeth austere and rigorous at the first view. But if you consider thoroughly of it, you shall find the same to be meek, gentle'.[7] Highly favourable portraits of the constant man are to be found, for instance, in Sir Henry Wotton's lyric 'How happy is he born and taught', or in numerous poems of Jonson, including the epigram 'To Sir Thomas Roe' (*Epigrams* 98,3–9):

> He that is round within himself and straight
>     Need seek no other strength, no other height;
> Fortune upon him breaks herself, if ill,
>     And what would hurt his virtue makes it still . . .
> Be always to thy gathered self the same.[8]

Such ideals left their mark on numerous biographies, or brief lives, of the period. An example is the portrait of Sir Horace Vere, in Thomas Fuller's *The Worthies of England* (1662). Vere was a soldier and royalist, of the family of the Earl of Oxford, who, Fuller claims, observed

> a constant tenor, neither elated nor depressed with success. Had one seen him returning from a victory, he would, by his silence, have suspected that he had lost the day; and had he beheld him in a retreat, he would have collected him a conqueror, by the cheerfulness of his spirit.

As one might expect, this sort of ideal had a particular affinity with the lives of soldiers and statesmen.[9] Mark Tapley in Dickens's *Martin Chuzzlewit*, with his immortal belief that adversity brings 'some credit in being jolly' is thus a late-born Stoic, presented in a comic mode.

For many moderns it requires an effort of the historical imagination to warm to the idea of the static personality. It conflicts with so much that our culture teaches us to admire. Stoic philosophers did not, of course, expect all men, or indeed many men, to stand as perfectly formed, unshakeable 'gathered selves' without having to undergo a transforming educational process, but change was not valued for its own sake; stability was always the goal. It is true that in the Renaissance the ideal of constancy was only one amid numerous available attitudes to life; and even its ardent admirers could see the humorous side. When Jonson, in the Induction to *Bartholomew Fair*, adjures each member of the audience to form his own opinion on a play, and then to stick to it, unswayed by the hubbub of varying opinions around him, he adds: 'He that will swear *Jeronimo* [i.e. *The Spanish Tragedy*] or *Andronicus* are the best plays yet shall pass unexcepted at here, as a man whose judgement shows it is constant, and hath stood still these five and twenty, or thirty years'. This sentence is nothing if not double-edged; but it must, nonetheless, be viewed within the perspective of Jonson's admiration, indeed longing, for the gathered self. He is joking at a cherished ideal, not slipping into a routine mockery of mindless conservatism.

Renaissance Stoicism was a therapeutic rather than an analytic philosophy. To an extent this had always been the case with Stoicism, and, in the terms of the ancient world, it was none the worse a philosophy for that. The neo-Stoics of the Renaissance were necessarily somewhat detached from the religious and scientific beliefs of the early Stoics, and what most interested them in their works was not any insight they might gain into the nature of the universe and man's place in it, but the teaching they could extract about the regulation of the troubled mind.[10] Stoicism was a philosophy which could help men to cope with changing values and expanding knowledge. The goal pursued was an inner balance and peace which was so complete in itself that for the person who had achieved it the changes and troubles of the world became not only tractable but irrelevant. It was a philosophy which responded to sorrow, and in many cases drew its own strength and inspiration from such depths. Its writings are a literature of consolation and had the power to appeal to the rigorous, intellectually troubled mind, to the simultaneously passionate and jaded (as Horatio appeals to Hamlet). It offers no easy sweetness as a reward but only uncompromising repose, removed from both misery and joy; happiness itself is suspect because so vulnerable to shifts in fortune. In fact the *De Constantia* includes 'joy' as one of the four principal affections – the others being 'desire, fear and sorrow' – which the Stoic must eschew.[11] This chilly ideal held sway over the mind of Seneca, trapped in the dangerous hothouse of Nero's court, involved, himself, in cynical political manoeuvrings and obsessed, as his works indicate, with images of torture and death. It pervaded too the writings of that 'violent, bitter man', Ben Jonson, who, in more senses than one, appeared to find, at least in imagination, some sweetness reared in stone. Lipsius himself is perhaps the most curious case of all. The man who taught the virtues of constancy to so many others was himself the living opposite of his ideal; he changed not only his abode and occupation but also his professed faith, time and again, seemingly unable, to the last, to settle into any loyalties. The *De Constantia* is partly a response to change and turmoil. It is based on an apparently autobiographical episode in which Lipsius was taking flight from the political and religious upheavals of the Low Countries, and was beginning a journey to Vienna, seeking quiet and rest. He stops on the way at Liège, where is he received by the revered sage, Charles Langius. Langius criticizes Lipsius' whole mode of procedure, and embarks on a course of treatment for the disturbed soul. During two dialogues, he probes the real springs of Lipsius' misery and expounds to him the antidotes which constancy would provide. It is fitting that Lipsius' teachings should be given through the mouth of another, as in practice constancy was so little his forte; even Stoicism was rejected in the end. Within his own lifetime he had become a byword for shifting opportunism.

The Stoicism of Lipsius and other Renaissance writers is partly one accommodated to a Christian culture. Lipsius at one point distinguishes contemporary adherents of Stoicism from the original Stoics, and argues that Christian followers of the doctrine, through their belief in God's providence, have an advantage over their predecessors which should stimulate them to greater success in the achieving of constancy. But on the whole he does not press the distinction very strongly, but rather amalgamates or bridges the two cultures with ease. The language which he gives Charles Langius to describe the healing operation of Stoic thought-processes has much in common with Christian penitential imagery, and it is also suggested that adversity is something sent by God for the chastisement of men, to make them more stable. It is striking, however, that, although

Stoicism can be blended without difficulty into a Christian consciousness, it sits uneasily with Christianity in its most specific forms. The religion of the *De Constantia*, like that of Boethius' *Consolation of Philosophy*, is a religion without Christ. From beginning to end, however much reference is made to God or to the religious conflicts of the Low Countries, mention of Christ is avoided, and avoided without any sense of strain or omission. It is worth bearing this particular spiritual balance in mind in relation to English Renaissance drama. The enforcedly secular stage was not without a spiritual dimension in many, perhaps in most cases; but it was not easy for a dramatist to find a way of expressing spirituality successfully through vehicles of non-specific Christianity. One of the factors in the 'wholeness' of Shakespeare's plays is their ability to contain a core of contemporary spirituality within secular or pagan vessels, and show little strain or discrepancy between the two.

Shakespeare's supposed 'universality' (that is, his transhistorical appeal) is partly his gift, beyond that of any other English poet, of making those of later ages, and with different belief systems, share, sympathetically, in alien or dead conceptions. Accordingly he will be our friendliest, most persuasive guide to the Renaissance ideal of constancy. Here it is necessary to combat a notion of Shakespeare's attitude to personality which threatens to become the *communis opinio*. To clarify the issue we want to take a model proposed by Thomas Greene, not because it is especially convincing, but because it is representative, in its placing of Shakespeare, of a wide range of scholarly opinions on the subject.[12] Greene suggests that a new interest in the flexibility of the self is characteristic of the Renaissance. He distinguishes two kinds of 'flexibility' which he terms 'lateral' and 'vertical'. Lateral flexibility entails a rich variety in a life at any single level of spiritual development, a variety of role, occupation and preoccupation, life-style and home. Vertical flexibility entails the belief that men have the capacity to alter their natures, their status as creatures, in an upward direction; through aspiration or education they can move towards the condition of angels, and, as a corollary, they can sink to the condition of beasts. Greene connects a belief in this vertical flexibility with the principles of humanist education, and cites various humanistic views including Erasmus' comment *homines non nascuntur, sed finguntur* ('men are not born but made'). On the other hand, in the works of Petrarch, especially the *Secretum*, the *Canzoniere* and the *Letters*, he traces an obsession with the lateral variety of the author's own life and psyche – the *varietas mortifera* as Petrarch himself described it. As the phrase suggests, Petrarch was often perturbed by the shifting qualities he observed in himself, and craved stability as a necessary stage in developing a communication with God and truth. Machiavelli is advanced as one who rejected the idealistic path of willed metamorphosis through intellectual discipline and espoused a pursuit of horizontal flexibility. He studied, as Greene puts it, 'the endless, inconclusive struggle between fortune and human resourcefulness',[13] and suggested that fortune could be best overcome by bending with it. This is the opposite to the way a Stoic would seek to deal with shifts of fortune, and is possibly designed as a refutation of the Stoic view. Greene also emphasizes the view of Montaigne (for example in *An Apology of Raymond Sebond*): Montaigne is preoccupied, like Petrarch, with the horizontal flexibility of man's shifting, unfixed nature, but, unlike Petrarch, he accepts this condition and is prepared to delight in it, since stability is unattainable and the pursuit of it vain.

When he comes to discuss Shakespeare, Greene tacitly allies him with Machiavelli and Montaigne; and Shakespeare has often been regarded as a wholehearted admirer of the shifting personality in one or other of its forms. Greene argues that Shakespeare admires adaptability, because he 'rewards' comic heroines, who disguise themselves and are generally resourceful, and punishes rigidity in tragic heroes. But it is inadequate to lump together the versatility of (say) Viola and Portia as comparable; it is even less satisfactory to equate Hamlet and Coriolanus as examples of fatal inflexibility. In any case, if a writer dismisses certain characters to happiness and brings others to grief, it does not necessarily mean that he approves the one and frowns upon the other. Furthermore a character who can adapt to circumstances and make the best of fortune is not necessarily unfixed in mind or spirit. Viola may disguise herself, fall in love rapidly, and tell a whole series of resourceful half-lies, but none of this can unseat the gentle repose which is the underlying substance of her nature. She retains this repose as she moves to and fro between households, and is pushed into one shift after another, while Orsino languishes at home with his soul at sea,

> unstaid and skittish in all motions else
> Save in the constant image of the creature
> That is beloved,

(II.iv.18–20)

and even this single constant image proves an idol of no substance. It is important to distinguish between a readiness to adapt in the face of unavoidable difficulties and a restless desire to make crafty manoeuvres – this leads to the gulf between the spirited or hopeful or resigned resourcefulness of Viola, Imogen, Helena, and the rootless scheming of Iago or Don John. When Shakespeare dramatizes stability or instability in his characters, they are qualities seen not so much in the actions in which they participate as in the roots of their longings and fears, and in the extent of their ability to be profitably single-minded.

Some writers have been able, with varying success, to present virtue in terms of stillness, repose and constancy, in a contrast with the hectic energy and movement of vice. This can be seen in the polarization of chaste heroines and villains in some of Jonson's comedies, or that of the Lady and Comus, and a similar structure lies behind Shakespeare's handling of Cordelia and Edmund. But on the whole it is true that Shakespeare does not reveal virtue through this kind of immovability. His plays are involved with the exploration of human weakness. It would be fair to claim that, as regards the Shakespearean kind of drama, there is more dramatic interest in the presentation of Brutus' failure to be as stable and disinterested as he would like than there could be in depicting a character who pursued similar ideals successfully. But Shakespeare can, at times, present achieved constancy with a startling emotional power.

## SHAKESPEARE AND THE CONSTANT (WO)MAN

### Sonnet 94

To illustrate Shakespeare's interest in this range of ideas we begin, not with one of the plays, but with a sonnet:

> They that have power to hurt, and will do none,
> That do not do the thing they most do show,
> Who, moving others, are themselves as stone,
> Unmoved, cold, and to temptation slow –
> They rightly do inherit heaven's graces,
> And husband nature's riches from expense,
> They are the lords and owners of their faces,
> Others but stewards of their excellence.
> The summer's flower is to the summer sweet,
> Though to itself it only live and die,

But if that flower with base infection meet
The basest weed outbraves his dignity:
  For sweetest things turn sourest by their deeds;
  Lilies that fester smell far worse than weeds.

The sestet is a relatively straightforward admonition on the principle *corruptio optimi pessima*; the octave is considerably less clear, and the effect of the combination is equally uncertain. Perhaps the most striking perplexity of the octave is whether the sort of people here described – those who seem to remain unaffected in the midst of all the effect they have on others – are presented as admirable or repellent. The poet appears, in the specific context of this sonnet, to be recommending emotional restraint as a vital safeguard against the corruption which accompanies an easy-going openness towards others. The conjunction of this poem with its neighbours in the sequence (92–96) certainly indicates that it arises out of a mood of disillusion consequent on infidelity, but it does not concentrate on such matters as directly as the other sonnets, and the intricacies of the sequence fail to resolve its particular difficulties. The bitterness of the situation entangles this poem too, but that does not necessarily cancel out Shakespeare's promotion of self-containment.

Some have argued that the behaviour here described should be seen as unattractive simply because Shakespeare loves to promote open-heartedness in his works, and dislikes this kind of restraint. They point out that the first seventeen of the sonnets (probably not part of the sequence anyway) recommend the broadcasting and multiplication of Nature's gifts, and a condemnation of niggardliness. But a moment's reflection lets us see that each strongly held view in Shakespeare is likely to have its opposite, expressed with equal conviction. In any case the ideal of self-containment is one which Shakespeare presents, in certain contexts, in tones of unambiguous approval. With sonnet 94 we have the problem of tackling the slipperiness of Shakespearean language without recourse to a detailed dramatic context.

The vocabulary and phraseology associated with the description of emotional restraint in this poem can easily prompt a hostile response. The poet describes those who are 'cold', 'unmoved' and like stone (cf. sonnet 11.6 'cold decay'). And then people who 'do not do the thing they most do show' and who are 'the lords and owners of their faces' are tantamount to the deceivers of the plays, those whose minds' construction cannot be found in their faces. Nevertheless we would suggest that within this poem they are being positively promoted, even if in a restrained and sober manner. Anyway, within the bounds of the sonnet's imagery, the chill and rigidity of stone is equated, it seems, with the softness and vulnerability of 'the summer's flower'. Such imagery of coldness can, in its own right, be expressive of beneficial qualities.

Twentieth-century psychological doctrines – especially those which are debased and popularized – have tended to see 'coldness' as a vicious trait, unpleasant for others and indicative of something maladjusted in the individual. The use of the word 'cold' in Renaissance English has a wider range of possibilities. It is not that there is a complete division in sensibility; for the most part lack of warmth emerges as unsympathetic in Renaissance literature as in so many others. But certain types of coldness are presented favourably. Any intense admiration of chastity, such as we find in Shakespeare's romances, is liable to entail some recommendation of coldness. Othello wails 'cold, cold, my girl! – /Even like thy chastity' (V.ii.276f.), but Desdemona, of course, is dead, and the word here piquantly combines positive and negative senses.[14] Milton's goddess Melancholy in *Il Penseroso* is thus exhorted:

> There held by holy passion still,
> Forget thyself to marble, till
> With a sad, leaden downward cast
> Thou fix them on the earth as fast.
>
> (41–44)

Milton is clearly recommending the mood of pensive melancholy, and here describes its embodiment in terms both of stone – the marble, as of a monument – and of lead. Lead too, in the period, frequently had unpleasant associations – dullness, deadness, oppressiveness. But Milton's depiction of the melancholy life connects with an atmosphere of pleasure and warmth. The poet says at the outset that the joys of melancholy would be lost on the non-devotee, that her

> saintly visage is too bright
> To hit the sense of human sight,
> And therefore to our weaker view
> O'erlaid with black, staid wisdom's hue.
>
> (13–16)

Of course the sonnet is much more difficult to interpret than *Il Penseroso*. It springs from a bitter, jaundiced mood, rather than an eager, or even a resigned one. Moreover it expresses not the serenity of a life 'sober, steadfast and demure' already embraced, but the very processes themselves of emotional control. This is reflected in the awkward, stumbling quality of phrasing in the second line – 'That do not do the thing they most do show' – and in the initial mention of the violent forces which are there to be restrained – 'They that have power to hurt, and will do none'. These processes of restraint show themselves to be difficult, and may well be unappealing, but they are certainly not negligible, nor confined to the realms of villainy.[15]

## Hamlet

Some of the sonnets – including number 94 – are unsuccessful as works of art precisely because, lacking a dramatic setting, their meaning floats uncontrollably. It is therefore with some relief that we turn to the plays themselves. *Hamlet* makes a number of gestures in the direction of Stoicism. Claudius' advice to his nephew in I.ii owes a certain amount to the Stoic *consolatio*, presumably via Renaissance intermediaries, although the fact that it is given in public helps to contribute to its somewhat suspect and insincere quality.[16] In the final act the poise of Hamlet, together with his fearlessness in the face of his own death, also has Stoic resonances, as the young prince grows up, and, in a conspicuous instance of tragic waste, dies just as he has achieved a full measure of maturity. In fact several codes jostle against each other in this play, as values emerge by turns Stoic, Christian and heroic (including the revenge ethos by which immoderate grief is seen as unmanly). The syncretism is characteristic of the age and of its drama, but the modern critic can point to fissures and inconcinnities in the amalgam, for example in V.ii.215–220, where the Biblical fall of a sparrow conjoins the Stoic 'the readiness is all'.[17]

But the chief Stoic ingredient is the way that the stability of Horatio is, for the audience as well as for the prince, a counterpoising relief to all that is hectic and inconstant and anguished. The emotional balance is rather like that described by Pope, towards the end of the *Epistle to a Lady*, and embodied by him in the structure of the poem as a whole:

> So when the sun's broad beam has tired the sight,
> All mild ascends the moon's more sober light;
> Serene in virgin modesty she shines,
> And, unobserved, the glaring orb declines.

(253–256)

Horatio, the man that is not passion's slave, is the balm of hurt minds, the sober light for tired eyes. By Shakespeare's sleight-of-hand his benign influence extends far beyond his physical presence in the play; this helps to solve the problem of how to present emotional control in a favourable light. Horatio's stillness gains its power to move audiences through Hamlet's longing for what he himself lacks.

## Macbeth

In *Macbeth* reactions to disaster involving both contempt of death and a readiness to accept whatever happens can be seen to some extent in the light of Stoic philosophy. According to Seneca, in his 26th letter to Lucilius, on old age and death, *egregia res est mortem condiscere* ('it is an excellent thing to learn how to die', 9). Language like this lies at the root of the description of the execution of the Thane of Cawdor, who dies 'as one that had been studied in his death,/To throw away the dearest thing he owed/As 'twere a careless trifle' (I.iv.9–11). Though Cawdor is a traitor, his courage is seen as admirable, and this helps to set the tone of this tough work, in which such courageous self-control is almost the only virtue one might dare to trust in or hope for. It to an extent redeems Cawdor's treachery, and in the end restores a certain stature to Macbeth, when he abandons the last vestiges of pretence and goes down fighting. Between these points are shown a series of responses to the news of a death which closely concerns the hearer. All of them, except the last, are in some way unbalanced, lacking the poise that can express true feeling for the deceased.

Macduff reacts to the discovery of Duncan's body in terms of Last Judgement imagery, mixed with horrified gasps (II.iii.62ff.). There is no personal sorrow here. One of the effects of Macbeth's actions is that a balanced individuality of grief is hardly achievable. Everything is swallowed up in enormity. Malcolm and Donalbain are quite unable to make any proper response to their father's death. Malcolm's immediate question 'O, by whom?' (98) is notorious for its inadequacy, but little else is possible. The answers multiply falsehood and speculation. When the brothers next speak, it is stealthily to each other. Their fear for their own lives preoccupies them; they feel in no mind to express any sorrow publicly, and even to themselves they can say nothing of emotional substance (117ff.).

Much deserved admiration has been accorded to the way Shakespeare portrays Macduff when he receives the news of the slaughter

of his family (IV.iii.199ff.). The episode is characterized by a powerful depiction of grief, from Macduff's initial inability to absorb the
news to his brushing aside of Malcolm's heroic exhortation to 'make
us medicines of our great revenge'. For all the human intelligibility of
Macduff's behaviour, however, it is not put forward as a model for
conduct, even in these circumstances. His response to the disaster is
complicated by his feelings of guilt about his contribution to it, and,
lacking a wholesome conscience, he is tossed between extremes of
fury and despair. If, as we are inclined to believe, because of the way it
fits into the immediate context, Macduff's exclamation 'He has no
children' (216) does refer to Macbeth, and to the impossibility of
effecting a proper vengeance because he has no children for Macduff
to kill, then it is a glimpse of a hell as deep, though brief, as any of
Macbeth's own. The enormity of what Macbeth has done proves
infectious in so many ways. And Macbeth himself, of course, can find
no other way to react to the news of his wife's death than an impatient
shrug, followed by an over-eloquent generalization on the human
condition, which tells us a great deal about himself, but expresses
nothing at all of loss or mourning (V.v.17ff.). There is no sense of any
communication, sharing of suffering, just of dissatisfaction in isolation. He does not even ask what happened.

The only balanced response in the play to news of death comes
near the end, in an episode which is often underestimated, both as
regards its structural importance and its intrinsic power to move. Old
Siward's immediate response to hearing of the death of his son in
battle is to ask how he died. On learning that Young Siward received
his wounds 'on the front', and therefore died fighting bravely, he says:

> Why then, God's soldier be he!
> Had I as many sons as I have hairs,
> I would not wish them to a fairer death!
> And so, his knell is knolled.

> (V.ix.13–16)

Old Siward should not be thought of as heartless. The grief which he
refuses to pour out in public is clearly hinted at by Malcolm: 'He's
worth more sorrow,/And that I'll spend for him'. But Old Siward
can cap this: 'He's worth no more;/They say he parted well and paid
his score:/And so, God be with him!' The sense of rightness and
fruition expressed here should not be easily brushed aside. At last the
time is free, and heroic response to loss is once more possible. Like
the Thane of Cawdor, Young Siward died well, but also had the

advantage of pursuing the good cause to the end. When the country is purged of Macbeth's wickedness, men can respond to death with a decent restraint and balance. Old Siward's reaction is that of a toughened, inured soldier, but then it is to a great extent on his type of standards that the play's moral foundations are laid.

## Coriolanus

*Coriolanus* is a play which deals centrally with notions of constancy and change. We continually see the inflexibility of Coriolanus himself, in his political opinions, clashing with the giddiness of the mob, which is a source of wonder even to the tribunes. Perhaps the most striking Stoic motif in the play is that of the futility of travel as a cure for discontent or failure. Coriolanus becomes a seeker after a new life, a fresh start, when he is banished from Rome; but what matter where, for him, if he be still the same? Seneca is clear that travel for the sake of recreation or refreshment is useless as long as the mind is oppressed. (The idea also appears in Horace, e.g. *Odes* II.16.17–20.) In *Letter* 28.1–2 he writes *animum debes mutare, non caelum* ('You need a change of attitude, not of climate') and *onus animi deponendum est; non ante tibi ullus placebit locus* ('You must lay down the burden of your mind; until then no place will please you'). He adds that if you undertake a change of scene while still lacking peace of mind, then 'whatever you do, you do against yourself; and you harm yourself by the very act of moving, for you are disturbing a sick person' (*quidquid facis, contra te facis et motu ipso noces tibi; aegrum enim concutis*, 3). This view is taken up by Lipsius, and indeed provides the basic structure for the *De Constantia*. The idea that travel is immaterial, and that the gathered self will remain unaffected by it, is powerfully expressed in Jonson's epigram 'To William Roe' (128.6ff.):

> there may all thy ends,
> As the beginnings here, prove purely sweet,
> And perfect in a circle always meet.
> So when we, blest with thy return, shall see
> Thyself, with thy first thoughts, brought home by thee,
> We each to other may this voice inspire:
> This is that good Aeneas, passed through fire,
> Through seas, storms, tempests, and embarked for hell
> Came back untouched. This man has travelled well.

(The penultimate word is a pun, both 'travelled' and 'travailed').

179

Coriolanus' farewell speech to Rome (III.iii.120ff.) is a curious mixture of Stoic attitude and extraordinarily unStoical feeling. He says to those who are casting him out 'I banish you'. This reflects Stoic belief that place is immaterial, that the right-thinking individual is a citizen of the world. Coriolanus suggests that he is self-sufficient enough to manage without Rome. But how does he express himself?

> You common cry of curs! whose breath I hate
> As reek of the common fens, whose loves I prize
> As the dead carcasses of unburied men
> That do corrupt my air – I banish you!

He is completely possessed by a splendid, invigorating, but certainly utterly unStoical anger, for which the Stoic statement is the climax. When he walks away saying 'There is a world elsewhere', his words are of complex significance. In one sense he is continuing his Stoic view that place is immaterial. But insofar as the statement is also a wish, or a hope, that a change of place will bring him a new lease of life and success, he is contradicting his Stoic pose even as he speaks the words.

Coriolanus has inflexible views – his constancy, if it may be so called, is of a somewhat brittle kind. Unwavering adherence to his political opinions and heroic pride lead him to commit the ultimate *volte-face* of turning against his state. He lacks any clear centre. One can cite the episode, after the capture of Corioles, where he begs, as the only favour he wishes, that a certain Volscian who had once befriended him should be given his freedom. He makes the noble gesture, but has forgotten the name of the man he wishes to help: 'By Jupiter, forgot!/I am weary, yea, my memory is tired;/Have we no wine here?' (I.ix.89–91) Plutarch does not bring the episode to this conclusion, but simply records Coriolanus' request and the approval which it arouses in all present; it is designed as an illustration of Coriolanus' nobility. But Shakespeare's piquant addition is a revelation of the swirling instability of Coriolanus' mind. He cannot with ease express himself in any way other than by fighting and his attempt at magnanimity fails. Likewise he refuses to act a part to the Roman people ('He would not flatter Neptune for his trident,/Or Jove's for's power to thunder. His heart's his mouth': III.i.254f.), but this attractive honesty is not so much a reflection of his inner self as something striven for with considerable pain. Even Volumnia thinks so: 'You might have been enough the man you are/With striving less to be so'

(III.ii.19f.). To a Stoic this inflexibility would be not constancy, but what Lipsius distinguishes as 'obstinacy or frowardness'.[18] Although Coriolanus attempts to adhere to a steady course of behaviour (even with a change of party in the middle), and to banish from himself the affections which might tie him to place or person, when he meets Virgilia for the last time in the tent of the Volscians, he gives expression to his irrepressible passions in a vein not wholly unlike Prospero's (V.iii.44f.): 'a kiss/Long as my exile, sweet as my revenge!' Thus the Stoic resonances in the play – and there are others, for example the 'precepts' underlying Coriolanus' words to his mother in IV.i.3ff., or the Second Watch's Stoic image for Coriolanus in V.ii.108f. 'He's the rock, the oak not to be wind-shaken' – are pregnant with a certain irony.

## Antony and Cleopatra

It would be easy to imagine that *Antony and Cleopatra* might contain a patchwork of Stoic ideas amongst its many richnesses. But in fact there are only a small number of definite Stoic statements in the play. Yet, if we were to seek throughout Shakespeare's Roman plays for a Stoic who is really worth the candle, we could do a great deal worse than settle, in the end, on Cleopatra herself. This may be dismissed as mere paradox-mongering, since Cleopatra is so often seen as the last word in pettiness and fickleness. Certainly she is of infinite variety: she can lose her temper to the extent of being capable of harming a messenger; she seems half-content to reassure herself about Antony's return on the basis of the most amusingly superficial investigations about Octavia; and neither Antony nor the audience, for that matter, is ever really sure about her political allegiance towards the end of the play. Nevertheless Cleopatra is always self-assured, and, in the play's second part, despite the mystery which comes to surround some of her actions, she is presented as intriguingly composed.

In the first main movement of *Antony and Cleopatra* (there is a definite break at the end of III.vi) the virtues of self-control and self-sufficiency are manifest, not so much in any of the major characters (if the terminology of 'major' and 'minor' characters is appropriate for this play), but in Sextus Pompey, who is not credited by Plutarch with the viciousness of which the tradition derived from Augustan propaganda accuses him. Admittedly Pompey is something of an independent adventurer, and associates with pirates, but this hardly sets him on a lower moral plane than Antony and

Caesar. And he refuses to take the pragmatic advice of the pirate Menas to slaughter the whole triumvirate while on his galley:

> this thou shouldst have done,
> And not have spoke on't! In me 'tis villainy,
> In thee it had been good service. Thou must know,
> 'Tis not my profit that does lead mine honour,
> Mine honour, it.
>
> (II.vii.72–76)

His wry attitude is hardly that of an unbending Stoic, but it has, for all that, its own measure of integrity. No matter how close he is to a stroke of good fortune, Pompey is not in the least tempted to bend his code of conduct and enforce what might have been. A little later, as the party on the galley begins to break up, Pompey shakes Antony by the hand with the words 'Antony,/You have my father's house. But what, we are friends?' (II.vii.125f.). Shakespeare alters the account in Plutarch, where Pompey makes his remark before the party, and means it as a taunt. In reply to Antony's question about where they might sup,

> There, said Pompey, and showed him his admiral galley which had six banks of oars: That, said he, is my father's house they have left me. He spake it to taunt Antonius, because he had his father's house, that was Pompey the Great.[19]

In Shakespeare's version the bitterness of Pompey's words is allayed, and the remark emerges as one calmer and more resigned, indeed companionable. As Menas had said earlier, 'Pompey doth this day laugh away his fortune' (II.vi.103). It is in his apparent contempt for fortune and success that Pompey displays virtue of a quasi-Stoic kind. He says of himself, to Lepidus' observation that he looks changed:

> Well, I know not
> What counts harsh Fortune casts upon my face,
> But in my bosom shall she never come,
> To make my heart her vassal.
>
> (II.vi.53–56)

This is as clear-cut a claim of moral strength as anything that Shakespeare's Brutus makes, and – something which is not true of Brutus – there is nothing that contradicts his words.

Pompey, of course, is destined for failure, as the world sees failure.

He dies out of sight and almost out of mind, the mention of his death creeping in, as it were, by the by. His virtue has to be its own reward. We would suggest that whatever virtue there is in the world of the play consists, in one form or another, of such scorn of worldly success. It is a combination of an acceptance of what fortune brings with a refusal, when it comes to the point, to transgress a few fundamental principles; and it is generally tinged, in this play, with a certain positive cheerfulness. There is nothing here of the sternness of Lucan's Cato, or the anguish of Shakespeare's Brutus. Pompey laughs away his fortune and later Scarus declares 'we have kissed away/Kingdoms and provinces' (III.10.7f.). Scarus, of course, is speaking in disgust at the loss of the first sea battle through Antony's seemingly uxorious pursuit of Cleopatra's fleeing ship. Scarus disapproves of kissing away kingdoms and provinces, as Menas disapproves of laughing away one's fortune. But both statements – like so many others in this play – have resonances and applications far beyond their immediate contexts, which can involve subsequent drastic reversals in meaning. What is intended as criticism of irresponsibility can change, when seen in a different perspective, into something more like a celebration of self-sufficiency.

Another example of this phenomenon will serve to adumbrate further the notion of virtue which can be seen in the play. In the opening scene, when Antony declares to Cleopatra:

> Let Rome in Tiber melt, and the wide arch
> Of the ranged empire fall! Here is my space –
> Kingdoms are clay,
>
> (I.i.33–35)

he is, in the immediate context, making an exuberantly hyperbolical pronouncement of the strength of his devotion to a woman, following a tradition of love poetry in making the beloved the counterpoise to the whole world. Even in its immediate context, it may be felt, this statement does not ring entirely true, not least since Antony's chosen way of making Cleopatra the world's equivalent is to use the measure of the world of power itself where his own interests lie. And it is not very long before we see him chasing again after his kingdom and going through various convolutions in pursuit of it. So his full-blooded assertion becomes increasingly tangled in a complex web of ironies. But, when seen in the context of the whole play, the view that kingdoms are clay is neither bombast, nor fleeting infatuation, nor a lie, but emerges as a universal truth – kingdoms *are* clay, in the perspective of time rather than of love, time where all comes down to the dungy earth, the nurse of Caesars and beggars, the dark towards which Iras calmly sets her gaze. The 'virtue' of this play, it seems to us, is contained in an attitude that is partly world-despising, but which becomes all the more attractive because its proponents are great lovers of the world in their way.

Antony's problem, like Hamlet's – much more than Hamlet's, indeed – is that he cannot make up his mind. He wavers and journeys between his two main courses of life, never content to surrender either of them. But Cleopatra, for all her superficial fickleness and moodiness, is undoubtedly single-minded. She knows what she wants; she may not always get her way, but at least she spares herself the anguish of wondering what that way should be. Despite her various complaints she never seems especially unhappy during Antony's absence. There is no great jolt when in the last stages of the play she starts to adopt a more dignified and, even, sterner mode of behaviour. One sort of self-possession leads easily to another.

Cleopatra is able to beat the Romans at their own game, and still enjoy herself in the process. It is the play's complete worldlings, Caesar and followers like Philo and Demetrius, who take the severe and joyless attitude to human conduct and who are almost exclusively wrapped up in the worldliness of political life and success. Cleopatra, although she does not seek out failure, is put into a position where she can and does gain considerable insight into its importance – or lack of it. Just after Antony has died she expresses a wish 'to rush into the secret house of death/'Ere death dare come to us', and of her proposed suicide she says 'Let's do it after the high Roman fashion,/And make death proud to take us' (IV.xv.81f.,87f.). There is a mixture of truth and falsehood surrounding these statements. She does eventually follow Roman example by choosing death rather than dishonour, and she dies in a dignified way, of which death, we daresay, might be proud. But her death has nothing of the stern contempt of pain which characterizes so many Roman suicides. Cleopatra has 'pursued conclusions infinite/Of easy ways to die' (V.ii.353f.), and she dies saying, 'As sweet as balm, as soft as air, as gentle' (V.ii.310). Yet how much more dignified is her death, surely, than that of Brutus who is reduced to begging and cajoling someone into holding the sword. And how much more deliberate and composed and necessary is her suicide than the impetuous mistake of Antony. What is more, Cleopatra does not rush into death at all. There has been much speculation on the reason for Cleopatra's delay in following Antony. But certainly one of its effects it to make her eventual farewell to the world ungrudging and untainted with momentary despair or bitterness: 'If thus thou vanishest, thou tell'st the world/It is not worth leave-taking' (V.ii.296f.). In terms of Stoic virtue it is certainly desirable not to rush into death. Non-Christian Stoics countenanced suicide, but not if committed in haste, or in despair, or in anything other than a state of composure. As Seneca tells Lucilius (*Letters* 24.24f.): 'Even when reason persuades one to finish one's life, the impulse must not be adopted rashly nor at headlong speed. A brave wise man ought not to flee from life but to make a proper exit (*vir fortis ac sapiens non fugere debet e vita sed exire*)'.

Cleopatra's most overtly Stoic statement is made at the beginning of the long final scene:

> My desolation does begin to make
> A better life; 'tis paltry to be Caesar –
> Not being Fortune he's but Fortune's knave,
> A minister of her will –; and it is great
> To do the thing that ends all other deeds,
> That shackles accidents and bolts up change.
>
> (V.ii.1–6)

The Arden editor gives a good gloss on 'a better life': 'a life in which Fortune's gifts are rightly estimated and despised, and the contemplation of one crowning and emancipating deed restores a sense of confidence, and superiority over Fortune's minion'.[20] In finding the ability to come to terms in this way with desolation, Cleopatra ensures her victory. This kind of triumph is expressed more tersely, but with a similar flavour, by Seneca (*Letters* 26.10): *Qui mori didicit, servire dedidicit* ('He who has learned to die has unlearned slavery'). After more twists and turns Cleopatra settles into her final resolution:

> now from head to foot
> I am marble-constant; now the fleeting moon
> No planet is of mine.
>
> (V.ii.238–240)

It is a source of very special excitement to hear Cleopatra of all people extol the splendours of constancy and find virtue through desolation. If she wishes to be as constant as cold stone this can in no sense turn her into a sternly inflexible personality. Instead, the marble itself is illumined and the virtue of marble-constancy is freed from its more inhuman connotations.

Shakespeare may have arrived at his conception of Cleopatra as a paradoxical Stoic on his own, but he could have found it in Horace. Baldwin has collected the evidence for Shakespeare's familiarity with at least some of the *Odes*,[21] and when writing about Cleopatra's death, Shakespeare could well have turned up Horace's treatment in *Odes* I.37,[22] or been directed to it by one of his more learned friends:

> Nunc est bibendum, nunc pede libero
> pulsanda tellus, nunc Saliaribus
>   ornare pulvinar deorum
>     tempus erat dapibus, sodales.
>
> antehac nefas depromere Caecubum
> cellis avitis, dum Capitolio
>   regina dementis ruinas
>     funus et imperio parabat
>
> contaminato cum grege turpium
> morbo virorum, quidlibet inpotens
>   sperare fortunaque dulci
>     ebria . sed minuit furorem
>
> vix una sospes navis ab ignibus
> mentemque lymphatam Mareotico
>   redegit in veros timores
>     Caesar ab Italia volantem
>
> remis adurgens, accipiter velut
> mollis columbas aut leporem citus
>   venator in campis nivalis
>     Haemoniae, daret ut catenis
>
> fatale monstrum: quae generosius
> perire quaerens nec muliebriter
>   expavit ensem nec latentis
>     classe cita reparavit oras,
>
> ausa et iacentem visere regiam
> voltu sereno, fortis et asperas
>   tractare serpentes, ut atrum
>     corpore conbiberet venenum,

deliberata morte ferocior,
saevis Liburnis scilicet invidens
privata deduci superbo
non humilis mulier triumpho.

*(Now we should drink, now with free foot*
*stamp the ground, now it is time to adorn*
*the gods' cushions with Salian feasts,*
*companions.*

*Once it was impiety to bring forth Caecuban wine*
*from ancestral stores, while a queen was preparing*
*mad ruin for the Capitol and doom for the*
*empire*

*with her flock of disgusting he-men corrupted by*
*perversion, she wild to hope for anything, and drunk*
*with sweet fortune. But there diminished her*
*frenzy*

*scarce one ship saved from the flames, and*
*Caesar brought back her brain watery with*
*Mareotic wine to justified fears, as she fled*
*from Italy*

*he pressing on her with oars, like a hawk soft*
*doves or a swift hunter the hare in the*
*plains of snowy Thessaly, to give to chains*

*a doom-bringing prodigy; she who more nobly*
*seeking to die neither feared the sword*
*woman-like nor took in exchange unseen shores*
*with swift fleet,*

*enduring both to see with face calm her*
*palace lying low and brave to handle rough*
*snakes, so as to drink in the black poison*
*with her body,*

*fiercer now she has resolved on death, doubtless scorning to*
*be carried a private person on savage*
*Liburnian galleys in proud – a not humble*
*woman – triumph.)*

Horace's poem displays a complex attitude towards its subject; it begins by abusing and ends by praising Cleopatra. The first half reflects hostile Augustan propaganda: mention of Antony is suppressed, so that the war can be presented not as a civil war but as one fought against a foreign enemy; Cleopatra, it is insinuated, was sexually lax; the battle is presented as a collision between traditional Roman virtue and Eastern decadence. The victory itself is grossly exaggerated – Antony managed to break out of the blockade with a reasonable number of ships – and Octavian did not immediately pursue the pair to Egypt, as the poet claims. However the historical distortions of the final stanzas work to the opposite effect; Cleopatra's suicide is implied, falsely, to have occurred shortly after Actium (nearly a year elapsed). The picture of Cleopatra gazing on the ruins of her palace (not in fact destroyed), with calm of mind all passion spent, has no basis in history but suggests her newly-attained poise. The shift in attitude begins in the simile which shows the velocity but also the violence of Caesar, figured in the hawk, the softness but also the pathetic vulnerability of the dove-like Cleopatra.

This new perspective, perhaps designed to provide Octavian with a worthy antagonist, is sustained by a series of precise reversals, centred on Actium. In stanza 2 Horace stresses the effeminacy of the Egyptians; *virorum* is ironic, since it refers to Cleopatra's eunuchs, men unmanned. In the final stanza Cleopatra is accorded man-like courage (*nec muliebriter*), and chooses death by her own hand rather than captivity and humiliation. She dies not for love, but as a proud queen of Egypt, 'fitting for a princess/Descended from so many royal kings'. Before Actium she is drunk, her mind crazed with Mareotic wine, but the battle restores her to sobriety and she dies by drinking in (*conbiberet*) the asp's poison with her body, a completion of the image-pattern. The final contrast is constructed by language with a philosophical colour. The phrase 'drunk with sweet fortune' establishes Cleopatra as an anti-Stoic, since, as we have seen, the good man was not elated by good fortune or downcast by bad. After defeat she attains a Stoic indifference to fortune, looking at her fallen palace with 'face serene'. Finally we see matters entirely through her eyes, as the pejorative adjectives *saevis* and *superbo*, used of the Romans, show. Rightly or wrongly Horace's ode can be read as radically dialectical, as the Marvell of the 'Horatian Ode' for Cromwell later saw, something which could obviously have attracted Shakespeare.[23]

In other plays the constant man has either been, in fact, a failure at the game, as is the case with Coriolanus – someone entirely lacking the wholeness and self-sufficiency to remain secure in any course; or he has acted as a foil to the more interesting inconstant men. Horatio, important as he is, is of no great interest as a personality in his own right. In a comparable way Old Siward helps to underline the failings of others, whether these be their own fault or that of the times in which they live. And Sextus Pompey provides an example of indubitable honour in an environment where honour is far from prevalent. But Cleopatra, sole constant woman, becomes the Stoic foil to her own fascinating changefulness, so achieving a paradoxical and moving combination of fleeting moon and marble-constancy.

# ABBREVIATIONS USED IN NOTES

**Baldwin**
Baldwin, T.W., *William Shakspere's Small Latine and Lesse Greeke*, 2 vols., Urbana, University of Illinois Press, 1944.
**Bullough**
Bullough, G. (ed.), *Narrative and Dramatic Sources of Shakespeare*, 8 vols, London and Henley, Routledge & Kegan Paul; New York, Columbia University Press, 1957–1975.
**Cunliffe**
Cunliffe, J.W., *The Influence of Seneca on Elizabethan Tragedy*, first published 1893, Hamden, CT, Archon Books, 1965.
**MacCallum**
MacCallum, M.W., *Shakespeare's Roman Plays and their Background*, first published 1910, reprinted with a foreword by T.J.B. Spencer, London and Melbourne, Macmillan, 1967.
**Root**
Root, R.K., *Classical Mythology in Shakespeare*, *Yale Studies in English* 19, first published 1903, reprinted New York, Gordian Press, 1965.
**Thomson**
Thomson, J.A.K., *Shakespeare and the Classics*, London, Allen & Unwin, 1952.

# NOTES

## 1 INTRODUCTION

1. George Watson (ed.), *John Dryden: Of Dramatic Poesie and Other Critical Essays*, 2 vols., London, Dent, 1962, vol. 2, p. 75; cf. Lawrence Lipking, *The Life of the Poet: Beginning and Ending Poetic Careers*, Chicago and London, University of Chicago Press, 1981, pp. 138–146.
2. See 'Conversations with William Drummond' in George Parfitt (ed.), *Ben Jonson: The Complete Poems*, Harmondsworth, Penguin, 1975, p. 462. Drummond, it is perhaps relevant to recall, said of Jonson that drink was 'one of the elements in which he liveth'.
3. For the details summarized in this section see Baldwin, vol. 1, pp. 1–74; Thomson, pp. 17–31.
4. See 'Introductory lecture' (1892) in Christopher Ricks (ed.), *A.E. Housman: Collected Poems and Selected Prose*, London, Allen Lane, Penguin, 1988, p. 265.
5. See 'English literature and the Latin tradition', in Dorothy Collins (ed.), *Chesterton on Shakespeare*, Henley-on-Thames, Darwen Finlayson, 1971, pp. 13–25 (the quotations are from pp. 13, 17f.).
6. Watson (ed.), op. cit. vol. 1, p. 67.
7. See Stuart Gillespie, *The Poets on the Classics: An Anthology of English Poets' Writings on the Classical Poets and Dramatists from Chaucer to the Present*, London and New York, Routledge, 1988, pp. 101, 104.
8. Reprinted in D. Nichol Smith (ed.), *Eighteenth Century Essays on Shakespeare*, 2nd edn, Oxford, Clarendon Press, 1963, pp. 151–202.
9. This vitiates e.g. Percy Simpson, 'Shakespeare's use of Latin authors' in *Studies in Elizabethan Drama*, Oxford, Clarendon Press, 1955, pp. 1–63.
10. From the 1765 *Preface* to his edition of Shakespeare see W.K. Wimsatt (ed.), *Dr. Johnson on Shakespeare*, Penguin Shakespeare Library, Harmondsworth, Penguin, 1969, pp. 76f.
11. Thomson, p. 153.
12. See Baldwin, vol. 1, pp. 374, 186f.
13. For a full discussion see Thomson, pp. 66–74, 186–188.

14. Connoisseurs of deconstruction, in its American guise, will relish J. Hillis Miller, 'Ariachne's broken woof', *Georgia Review*, vol. 31, 1977, pp. 40–60, a classic of its kind.

15. See Lizette Andrews Fisher, 'Shakspere and the Capitol', *Modern Languages Notes*, vol. 22, 1907, pp. 177–182.

16. See J. Dover Wilson, 'Shakespeare's "small Latin" – how much?', *Shakespeare Survey*, vol. 10, 1957, pp. 12–26 (p. 17). This article adopts a neo-Farmerian stance.

17. Bruce Harbert, 'Chaucer and the Latin Classics', in Derek Brewer (ed.), *Geoffrey Chaucer*, Writers and Their Background, London, G. Bell, 1974, pp. 137–153 (p. 146).

18. C.S. Lewis, *Surprised by Joy: The Shape of My Early Life*, London, Bles, 1955, p. 56f.

19. Quoted by Thomas M. Greene, *The Light in Troy: Imitation and Discovery in Renaissance Poetry*, New Haven and London, Yale University Press, 1982, p. 28.

20. Cf. Dover Wilson, op.cit., p. 19.

21. See e.g. Kenneth Muir, 'Shakespeare among the commonplaces', *Review of English Studies*, vol. 10, 1959, pp. 282–289 (on Shakespeare's use of Erasmus' *Adages*); Walter J. Ong, 'Commonplace rhapsody: Ravisius Textor, Zwinger and Shakespeare', in R.R. Bolgar (ed.), *Classical Influences on European Culture AD 1500–1700*, Cambridge University Press, 1976, pp. 91–126, an illuminating study.

22. See Frank Kermode, 'Shakespeare's Learning', in *Shakespeare, Spenser, Donne: Renaissance Essays*, London, Routledge & Kegan Paul, 1971, pp. 181–199 (p. 183).

23. See Baldwin, vol. 1, pp. 652–673 (Palingenius) (but cf. J.A. Burrow, *The Ages of Man: A Study in Medieval Writing and Thought*, Oxford, Clarendon Press, 1986, pp. 50–54); p. 622 (fable).

24. For the possible influence of school Latin on Shakespeare's language see Hilda M. Hulme, *Explorations in Shakespeare's Language: Some Problems of Lexical Meaning in the Dramatic Text*, ch. 5, '"Latin" reference in Shakespearean English', London, Longmans, 1962, pp. 151–201.

25. See T.W. Baldwin, *On the Literary Genetics of Shakspere's Poems and Sonnets*, Urbana, University of Illinois Press, 1950, pp. 384, 381.

26. Greene, op.cit., pp. 267, 45, 86.

27. See the sensitive remarks of A.D. Nuttall, *William Shakespeare: The Winter's Tale*, Studies in English Literature, no. 26, London, Edward Arnold, pp. 40f.

28. For this play and its sources see T.W. Baldwin, *On the Compositional Genetics of 'The Comedy of Errors'*, Urbana, University of Illinois Press, 1965; introduction to R.A. Foakes's revised Arden edition, London, Methuen, 1962, pp. xxiv ff., citing further studies. For Shakespeare's Christianizing of Plautus see also John Arthos, 'Shakespeare and the ancient world', *Michigan Quarterly Review*, vol. 10, 1971, pp. 149–163 (pp. 149–158).

29. For Shakespeare's possible use of Mirandula, see Baldwin, vol. 2, pp. 408–414.
30. We cite from an edition published at Lyons in 1620 (copy in Bodleian Library).
31. Cited by Cunliffe, p. 106 (text emended).
32. See Baldwin, vol. 1, p. 154.
33. See Frank Kermode's Arden edition, London, Methuen, 1954 (repr. 1964), Appendix D, pp. 147–150; Baldwin, vol. 2, pp. 443–452.
34. For a comparison of Shakespeare and Dryden see F.R. Leavis, 'Antony and Cleopatra and All For Love: a critical exercise', Scrutiny, vol. 5, 1936–7, pp. 158–169. For Shakespeare's use of Plutarch see MacCallum, and C.B.R. Pelling's edition of Life of Antony, Cambridge University Press, 1988, pp. 37–45. J. Leeds Barroll, 'Enobarbus' description of Cleopatra', University of Texas Studies in English, vol. 37, 1958, pp. 61–78 adopts an iconographic approach: Cleopatra is a Voluptas figure, Antony like Hercules made effeminate by Omphale (perhaps the strongest piece of evidence for his thesis is Antony's transvestism in II.v.22). Some of the material is suggestive, but Barroll presses the idea too hard. See too on Venus and Mars and Shakespeare's iconographic use of myth, Janet Adelman, The Common Liar: An Essay on 'Antony and Cleopatra', New Haven and London, Yale University Press, 1973, pp. 80–101.
35. See D.A. Russell, 'De imitatione', in David West and Tony Woodman (eds), Creative Imitation and Latin Literature, Cambridge University Press, 1979, pp. 1–16 (p. 16).
36. Watson (ed.), op. cit., vol. 1, p. 69.
37. See G.K. Hunter, 'Seneca and the Elizabethans: a case-study in influence', Shakespeare Survey, vol. 20, 1967, pp. 17–26 (pp. 21,24) (hereafter Hunter 1967); 'Seneca and English Tragedy', in C.D.N. Costa (ed.), Seneca, London and Boston, Routledge & Kegan Paul, 1974, pp. 166–204, (hereafter Hunter 1974). For a similar view see Howard Baker, Induction to Tragedy: A Study in a Development of Form in Gorboduc, The Spanish Tragedy and Titus Andronicus, 1939, repr. New York, Russell & Russell, 1965. For a survey of the dispute see Anna Lydia Motto and John R. Clark, 'Senecan tragedy: a critique of scholarly trends', review article, Renaissance Drama, vol. 6, 1973, pp. 219–235 (pp. 225–259).
38. See T.W. Baldwin, Shakspere's Five-Act Structure: Shakspere's Early Plays on the Background of Renaissance Theories of Five-Act Structure From 1470, Urbana, University of Illinois Press, 1947.
39. See Cunliffe, Appendix 2, pp. 130–155.
40. Baldwin, vol. 1, p. 382.
41. See Hunter 1967, p. 25, note 10.
42. Cf. Catherine Belsey, 'Senecan vacillation and Elizabethan deliberation: influence or confluence?', Renaissance Drama, vol. 6, 1973, pp. 65–88. A similar moderate position is adopted by Henry W. Wells, 'Senecan influence on Elizabethan tragedy: a re-estimation', Shakespeare Association Bulletin, vol. 19, 1944, pp. 71–84. See also

Emrys Jones, *The Origins of Shakespeare*, Oxford, Clarendon Press, 1977, Appendix A, 'Shakespeare and Seneca', pp. 267–272 (not all his parallels convince). Less judicious, though still useful, is Joost Daalder's introduction to his edition of Jasper Heywood's *Thyestes* of 1560, London, Ernest Benn; New York, Norton, 1982 (Daalder's discussion is marred by the vagueness of some of the supposed analogies and overestimation of Heywood's translation). For a sober account of the background to the developed form of Elizabethan tragedy, see J.M.R. Margeson, *The Origins of English Tragedy*, Oxford, Clarendon Press, 1967; more stimulating on immediately pre-Shakespearean tragedy is Wolfgang Clemen, *English Tragedy Before Shakespeare: The Development of Dramatic Speech*, trans. T.S. Dorsch, London, Methuen, 1961, especially pt. 3 (both writers take a moderate view on Senecan influence).

43. Text in Marie Axton (ed.), *Three Tudor Classical Interludes*, Cambridge, D.S Brewer, Rowman & Littlefield, 1982. The volume also contains *Thersites* and *Horestes*.
44. Text in Peter Happé (ed.), *Tudor Interludes*, Harmondsworth, Penguin, 1972.
45. See Gordon Braden, *Renaissance Tragedy and the Senecan Tradition: Anger's Privilege*, New Haven and London, Yale University Press, 1985, pp. 181,37. This is the most stimulating study of the subject yet to appear.
46. Text in Arthur H. Nethercot, Charles R. Baskervill, Virgil B. Heltzel (eds), *Elizabethan Plays*, New York, Holt Rinehart & Winston, 1971. This volume also contains *Gorboduc*.
47. Clemen, op.cit., pp. 253–257 (Clemen does not, in our opinion, do justice to the rhetorical advances achieved in this play).
48. Hunter 1974, pp. 187,192.
49. See Clemen, op.cit., p. 25.
50. See C.D.N. Costa, 'Polonius, Seneca and the Elizabethans', *Proceedings of the Cambridge Philological Society*, n.s. vol. 21, 1975, pp. 33–41.
51. See Albert Feuillerat's edition of *The Defence of Poetry*, Cambridge University Press, 1963, p. 38 (vol. 3 of *The Prose Works of Sir Philip Sidney*).
52. See Clemen, op.cit., p. 84.
53. See Preface to Robert Greene, *Menaphon* (1589), in Ronald B. McKerrow (ed.), *The Works of Thomas Nashe*, 5 vols, Oxford, Basil Blackwell, 1966; vol. 3, pp. 315f.
54. See Clemen, op.cit., p. 250. For *Othello* V.ii.275ff. (a version of the prayer to the Furies) see p. 245.
55. See Braden, op.cit., p. 67f.
56. T.S. Eliot, 'Shakespeare and the Stoicism of Seneca' (1927), in *Selected Essays*, London, Faber & Faber, 1951, pp. 126–140 (p. 129). Braden, op. cit., (p. 178) modifies to 'cosmic self-dramatization'.
57. Statistics from Root, p. 128.
58. See Clemen, op.cit., pp. 236–238.

59. See Thomson, p. 127.
60. See the note in M.R. Ridley's Arden edition, London, Methuen, 1958, p. 121. For the passage as Senecan cf. Braden, op.cit., pp. 175–177.
61. See John Freeman (ed.), *Thomas Fuller, The Worthies of England*, London, Allen & Unwin, 1952, p. 180.
62. Thomson, p. 124.
63. See e.g. Kenneth Muir, *Notes and Queries*, vol. 194, 1949, pp. 214–216; vol. 201, 1956, pp. 243f; Bullough, vol. 7, pp. 451–455, 521–523; J.M. Nosworthy, 'The bleeding captain scene in *Macbeth*', *Review of English Studies*, vol. 22, 1946, pp. 126–130. Cf. R.J. Kaufman, 'The Seneca perspective and the Shakespearean poetic', *Comparative Drama*, vol. 1, 1967, pp. 182–198 (p. 183). For a clear imitation of *Hercules Furens* 1258–1261 see Chapman, *Byron's Tragedy* (1608), V.iv.69–72:

> Why should I keep my soul in this dark light,
> Whose black beams lighted me to lose myself,
> When I have lost my arms, my fame, my mind,
> Friends, brother, hopes, fortunes, and even my fury?

For another possible parallel compare *Hercules Furens* 735f. and *Macbeth* I.vii.8ff. (Cunliffe p. 82).
64. See Inga-Stina Ewbank, 'The fiend-like queen: a note on *Macbeth* and Seneca's *Medea*', *Shakespeare Survey*, vol. 19, 1966, pp. 82–94.
65. See David Norbrook, '*Macbeth* and the politics of historiography', in Kevin Sharpe and Steven N. Zwicker (eds), *Politics of Discourse: the Literature and History of Seventeenth-Century England*, Berkeley, Los Angeles and London, University of California Press, 1987, pp. 78–116 (pp. 112–115).
66. See e.g. C.J. Herington, 'Senecan tragedy', in E.J. Kenney and W.V. Clausen (eds), *The Cambridge History of Classical Literature*, vol. 2, *Latin Literature*, Cambridge University Press, 1982, pp. 519–530.
67. Jones, op.cit., pp. 26–28. The results, of course, are different – Shakespeare 'converts Claudius' "scatterbrainedness" into a profound self-alienation' (p. 27).
68. See W.A. Armstrong, 'The influence of Seneca and Macchiavelli on the Elizabethan tyrant', *RES*, vol. 24, 1948, pp. 19–35.
69. W.R. Johnson, *The Idea of Lyric: Lyric Modes in Ancient and Modern Poetry*, Berkeley, Los Angeles and London, University of California Press, 1982, p. 151.
70. See Braden, op.cit., pp. 40,57,184.
71. See Graham Bradshaw, *Shakespeare's Scepticism*, Brighton, Harvester, 1987, p. 252; Erich Auerbach, *Mimesis: The Representation of Reality in Western Literature*, trans. by W.R. Trask, Princeton University Press, p. 71.
72. See Kenneth Muir's Arden edition, London, Methuen, 1951, Introduction p. xx.
73. Bradshaw, op.cit., p. 223.

74. Emrys Jones, *Scenic Form in Shakespeare*, Oxford, Clarendon Press, 1971, p. 195.
75. T.S. Eliot, 'Seneca in Elizabethan translation' (1927), in *Selected Essays*, pp. 65–105 (pp. 68, 74).
76. Cf. Wolfgang Clemen, *The Development of Shakespeare's Imagery*, 2nd edn., London, Methuen, 1977, p. 95.
77. E.g. John Harvey, 'A note on Shakespeare and Sophocles', *Essays in Criticism*, vol. 27, 1977, pp. 259–270.
78. Baldwin, vol. 1, p. 392.
79. See the note in J.C. Maxwell's Arden edition, London, Methuen, 1953, p. 22.
80. See Cunliffe, p. 7.
81. See Clemen, *English Tragedy*, p. 27.
82. Quoted by Cunliffe, p. 9f.
83. Jones, *Origins of Shakespeare*, chs 3 and 4 'Shakespeare and Euripides', pp. 85–118. Although we disagree with the conclusions, these chapters are in our view essential reading.
84. See A.D. Nuttall, *Timon of Athens*, New Critical Introductions to Shakespeare, Hemel Hempstead, Harvester, 1989, pp. 106f.

## 2 SHAKESPEARE'S OVID

1. The starting point for any study of Shakespeare and Ovid must be Baldwin, vol. 2, ch. 42, pp. 417–455. The most general literary discussion is Leonard Barkan, *The Gods Made Flesh: Metamorphosis and the Pursuit of Paganism*, New Haven and London, Yale University Press, 1986, ch. 6, pp. 243–288, with up-to-date bibliography (but see Charles Martindale's review in *Comparative Literature*, vol. 41, 1989, pp. 177–182). Still worth reading is M.C. Bradbrook, *Shakespeare and Elizabethan Poetry: A Study of his Earlier Work in Relation to the Poetry of the Time*, London, Chatto & Windus, 1951, ch.4, pp. 51–74; ch.7, pp. 104–122.
2. Baldwin, vol. 2, p. 418.
3. Quoted from the *ABC of Reading* by John Frederick Nims in the introduction to his edition of Golding, New York, Macmillan, 1965, p. xiii. For Golding see also Gordon Braden, *The Classics and English Renaissance Poetry: Three Case Studies*, New Haven, Yale University Press, 1978, pp. 1–54. For Spenser and Golding see Anthony Brian Taylor, 'When did Spenser read Golding?', *Notes and Queries*, vol. 233, 1988, pp. 38–40 and the earlier articles listed in note 2.
4. 'On the study of Celtic literature', in R.H. Super (ed.), *Lectures and Essays in Criticism*, Ann Arbor, University of Michigan Press, 1962, p. 380 (vol. 3 of *The Complete Prose Works*): Arnold is talking about various ways of handling nature. For the links with Chaucer see Ann Thompson, *Shakespeare's Chaucer: A Study in Literary Origins*, Liverpool University Press, 1978, pp. 67ff.
5. *Palladis Tamia*, London, 1598, pp. 281f.
6. For Ovid and Spenser see Colin Burrow, 'Original fictions:

metamorphoses in the *Faerie Queene'*, in Charles Martindale (ed.), *Ovid Renewed: Ovidian Influences on Literature and Art from the Middle Ages to the Twentieth Century*, Cambridge University Press, 1988, pp. 99–119.

7. In what follows we assume that *Titus* is wholly the work of Shakespeare. If it is not, some adjustment to the argument would obviously be necessary. Little about Shakespeare is uncontroversial; but if we had everywhere hedged this book about with the appropriate provisos and overloaded it with references to modern discussions, it would have been difficult to achieve either brevity or readability. We hope that our readers will bear this in mind if at some points we seem incautious or unduly dogmatic. In particular on technical matters (questions of date, text, authorship etc.) we claim no especial expertise or authority.

8. The best account of the relationship of *Titus* and Ovid remains Eugene M. Waith, 'The metamorphosis of violence in *Titus Andronicus*', *Shakespeare Survey*, vol. 10, 1957, pp. 39–49; cf. the introduction to his edition in the Oxford Shakespeare series, Oxford, Clarendon Press, 1984. He modifies his view somewhat in *Patterns and Perspectives in English Renaissance Drama*, London and Toronto, Associated University Presses; Newark, University of Delaware Press, 1988, pp. 10f; 138–147 (142f.). Other studies include: Andrew V. Ettin, 'Shakespeare's first Roman tragedy', *English Literary History*, vol. 37, 1970, pp. 325–341 (in taking the play to be a critique of Roman tradition, Ettin assumes that Elizabethan values resembled modern 'liberal' ones); D.J. Palmer, 'The unspeakable in pursuit of the uneatable: language and action in *Titus Andronicus*', *Critical Quarterly*, vol. 14, 1972, pp. 320–339; H.T. Price, 'The authorship of *Titus Andronicus*', *Journal of English and Germanic Philology*, vol. 42, 1943, pp. 55–81; Grace Starry West, 'Going by the book: classical allusions in Shakespeare's *Titus Andronicus*', *Studies in Philology*, vol. 79, 1982, pp. 62–77 (the article's main thesis, that the play is a critique of Roman education, is implausible). A book on the play, by Maurice Charney, is shortly to appear in Harvester's New Critical Introductions to Shakespeare series. For the view that Shakespeare was influenced by Golding as well as by Ovid see Antony Brian Taylor, 'Golding's *Metamorphoses* and *Titus Andronicus*', *Notes and Queries*, vol. 223, 1978, pp. 117–120.

9. For the contrary view see Martin Helzle, 'Seneca and the Elizabethan revenge tragedy: aspects of Thomas Kyd's *The Spanish Tragedy* and Shakespeare's *Titus Andronicus*', *Antike und Abenland*, vol. 31, 1985, pp. 137–152.

10. For Latin quotations in Shakespeare see J.W. Binns, 'Shakespeare's Latin citations: the editorial problem', *Shakespeare Survey*, vol. 35, 1982, pp. 119–128.

11. For further examples see Price, op.cit., pp. 63, 68.

12. It has been suggested that this speech is modelled on Seneca, *Troades* 142–164 (Cunliffe, p. 71f.), but the similarity is vague.

13. Wolfgang Clemen, *The Development of Shakespeare's Imagery* (1951), 2nd edn, London, Methuen, 1977, p. 26.

14. Preface to *Fables Ancient and Modern* (1700), in George Watson (ed.), *John Dryden: Of Dramatic Poesie and Other Critical Essays*, 2 vols, London, Dent, 1962, vol. 2, pp. 271f.; 277–280.

15. Cf. the love scene between Bel Imperia and Horatio in Kyd's *Spanish Tragedy*, II.iv. See too Taylor, 'Golding's *Metamorphoses*', p. 117f.

16. Two references to Dido linking her with the destruction of Troy are III.ii.27f.; V.iii.80–7. For another, more fugitive echo of the hunting scene in *Aeneid* IV see *1 Henry IV* III.i.36f. For the view that Virgil is an important presence in *Titus* see Ettin, op.cit., pp. 326–328, 341.

17. John W. Velz, 'The ancient world in Shakespeare: authenticity or anachronism? A retrospect', *Shakespeare Survey*, vol. 31, 1978, pp. 1–12 (p. 12). Robert S. Miola's *Shakespeare's Rome*, Cambridge University Press, 1983, is seriously marred by its over-emphasis on Virgil. For a brief, more lucid statement of his position see 'Vergil in Shakespeare: from allusion to imitation', in John D. Bernard (ed.), *Vergil at 2000: Commemorative Essays on the Poet and his Influence*, New York, AMS Press, 1986, pp. 241–258.

18. Cf. Root, Introduction pp. 4f. If the passage about 'the floor of heaven' in *Merchant of Venice* V.i.58ff. was really inspired by Virgil *Aeneid* VI.730ff. (Anchises' speech), it only confirms the profound difference in sensibility. More Virgilian is the description of the bees in *Henry V* I.ii.187–204, which clearly derives from *Georgics* IV: see John H. Betts, 'Classical allusions in Shakespeare's *Henry V* with special reference to Virgil', *Greece and Rome*, vol. 15, 1968, pp. 147–163. For Virgil and Shakespeare generally see Baldwin, vol. 2, ch. 43, pp. 456–496. For a more comparative approach see A.D. Nuttall, 'Virgil and Shakespeare', in Charles Martindale (ed.) *Virgil and His Influence: Bimillennial Studies*, Bristol Classical Press, 1984, pp. 71–93. For the influence of Marlowe's *Dido, Queen of Carthage* on *Antony and Cleopatra* see Janet Adelman, *The Common Liar: An Essay on Antony and Cleopatra*, New Haven and London, Yale University Press, 1973, pp. 76–78, Appendix B, pp. 177–183. Cf. Barbara J. Bono, *Literary Transvaluation: From Vergilian Epic to Shakespearean Tragicomedy*, Berkeley, Los Angeles and London, University of California Press, 1984.

19. Alexander Ross, *Mystagogus Poeticus, or the Muses' Interpreter*, London, 1647, p. 252. While this postdates Shakespeare, its traditional character makes it relevant to an understanding of the earlier period.

20. See R.J. Schark, 'Allusion, theme, and characterization in *Cymbeline*', *SP*, vol. 69, 1972, pp. 210–216 (212f.); Barkan, op.cit., pp. 244ff.

21. See James Nosworthy's introduction to the Arden edition, Methuen, London, 1955, repr. 1969, pp. lxviiff.; Ann Thompson, 'Philomel in *Titus Andronicus* and *Cymbeline*', *Shakespeare Survey*, vol. 31, 1978, pp. 23–32. Keats explores the connections in 'The Eve of St Agnes': so 'a tongueless nightingale' (206) and the echoes of *Cymbeline* in 244ff; cf. Jack Stillinger, 'The hoodwinking of Madeline: scepticism in "The

Eve of St. Agnes"', *Studies in Philology*, vol. 58, 1961, pp. 533–555 (pp. 541–543). The betrayal of Troy by Sinon, featured in the *ecphrasis* in *Lucrece*, also duly makes its reappearance in *Cymbeline* (III.iv.60–62). Another Ovidian parallel occurs in I.iv.8ff. (cf. *Metamorphoses*. XI.463ff., the departure of Ceyx from Alcyone), where again Shakespeare is even more mannered than his model and the imagery more elaborate and conceited.

22. For the epyllion see Laurence Lerner, 'Ovid and the Elizabethans', in Martindale, (ed.), *Ovid Renewed: Ovidian Influences on Literature and Art From the Middle Ages to the Twentieth Century*, Cambridge University Press, 1988, pp. 121–135; Douglas Bush, *Mythology and the Renaissance Tradition in English Poetry*, Minneapolis, University of Minnesota Press; London, Oxford University Press, 1932, *passim*.

23. Illustrated in colour in Charles Hope, *Titian*, London, Jupiter Books, 1980, plate 28.

24. All discussion of the relation of the poems to their sources must begin with T.W. Baldwin, *On the Literary Genetics of Shakspere's Poems and Sonnets*, Urbana, University of Illinois Press, 1950, pp. 1–93 (*Venus and Adonis*), 97–153 (*Lucrece*). For critical accounts see Bush, op.cit., pp. 139–155; William Keach, *Elizabethan Erotic Narratives: Irony and Pathos in the Ovidian Poetry of Shakespeare, Marlowe and their Contemporaries*, Hassocks, Harvester, 1977. See also the introductions of the Arden edition (ed. F.T. Prince, London, Methuen, 1960) and the New Shakespeare edition (ed. J.C. Maxwell, Cambridge University Press, 1969).

25. For example, it is cited at the beginning of later editions of Mirandula's *Flores*.

26. For this poem, which survives in a single copy in the British Library, see Robert Kilburn Root, 'Some notes on Shakespeare', *Journal of English and German Philology*, vol. 4, 1902, pp. 452–459 (pp. 454f.); M.C. Bradbrook, 'Shakespeare's recollections of Marlowe', in Philip Edwards, Inga-Stina Ewbank, G.K. Hunter (eds), *Shakespeare's Styles: Essays in Honour of Kenneth Muir*, Cambridge University Press, 1980, pp. 191–203 (pp. 197f.). (We would like to thank Katherine Duncan-Jones for her guidance here.) Bradbrook has also argued that *Venus and Adonis* is a response to Greene's criticism of Shakespeare: see 'Beasts and gods: Greene's *Groatsworth of Witte* and the social purpose of *Venus and Adonis*', *Shakespeare Survey*, vol. 15, 1962, pp. 62–72. Maurice Evans in his admirable New Penguin edition of *The Narrative Poems* (London, Penguin Books, 1989) suggests that the allegorical horse of Blind Desire in *Narcissus* might have prompted the episode with the horse in Shakespeare (intr. pp. 4–5). His summary of the poem is not, however, quite accurate.

27. For Erasmus and *copia* see e.g. Marion Trousdale, *Shakespeare and the Rhetoricians*, London, Scolar Press, 1982.

28. Terence Hawkes (ed.), *Coleridge on Shakespeare*, Penguin Shakespeare Library, Harmondsworth, Penguin, 1969, p. 70.

29. The idea is a commonplace, and Shakespeare's source in *Venus and*

*Adonis* may be a passage in George Buchanan, whose Venus 'is the bond of the universe, keeping it from a return to chaos' (Baldwin, *On the Literary Genetics*, pp. 49–55 (p. 51)).

30. The conceit derives ultimately from an Anacreontic poem about the dead Adonis (26–31), wrongly attributed to Theocritus, first translated into English in 1588, but widely disseminated through literary sources; for the text and a translation see J.M. Edmond's Loeb edition of *The Greek Bucolic Poets*, London, Heinemann, 1912, pp. 480–483 (the Arden and New Shakespeare editions are misleading on this reference). See also A.T. Hatto, '"Venus and Adonis" and the boar', *Modern Language Review*, vol. 41, 1946, pp. 353–361. The sexual link is clinched by the 'full-acorned boar' in *Cymbeline* II.iv.168.

31. In Renaissance versions (including Titian's painting in The Prado) Venus is usually the more active of the two. For the conflation with Salmacis and Hermaphroditus see Thomson, pp. 60–62, and especially cf. *Shrew*, Introduction ii.52–55. M.A. Palmatier, 'A suggested new source in Ovid's *Metamorphoses* for Shakespeare's *Venus and Adonis*', *Huntington Library Quarterly*, vol. 24, 1960/1, pp. 163–169, suggests that Shakespeare may have been influenced by the idea, present in Ovid, that Venus is being punished for the sufferings she caused Myrrha, Adonis' mother.

32. See *Polyanthea* under *equus*, where only two passages from poetry are cited (the other is from Georgius Scotus).

33. For a more favourable estimate, in which merits and demerits are well stated, see C.S. Lewis, *English Literature in the Sixteenth Century excluding Drama*, Oxford, Clarendon Press, 1944, pp. 499–502. For what were obviously partly temperamental reasons, connected with his attitude to sexuality, Lewis disliked *Venus and Adonis*.

34. Prince, op.cit., intr. p. xxxvi.

35. See A.G. Lee, 'Ovid's Lucretia', *Greece and Rome*, vol. 22, 1953, pp. 107–118.

36. Ian Donaldson, *The Rapes of Lucretia: A Myth and its Transformations*, Oxford, Clarendon Press, 1982, p. 44.

37. See D.C. Allen, 'Some observations on *The Rape of Lucrece*', *Shakespeare Survey*, vol. 15, 1962, pp. 89–98 (pp. 94–97) argues that traditional allegorizations of *Aeneid* II help to account for Shakespeare's linking of Lucretia and Troy. We remain sceptical; Shakespeare is in general no great allegorizer of myth. For the *ecphrasis* see Clarke Hulse, *Metamorphic Verse: The Elizabethan Minor Epic*, Princeton University Press, 1981, pp. 175–194.

38. See Harold F. Brooks' Arden edition,London, Methuen, 1979, intro. lviiiff. For the view that Ovid's influence could have been indirect see Leah Scragg, 'Shakespeare, Lyly and Ovid: the influence of *Gallathea* on *A Midsummer Night's Dream*', *Shakespeare Survey*, vol. 30, 1977, pp. 125–134. But, while the whole climate of Elizabethan Ovidianism is important, there can be no doubt of Shakespeare's love and knowledge of the original.

39. Niall Rudd, 'Pyramus and Thisbe in Shakespeare and Ovid: *A Midsummer Night's Dream* and *Metamorphoses* 4.1–166', in David West and Tony Woodman (eds), *Creative Imitation and Latin Literature*, Cambridge University Press, 1979, pp. 173–193 (p. 193).

40. But for the ass's head in popular entertainments see Robert Weimann, *Shakespeare and the Popular Tradition in the Theater: Studies in the Social Dimension of Dramatic Form and Function*, ed. Robert Schwartz, Baltimore and London, Johns Hopkins University Press, 1978, p. 50. For Shakespeare and Apuleius see James A.S. McPeek, 'The Psyche myth and *A Midsummer Night's Dream*', *Shakespeare Quarterly*, vol. 23, 1972, pp. 69–79: John J.M. Tobin, 'Apuleius and the Bradleian Tragedies', *Shakespeare Survey*, vol. 31, 1978, pp. 33–43, with note 5, p. 33, for earlier literature. Both these articles seem to us to illustrate the excesses of source criticism; for example, it is unlikely that Shakespeare read Apuleius in the original very demanding Latin. Shakespeare also extracted some amusing material about asses' heads from Reginald Scot's *Discovery of Witchcraft* (1584).

41. See David P. Young, *Something of Great Constancy: The Art of 'A Midsummer Night's Dream'*, New Haven and London, Yale University Press, 1966, pt. 3, 'Bottom's Dream', pp. 111–166.

42. The best-known work on the whole subject is Anne Righter, *Shakespeare and the Idea of the Play*, first published 1962, Penguin Shakespeare Library, Harmondsworth, Penguin, 1967.

43. Christine Rees, 'The metamorphosis of Daphne in sixteenth- and seventeenth-century English poetry', *Modern Language Review*, vol. 66, 1971, pp. 251–263 (p. 263). For Ovid and art see Martindale (ed.), *Ovid Renewed*, op.cit., Introduction, pp. 14ff.; Joseph B. Solodow, *The World of Ovid's Metamorphoses*, Chapel Hill and London, University of North Carolina Press, 1988, especially ch. 6.

44. For an interesting discussion see Graham Bradshaw, *Shakespeare's Scepticism*, Brighton, Harvester, 1987, pp. 39ff. See too R.W. Dent, 'Imagination in *A Midsummer Night's Dream*', *Shakespeare Quarterly*, vol. 15, 1964, pp. 115–119. There is a likely parallel for Theseus' observations on poetry in Horace, *Epistles* II.1.210–213:

> ille per extentum funem mihi posse videtur
> ire poeta, meum qui pectus inaniter angit,
> irritat, mulcet, falsis terroribus implet,
> ut magus, et modo me Thebis, modo ponit Athenis.

This certainly reminded the Loeb translator of the *Dream*: 'methinks that poet is able to walk a tight rope, who with airy nothings (*inaniter*) wrings my heart, inflames, soothes, fills it with vain alarms like a magician, and sets me down now at Thebes, now at Athens' (H. Rushton Fairclough, *Horace: Satires, Epistles and Ars Poetica*, London, Heinemann, 1929, p. 415). For Shakespeare's likely knowledge of these lines see Baldwin, vol. II, p. 519f. Here we have the power of the poet to move and deceive, linked with magic, and a setting at Athens. Could this passage, perhaps lodged deep in Shakespeare's memory from his school days, be part of the genesis of the play?

45. See Robert F. Willson, 'Golding's *Metamorphoses* and Shakespeare's burlesque method in *A Midsummer Night's Dream*', *English Language Notes*, vol. 7, 1969, pp. 18–25. But Shakespeare is not parodying Golding explicitly, rather a manner of writing.

46. See Kenneth Muir, 'Pyramus and Thisbe: a study in Shakespeare's Method', *Shakespeare Quarterly*, vol. 5, 1954, pp. 141–153. But cf. David P. Young, op. cit., p. 41, where the material adduced is designed 'not so much to identify Shakespeare's sources as to indicate the kind of conventions he was satirizing'.

47. For other examples see the introduction to Brooks's Arden edition, pp. xlv.ff., where the relevant figures are named.

48. So Walter F. Staton Jr., 'Ovidian elements in *A Midsummer Night's Dream*', *Huntington Library Quarterly*, vol. 26, 1962/3, pp. 165–178; Baldwin, vol. 2, p. 446.

49. So Stephen Medcalf, 'Virgil at the turn of time', in Martindale (ed.), *Virgil and his Influence*, op.cit., pp. 215–244 (p. 235).

50. There is a fairly close parallel in Thomas Heywood's 'Apollo and Daphne': *The Dramatic Works*, 6 vols., New York, Russell & Russell, 1964, vol. 6, p. 293.

51. Barkan, op.cit., p. 281; for the iconography see John M. Steadman, 'Falstaff as Actaeon: a dramatic emblem', *Shakespeare Quarterly*, vol. 14, 1963, pp. 230–244 (in our view Steadman overstates the iconographic case).

52. E.g. Robert Wiltenburg, 'The *Aeneid* in *The Tempest*', *Shakespeare Survey*, vol. 39, 1986, pp. 159–168. For the evidence see J.M. Nosworthy, 'The Narrative Sources of *The Tempest*', *RES*, vol. 24, 1948, pp. 281–294 (288–294). For the *Naufragium* see Thomson, p. 135f.

53. See A.D. Nuttall, 'Ovid's Narcissus and Shakespeare's Richard II: the reflected self', in Martindale (ed.), *Ovid Renewed*, op.cit., pp. 137–150.

54. See Jane M. Miller, 'Some versions of Pygmalion', in Martindale (ed.), *Ovid Renewed*, pp. 205–214.

55. George Sandys, *Ovid's Metamorphoses, Englished, Mythologized and Represented in Figures*, Oxford, 1632, photographic reprint, ed. Stephen Orgel, New York and London, Garland Publishing, 1976; see also the edition by Karl K. Hulley and Stanley T. Vandersall, Lincoln, University of Nebraska Press, 1970, p. 484f.

56. Jasper Griffin, *Latin Poets and Roman Life*, London, Duckworth, 1985, p. 136f.

57. So Barbara Roche Rico, 'From "speechless dialect" to "prosperous art": Shakespeare's recasting of the Pygmalion image', *Huntington Library Quarterly*, vol. 48, 1985, pp. 285–295. In *Measure for Measure* III.ii.414 Lucio refers to prostitutes as 'Pygmalion's images'. There is a curious version of the Pygmalion story in *A Petite Pallace*

*of Pettie His Pleasure*, edited by I. Gollancz, 2 vols, London, Chatto & Windus, 1908, vol. 2, pp. 108ff., with liberal advice for 'gentlewomen'.

58. So, in a sensitive article, Martin Mueller, 'Hermione's wrinkles, or, Ovid transformed: an essay on *The Winter's Tale*', *Comparative Drama*, vol. 5, 1971, pp. 226–239 (p. 234f.).

59. Bradshaw makes the passage more reflexive by taking 'we' to refer in part to the audience, op.cit., p. 93f., cf. p. 86f.: *The Winter's Tale* 'pointedly reminds that it is a fiction', so that we 'find that the play we are watching is watching us'. This is an ingenious reading, quintessentially a critic's reading, but the subversive irony would leave little reason for the audience to be absorbed and moved.

60. For the contrary view see e.g. William C. Carroll, *The Metamorphoses of Shakespearean Comedy*, Princeton University Press, 1985, pp. 212ff. (citing a theatre reaction); cf. Nevill Coghill, 'Six points of stagecraft in *The Winter's Tale*', *Shakespeare Survey*, vol. 11, 1958, pp. 31–41 (p. 40); Rosalie L. Colie, *Shakespeare's Living Art*, Princeton University Press, 1974, pp. 278–283. For an essay on mythic patterns in the romances, see D.G. James, *Scepticism and Poetry: An Essay on the Poetic Imagination*, London, Allen & Unwin, 1937, ch.7, pp. 205–241 'The failure of the ballad-makers'.

61. For a version of the story without Hercules see *A Petite Pallace*, op.cit., vol. 1, pp. 169ff. Alcestis is restored to life by Proserpina. Cooper's *Thesaurus* under 'Admetus' has a summary, again without Hercules.

62. See A.D. Nuttall, 'Two unassimilable men', in Malcolm Bradbury and David Palmer (eds.), *Shakespearean Comedy*, Stratford-upon-Avon Studies 14, London, Edward Arnold, 1972, pp. 210–240 (pp. 216–224).

63. Root, op.cit., Introduction, pp. 8–13.

64. Root, op.cit., p. 128. We take all figures from Root.

65. For the romantic use of the merchandise image cf. Spenser, *Amoretti* XV.

66. Barkan, op.cit., p. 206. For further parallels see Douglas Bush, 'Notes on Shakespeare's Classical mythology', *Philological Quarterly*, vol. 6, 1927, pp. 295–302 (p. 295). A. Ross, op.cit., p. 5, applies the story to lovers: 'They who look upon women, and lust after them, lose their reason, and are devoured by their own lusts' (one of numerous contradictory allegorizations).

67. See Bush, op.cit., p. 296, citing the Renaissance mythographer, Natalis Comes, *per incredibilem florum varietatem et amoenitatem*; cf. Ross, op.cit., p. 83 (of Elysium): 'there are the flowers of all divine graces'.

68. So Sandys, op.cit., p. 254.

69. See Charles Martindale, *John Milton and the Transformation of Ancient Epic*, London and Sydney, Croom Helm, 1986, pp. 171–181.

70. See Baldwin, vol. 2, pp. 465ff., quoting Servius' gloss *amantium tinctas colore*: 'The modest Perdita is offering the pale flowers of

maidenly love' (p. 468). For the primroses see J.H.P. Pafford's Arden edition, Methuen, London, 1963, pp. 170–172.
71. Cooper's *Thesaurus* gives as a translation of *currus* both 'waggon' and 'chariot', but even Golding prefers the latter in this context.

## 3 SHAKESPEARE'S TROY

1. Gilbert Highet, *The Classical Tradition: Greek and Roman Influences on Western Literature*, New York and London, Oxford University Press, 1949, reprinted 1987, p. 197.
2. T.J.B. Spencer, '"Greeks" and "merrygreeks": a background to *Timon of Athens* and *Troilus and Cressida'*, in Richard Hosley (ed.), *Essays on Shakespeare and Elizabethan Drama in Honor of Hardin Craig*, Columbia, University of Missouri Press, 1962, pp. 223–233. 'Greek' is also used to mean 'cheat' (p. 229).
3. Patricia Thomson, 'Rant and cant in *Troilus and Cressida'*, *Essays and Studies*, 1969, n.s. vol. 22, pp. 33–56 (p. 49).
4. Spencer, op.cit., p. 227 (translation our own).
5. Sir Thomas Elyot, *The Book Named the Governor*, edited by S.E. Lehmberg, London, Dent, 1962, p. 30. For Erasmus see e.g. *De Copia*, in *Collected Works of Erasmus*, vol. 24, ed. Craig R. Thompson, Toronto, Buffalo and London, University of Toronto Press, 1978, pp. 649, 654f. Two other important pro-Greek voices were Sidney (*Apology*) and Spenser (*Letter to Raleigh*).
6. For Dryden's 'Preface, the grounds of criticism in tragedy, prefixed to *Troilus and Cressida'* (1679), see George Watson (ed.), *John Dryden: Of Dramatic Poesy and Other Critical Essays*, 2 vols., London, Dent, 1962, vol. 1, pp. 238–261. The quotations are from the play's prologue (7, 13), spoken by Shakespeare's ghost.
7. For an informative account of the play more sympathetic than ours see Alan Roper (ed.), *The Works of John Dryden*, vol. 13, (*All for Love*; *Oedipus*; *Troilus and Cressida*), Berkeley, Los Angeles and London, University of California Press, 1984, pp. 497ff.
8. For the view that *Troilus and Cressida* belongs to the tradition of 'comical satire' (a term of Jonson), centred on the derisive censure of vice and folly, see Oscar James Campbell, *Comicall Satyre and Shakespeare's Troilus and Cressida*, San Marino, Calif., Huntington Library Publications, 1965. However, the Jonsonian examples are not very like *Troilus* (*Poetaster* is closest).
9. So Barbara Everett, 'The inaction of *Troilus and Cressida'*, *Essays in Criticism*, 1982, vol. 32, pp. 119–139.
10. For Shakespeare and Chaucer see Ann Thompson, *Shakespeare's Chaucer: A Study in Literary Origins*, Liverpool University Press, 1978.
11. For the background see Robert Kimbrough, *Shakespeare's Troilus and Cressida and its Setting*, Cambridge, MA, Harvard University Press, 1964; Robert K. Presson, *Shakespeare's Troilus and Cressida and the*

*Legends of Troy*, Madison, University of Wisconsin Press, 1953; John S.P. Tatlock, 'The siege of Troy in Elizabethan literature, especially in Shakespeare and Heywood', *PMLA*, 1915, vol. 30, pp. 673–770. Two classical sources which Shakespeare knew are Virgil, *Aeneid* II, with its generally hostile presentation of the Greeks, and Ovid, *Metamorphoses* XIII, with its contrast between the wily and rhetorically skilled Ulysses and the oafish Ajax. The 'Euripidean' character of *Troilus* may derive from Ovid. For the sources see Kenneth Palmer's Arden edition, London and New York, Methuen, 1982, pp. 22ff.

12. For these translations see Henry Burrowes Lathrop, *Translations from the Classics into English from Caxton to Chapman 1477–1620*, University of Wisconsin Studies in Language and Literature, 35, Madison, 1933; for Hall pp. 146–150; for Chapman pp. 282–291. See too Millar MacLure, *George Chapman: A Critical Study*, University of Toronto Press, 1966, pp. 158–191. Earlier Thomas Drant had attempted a version.

13. See Douglas Bush, 'Notes on Shakespeare's classical mythology', *Philological Quarterly*, 1927, vol. 6, pp. 295–302 (pp. 298f.). For the text of *Thersites* see Marie Axton (ed.), *Three Tudor Classical Interludes*, Cambridge, D.S. Brewer, Rowman & Littlefield, 1982 (Introduction p. 5 for the quotation from Cox).

14. C.S. Lewis, *A Preface to Paradise Lost*, London, Oxford University Press, 1942, p. 37.

15. Chapman's *Seven Books* is not currently in print, though easily available on microfilm. We have consulted the copy in the Bodleian Library, but for ease of reference we give citations as follows: for the final version Allardyce Nicholl (ed.), *Chapman's Homer*, 2 vols, London, Routledge & Kegan Paul, 1957, vol. 1; for books I–II of the *Seven Books*, included in Nicholl, pp. 503ff., we also cite from his text. For the other five books we give the page references to Bullough's selected extracts, vol. 6, pp. 123ff. (the original edition has no line numbers).

16. This is attempted, if in a rather impressionistic way, in a fine essay, which deserves to be better known, by G.K. Hunter, '"Troilus and Cressida": a tragic satire', *Shakespeare Studies (Tokyo)*, vol. 13, 1974–5 (published 1977), pp. 1–23. See too Richard S. Ide, *Possessed With Greatness: the Heroic Tragedies of Chapman and Shakespeare*, London, Scolar Press, 1980, pp. 20–49. For a list of possible parallels with Chapman see the Arden edition, pp. 35ff.

17. So Jasper Griffin, *Homer on Life and Death*, Oxford, Clarendon Press, 1980, ch.4.

18. So (oversimplifying) M.C. Bradbrook, 'What Shakespeare did to Chaucer's *Troilus and Criseyde*', *Shakespeare Quarterly*, vol. 9, 1958, pp. 311–319, reprinted in *Muriel Bradbrook on Shakespeare*, Brighton, Harvester, 1984, pp. 99–109.

19. E.g. James M. Redfield, *Nature and Culture in the Iliad: The Tragedy of Hector*, Chicago and London, University of Chicago Press, 1975.

20. Winifred M.T. Nowottny, '"Opinion" and "value" in *Troilus and Cressida*', *Essays in Criticism*, vol. 4, 1954, pp. 282–296 (p. 291).
21. So Adam Parry, 'The language of Achilles', *Transactions and Proceedings of the American Philological Association*, vol. 87, 1956, pp. 1–7, reprinted in G.S. Kirk (ed.), *The Language and Background of Homer*, Cambridge, W. Heffer, 1964, ch.3.
22. Graham Bradshaw, *Shakespeare's Scepticism*, Brighton, Harvester, 1987, ch.4 'The genealogy of ideals: *Troylus and Cressida*', pp. 126–164 (p. 135).
23. Bradshaw, op.cit., p. 152f.
24. Cf., on the contradictions of the speech, Jonathan Dollimore, *Radical Tragedy: Religion, Ideology and Power in the Drama of Shakespeare and his Contemporaries*, Brighton, Harvester, 1984, pp. 42f.
25. For the classic discussion see Arthur W.H. Adkins, *Merit and Responsibility: A Study in Greek Values*, Oxford, Clarendon Press, 1960, ch. 3, although his picture has to be qualified in the light of subsequent criticisms (e.g. Hugh Lloyd-Jones, *The Justice of Zeus*, Berkeley, Los Angeles and London, University of California Press, 1971, ch. 1). The quotations are from p. 49.
26. For value in *Troilus* see, in addition to other works cited, Frank Kermode, 'Opinion, truth and value', *Essays in Criticism*, vol. 5, 1955, pp. 181–187. For the imagery of reflection producing scepticism about knowledge and value cf. *Julius Caesar* I.ii.50ff. and William O. Scott, 'The speculative eye: problematic self-knowledge in *Julius Caesar*', *Shakespeare Survey*, vol. 40, 1987, pp. 77–89, with further references.
27. So Richmond Lattimore, *The Odyssey of Homer*, New York, Evanston and London, Harper & Row, 1965, introduction p. 19.
28. Stephen Medcalf (ed.), *The Later Middle Ages: The Context of English Literature*, London, Methuen, 1981, pp. 291–303 (p. 302); cf. Charles Williams, '*Troilus and Cressida* and *Hamlet*', from *The English Poetic Mind* (1932), in Anne Ridler (ed.), *Shakespeare Criticism 1919–1935*, London, Oxford University Press, 1936, pp. 188–208; John Bayley, *The Uses of Division: Unity and Disharmony in Literature*, London, Chatto & Windus, 1976, pp. 185–210.
29. So, rightly, Margaret J. Arnold, '"Monsters in love's train": Euripides and Shakespeare's *Troilus and Cressida*', *Comparative Drama*, vol. 18, 1984, pp. 38–53, even if her argument is rather impressionistic. Such discontinuities are certainly characteristic of Euripides, though Ovid, his heir, may be the *direct* influence.
30. Adam Parry, 'Have we Homer's *Iliad*?', in John Wright (ed.), *Essays on the Iliad: Selected Modern Criticism*, Bloomington and London, Indiana University Press, 1978, pp. 1–27 (first published in *Yale Classical Studies*, vol. 20, 1966, pp. 175–216), p. 10.
31. So J.B. Hainsworth, *Homer, Greece and Rome: New Surveys in the Classics* 3, Oxford, Clarendon Press, 1969, p. 39.
32. See Palmer op.cit. While we do not always agree with his conclusions, we have learnt much from his discussion of the play.
33. Medcalf, op.cit., p. 302.

34. Watson (ed.), op.cit. vol. 1, p. 257f. The phrase 'Trojan style' was apparently used in a lecture by Neville Coghill (I owe this information to A.D. Nuttall).
35. For the view (in our opinion mistaken) that Shakespeare is directly imitating Lucan, see Thomson, p. 230f. and Emrys Jones, *The Origins of Shakespeare*, Oxford, Clarendon Press, 1977, pp. 275–277.
36. See J.C. Maxwell, 'Virgilian half-lines in Shakespeare's "heroic narrative"', *Notes and Queries*, vol. 198, 1953, p. 100.
37. For an interesting, if at times unfocussed, discussion see Harry Levin, 'An explication of the player's speech: *Hamlet* (II.ii.472–541)', *Kenyon Review*, vol. 12, 1950, pp. 273–296.
38. So, perhaps over-ingeniously, Bradshaw, op.cit., p. 65f.
39. Harold Jenkins (ed.), *Hamlet*, The Arden Shakespeare, London and New York, Methuen, 1982, p. 263. For the *topos* see Marvin T. Herrick, 'Hyrcanian tigers in Renaissance tragedy', in Luitpold Wallach (ed.), *The Classical Tradition: Literary and Historical Studies in Honor of Harry Caplan*, Ithaca, NY, Cornell University Press, 1966, pp. 559–571.
40. See Charles Martindale, *John Milton and the Transformation of Ancient Epic*, London and Sydney, Croom Helm, 1986, pp. 96f. and 218f.
41. Bradshaw, op.cit., p. 127f.
42. T. McAlindon, 'Language, style and meaning in *Troilus and Cressida*', *PMLA*, vol. 84, 1969, pp. 23–43 (pp. 31, 37, 41). For a position rather closer to our own see Kenneth Muir (ed.), *Troilus and Cressida*, The Oxford Shakespeare, Oxford, Clarendon Press, 1982, p. 25f. For some brief remarks on the style see Jane Adamson, *Troilus and Cressida*, Harvester (New Critical Introductions to Shakespeare), Brighton, Harvester, 1987, pp. 24–27.
43. E.g. Brian Vickers, *The Artistry of Shakespeare's Prose*, London, Methuen, 1968, p. 253 finds it 'portentously diffuse'.

## 4 SHAKESPEARE'S ROME

1. The starting point for any investigation of the subject should be two seminal articles: T.J.B. Spencer, 'Shakespeare and the Elizabethan Romans', *Shakespeare Survey*, vol. 10, 1957, pp. 27–38; John W. Velz, 'The ancient world in Shakespeare: authenticity or anachronism? A retrospect', *Shakespeare Survey*, vol. 31, 1978, pp. 1–12. There are a number of books on the Roman plays, but nothing which has yet fully superseded MacCallum. Vivian Thomas, *Shakespeare's Roman Worlds*, (London and New York, Routledge, 1989) includes careful accounts of Shakespeare's modifications of the source material, and he writes well on the way in which historical readings are constructed, and on class struggle and the internalizing of traditional Roman values in *Coriolanus*.
2. This paragraph owes a certain amount to a lecture given some years ago by Christopher Ricks at the University of Sussex.

3. A. Pope, Preface to *The Works of Shakespeare* (1725) in Paul Hammond (ed.), *Selected Prose of Alexander Pope*, Cambridge University Press, 1987, p. 164. Cf. Johnson's *Preface to Shakespeare* (1765), in W.K. Wimsatt (ed.), *Dr. Johnson on Shakespeare*, Penguin Shakespeare Library, Harmondsworth, Penguin, 1969, p. 66.
4. Wimsatt (ed.), op.cit., pp. 66, 61.
5. But for a defence of Johnson see G.F. Parker, *Johnson's Shakespeare*, Oxford, Clarendon Press, 1989, especially chapter 2.
6. See Madeleine Doran, *Endeavors of Art: A Study of Form in Elizabethan Drama*, Madison, University of Wisconsin Press, 1954, pp. 72–77. For anachronism see also the useful article by Kenneth Muir, 'The dramatic function of anachronism', *Proceedings of the Leeds Philosophical and Literary Society*, vol. 6(II) VIII, 1951, pp. 529–533.
7. Andrew Martindale, *The Triumphs of Caesar by Andrea Mantegna*, London, Harvey Miller Publishers, 1978, especially chapter 5, pp. 56–74, 'The *Triumphs of Caesar* and classical antiquity'. The quotation is from p. 101.
8. So Ronald Lightbown, *Mantegna*, Oxford, Phaidon-Christie's, 1986, chapter 8, pp. 140–153 (p. 152).
9. Michael Levey, *Giambattista Tiepolo: His Life and Art*, New Haven and London, Yale University Press, chapter 7, pp. 143–166 (p. 164).
10. Illustrated e.g. in Eugene M. Waith (ed.), *Titus Andronicus*, The Oxford Shakespeare, Clarendon Press, Oxford, 1984, p. 21 (with a full discussion). For costume see W.M. Merchant, 'Classical costumes in Shakespearian productions', *Shakespeare Survey*, vol. 10, 1957, pp. 71–76; Hal H. Smith, 'Some principles of Elizabethan stage costume', *Journal of the Warburg and Courtauld Institutes*, vol. 25, 1962, pp. 240–257 (p. 252f.).
11. Bullough, vol. 5, p. 512.
12. G.K. Hunter, 'A Roman thought: Renaissance attitudes to history exemplified in Shakespeare and Jonson', in Brian S. Lee (ed.), *An English Miscellany: Presented to W.S. Mackie*, Cape Town, London, New York, Oxford University Press, 1977, pp. 93–118 (p. 94). This important essay is too little known.
13. So David L. Kranz, 'Shakespeare's new idea of Rome', in P.A. Ramsey (ed.), *Rome in the Renaissance: The City and the Myth*, Medieval and Renaissance Texts and Studies, Binghampton, NY, 1982, pp. 371–380.
14. For suicide in Shakespeare see Rowland Wymer, *Suicide and Despair in the Jacobean Drama*, Brighton, Harvester, 1986; also Maurice Charney, *Shakespeare's Roman Plays: The Function of Imagery in the Drama*, Cambridge, MA, Harvard University Press, 1961, appendix, pp. 209–214; James Holly Hanford, 'Suicide in the plays of Shakespeare', *PMLA*, vol. 27, 1912, pp. 380–397.
15. 'An apology of Raymond Sebond', *The Essays of Montaigne Done into English by John Florio* (1603), with an introduction by George Saintsbury, first published London, 1893, reprinted New York, AMS Press, 1967, vol. 2, p. 266.

16. Wymer, op.cit., p. 3.
17. Spencer, op.cit., p. 33.
18. Quoted by Joanna Martindale (ed.), *English Humanism: Wyatt to Cowley*, London, Croom Helm, 1985, introduction p. 35.
19. Quoted by Hunter, op.cit., p. 103 (reported by Diggory Whear, 1633).
20. ibid., p. 106.
21. See MacCallum, p. 116.
22. See MacCallum, pp. 184f. for an example. The mistake in *Coriolanus*, III.iii.9ff. about Roman elections is also due to North. See also Paul Stapfer, *Shakespeare and Classical Antiquity*, translated by Emily J. Carey, London, C. Kegan Paul, 1880, pp. 78–81.
23. Bullough, vol. 5, p. 316.
24. For some interesting remarks on this passage see Terence Hawkes, *That Shakespeherian Rag: Essays on a Critical Process*, London and New York, Methuen, 1986, pp. 81–85.
25. Figures from David Nathan Fishel's useful thesis, *The Image of Rome in Elizabethan and Jacobean Drama*, B.Litt. dissertation, Oxford, 1978 (MS M.Litt. c.465); appendix B, pp. 179f. for a list. We are also indebted to his sketch of the context for Shakespeare's Roman plays.
26. See the edition of Joseph W. Houppert, Regents Renaissance Drama Series, London, Edward Arnold, 1970.
27. MacCallum, p. 66.
28. David Bevington, *Tudor Drama and Politics: A Critical Approach to Topical Meaning*, Cambridge, MA, Harvard University Press, 1968, pp. 234–236 (p. 234). See too Fishel, op.cit., pp. 42f.; pp. 115ff.
29. See the edition of Jonas A. Barish, New Haven and London, Yale University Press, 1965, with helpful introduction and notes (p. 27). See too J.A. Bryant, Jr, 'The significance of Ben Jonson's first requirement for tragedy: "truth of argument"', *Studies in Philology*, vol. 49, 1952, pp. 195–213; A. Richard Dutton, 'The sources, text, and readers of *Sejanus*: Jonson's "integrity in the story"', *Studies in Philology*, vol. 75, 1978, pp. 181–198.
30. See W. Gordon Zeeveld, '*Coriolanus* and Jacobean politics', *Modern Language Review*, vol. 57, 1962, pp. 321–334 (p. 327).
31. H.A. Mason, 'Is Juvenal a classic?', in J.P. Sullivan (ed.), *Critical Essays on Roman Literature: Satire*, London, Routledge & Kegan Paul, 1963, pp. 93–176 (pp. 111–113).
32. See the helpful edition and notes by W.F. Bolton and Jane F. Gardner, London, Edward Arnold, 1973, especially appendix B on Jonson's classical sources, pp. 176–193.
33. See the introduction by Maximillian E. Novak in *The Works of John Dryden*, vol. 13, general editor Alan Roper, Berkeley, Los Angeles, London, University of California Press, 1984, pp. 363–440.
34. See A.D. Nuttall, *A New Mimesis: Shakespeare and the Representation of Reality*, London and New York, Methuen, 1983, pp. 99–120. Other studies, not mentioned elsewhere in these notes, include Paul A. Cantor, *Shakespeare's Rome: Republic and Empire*, Ithaca, NY, Cornell University Press, 1976; Joanna Martindale,

'Shakespeare's Rome', *Omnibus*, vol. 9, March 1985, pp. 1–4; Kenneth Muir, 'Shakespeare's Roman world', *Literary Half Yearly* (Mysore, India), vol.15, 1974, pp. 45–63. For some remarks on Shakespeare's view of history see Richard Dutton, *William Shakespeare: A Literary Life*, Houndmills and London, Macmillan, 1989, pp. 74ff.

35. Hunter, op.cit., p. 108.

36. So David M. Bergeron, '*Cymbeline*: Shakespeare's last Roman play', *Shakespeare Quarterly*, vol. 31, 1980, pp. 31–41; Robert S. Miola, *Shakespeare's Rome*, Cambridge University Press, 1983, chapter 7, pp. 206–235.

37. Howard Erskine-Hill, *The Augustan Idea in English Literature*, London, Edward Arnold, 1983, p. 135. Ernest Schanzer, *The Problem Plays of Shakespeare: A Study of* Julius Caesar, Measure for Measure, Antony and Cleopatra, London, Routledge & Kegan Paul, 1963, also stresses the ambivalence of Shakespeare's presentation of Roman history (pp. 10–70 for *Julius Caesar*; 132–83 for *Antony and Cleopatra*), but his appropriation of the term 'problem play' is unhelpful.

38. Hereward T. Price, 'The language of *Titus Andronicus*', *Papers of the Michigan Academy of Science, Arts and Letters*, vol. 21, 1935, pp. 501–507 (p. 507).

39. Spencer, op.cit., p. 32.

40. G.K. Hunter, 'Sources and meanings in *Titus Andronicus*', in J.C. Gray (ed.), *Mirror up to Shakespeare: Essays in Honour of G.R. Hibbard*, Toronto, Buffalo and London, University of Toronto Press, 1984, pp. 171–188 (pp. 182–8).

41. Spencer, op.cit., p. 32.

42. See Emrys Jones, 'Stuart Cymbeline', *Essays in Criticism*, vol. 11, 1961, pp. 84–99.

43. Quoted e.g. by John Wilders, *The Lost Garden: A View of Shakespeare's English and Roman History Plays*, London and Basingstoke, Macmillan, 1978, p. 8.

44. Cf. S.P. Zitner, 'Shakespeare's *Coriolanus* and the Aristotelian modes of pathos', in Martin Cropp, Elaine Fantham and S.E. Scully (eds), *Greek Tragedy and its Legacy: Essays Presented to D.J. Conacher*, University of Calgary Press, 1986, pp. 295–312 (p. 300).

45. Quoted by Parker, op.cit., p. 101.

46. MacCallum, p. 280, note 1.

47. Quoted by Marilyn L. Williamson, *Infinite Variety: Antony and Cleopatra in Renaissance Drama and Earlier Tradition*, Mystic, CT, Lawrence Verry, 1974, p. 182; Robert Ornstein, 'The ethic of the imagination: love and art in *Antony and Cleopatra*', in John Russell Brown and Bernard Harris (eds), *Later Shakespeare*, Stratford-Upon-Avon Studies 8, London, Edward Arnold, 1966, pp. 31–46. Cf. Ruth Nevo, 'The masque of greatness', *Shakespeare Studies*, ed. J. Leeds Barroll, vol. 3, 1967, pp. 111–128. The standard treatment of Shakespeare's use of theatrical imagery is Anne Righter, *Shakespeare*

*and the Idea of the Play* (1962), reprinted Penguin Shakespeare Library, Harmondsworth, Penguin, 1967.

48. So e.g. J. Leeds Barroll, 'Shakespeare and Roman History', *MLR*, vol. 53, 1958, pp. 327–343.
49. This is the thesis of J.L. Simmons, *Shakespeare's Pagan World: The Roman Tragedies*, Charlottesville, University Press of Virginia, 1973. See too Paul N. Siegel, *Shakespeare's English and Roman History Plays: A Marxist Approach*, London and Toronto, Associated University Presses, 1986, chapter 8, 'Shakespeare's view of Roman history', pp. 100–134.
50. So Donna B. Hamilton, '*Antony and Cleopatra* and the tradition of noble lovers', *Shakespeare Quarterly*, vol. 24, 1973, pp. 245–251; Williamson, op.cit.; Janet Adelman, *The Common Liar: An Essay on Antony and Cleopatra*, New Haven and London, Yale University Press, 1973, chapter 2, pp. 53–101.
51. Emrys Jones, *Scenic Form in Shakespeare*, Oxford, Clarendon Press, 1971, p. 239.
52. L.C. Knights, 'On the tragedy of Antony and Cleopatra', *Scrutiny*, vol. 16, 1949, pp. 318–323 (p. 322); cf. Derek Traversi, *Shakespeare: The Roman Plays*, Stanford, CA, Stanford University Press, 1963. Knights's interpretation illustrates how 'morality' has filled the gap left by the death of religion amongst the majority of critics in twentieth-century England. Leavis in particular made literary criticism into a substitute for religion. The same defect can also be seen in much contemporary 'radical' criticism.
53. Hunter, 'A Roman thought', p. 107.
54. Wilders, op.cit., p. 138.
55. Quoted by M.L. Clarke, *The Noblest Roman: Marcus Brutus and His Reputation*, London, Thames & Hudson, 1981, p. 92.
56. Bullough, vol. 5, p. 195 (his translation).
57. Pope, *Preface*, in Hammond, op.cit., p. 162.
58. MacCallum, p. 83.
59. Spencer, op.cit., p. 35.
60. Bullough, vol. 5, p. 506.
61. See Kenneth Muir, *The Sources of Shakespeare's Plays*, London, Methuen, 1977, pp. 238ff.
62. Terence Hawkes (ed.), *Coleridge on Shakespeare*, Penguin Shakespeare Library, Harmondsworth, Penguin, 1969, p. 275.
63. So Janette Dillon, '"Solitariness": Shakespeare and Plutarch', *Journal of English and Germanic Philology*, vol. 78, 1979, pp. 325–344 (pp. 337–342).
64. For Jonson's hostility to *Julius Caesar* see J. Dover Wilson, 'Ben Jonson and *Julius Caesar*', *Shakespeare Survey*, vol. 2, 1949, pp. 36–43.
65. Velz, op.cit., pp. 9f. For the thrasonical Caesar see Harry Morgan Ayres, 'Shakespeare's *Julius Caesar* in the light of some other versions', *PMLA*, vol. 25, 1910, pp. 183–227.
66. Quoted e.g. by Arthur Humphreys, *Julius Caesar*, The Oxford Shakespeare, Clarendon Press, Oxford, 1984, p. 1.

67. *Coleridge on Shakespeare*, p. 268.
68. Virgil K. Whitaker, *Shakespeare's Use of Learning: An Enquiry into the Growth of his Mind and Art*, San Marino, CA, The Huntington Library, 1953, p. 238. The whole chapter, pp. 224–250, is worth reading in this connection.
69. Quoted by MacCallum, pp. 22f. (translation adjusted).
70. So W. Warde Fowler, 'The tragic element in Shakespeare's *Julius Caesar*', *Roman Essays and Interpretations*, Oxford, Clarendon Press, 1920, pp. 268–287. For Brutus' response to Portia's death and its significance see Thomas Clayton, '"Should Brutus Never Taste of Portia's death but once?": text and performance in *Julius Caesar*', *Studies in English Literature 1500–1900*, vol. 23, 1983, pp. 237–255, with note 5 for earlier treatments. See also the excellent discussion in Nuttall, op.cit., pp. 111–113.
71. Bullough, vol. 5, p. 268f.
72. *Johnson on Shakespeare*, p. 134.
73. For the style of this play see Humphreys's edition, op.cit., pp. 42–48; John W. Velz, '*Orator* and *Imperator* in *Julius Caesar*: style and the process of Roman history', *Shakespeare Studies*, vol. 15, 1982, pp. 55–75. For the style of the Roman plays in general see Charney, op.cit. For oratory in Shakespeare see Milton Boone Kennedy, *The Oration in Shakespeare*, Chapel Hill, NC, The University of North Carolina Press, 1942.
74. R.W. Zandvoort, 'Brutus' forum speech in *Julius Caesar*', *Review of English Studies*, vol. 16, 1940, pp. 62–66 (p. 65).
75. Bullough, vol. 5, p. 91.
76. ibid., introduction pp. 7, 45f.
77. R.G.M. Nisbet, 'The speeches', in T.A. Dorey (ed.), *Cicero*, London, Routledge & Kegan Paul, 1964, pp. 47–79 (p. 52).
78. John Bayley, *The Uses of Division: Unity and Disharmony in Literature*, London, Chatto & Windus, 1976, p. 241. For the style of *Antony and Cleopatra* see also Adelman, op.cit., pp. 102–168.
79. *Coleridge on Shakespeare*, p. 269.
80. Jones, op.cit., p. 236.
81. Emrys Jones (ed.), *Antony and Cleopatra*, New Penguin Shakespeare, Harmondsworth, Penguin, 1977, Introduction, pp. 45f. (p. 46).
82. We take this example from L.P. Wilkinson, *Horace and his Lyric Poetry*, Cambridge University Press, 1945, p. 126; cf. J.B. Leishman, *Translating Horace*, Oxford, Cassirer, 1956, pp. 74ff. Occasionally, it is true, Horace plays his habitual precision against a sudden mystery, e.g. *Odes* IV.1.37–40.
83. Quoted by Wilkinson, op.cit., p. 4.
84. Quoted by Rolfe Humphries, 'Latin and English verse – some practical considerations', in Reuben A. Brower (ed.), *On Translation*, Cambridge, MA, Harvard University Press, 1959, pp. 57–66, p. 57.
85. See Philip Brockbank's Arden edition, London, Methuen, 1976, note *ad loc.*, p. 290.
86. See the useful New Penguin Shakespeare edition of *Coriolanus* by

G.R. Hibbard, Harmondsworth, Penguin, 1967, pp. 213–215. We
have not seen Richard C. Crowley, 'Coriolanus and the epic genre', in
Richard C. Tobias and Paul G. Zolbrod (eds), Shakespeare's Last
Plays: Essays in Honor of Charles Crow, Athens, OH, Ohio
University Press, 1974, pp. 114–130. A recent study of the play is
Adrian Poole, Coriolanus, Harvester New Critical Introductions to
Shakespeare, New York and London, Harvester-Wheatsheaf, 1989,
with full bibliography. For the view that there is a significant Virgilian
presence in Coriolanus see John W. Velz, 'Cracking strong curbs
asunder: Roman destiny and the Roman hero in Coriolanus', English
Literary Renaissance, vol. 13, 1983, pp. 58–69; for supposed Livian
elements see Anne Barton, 'Livy, Machiavelli and Shakespeare's
Coriolanus', Shakespeare Survey, vol. 38, 1985, pp. 115–129 (both
authors press the analogies too hard).

## 5 SHAKESPEARE'S STOICISM

1. See Baldwin, vol. 2, pp. 578ff.
2. Gilles D. Monsarrat, Light from the Porch: Stoicism and English
   Renaissance Literature, Études Anglaises 86, Paris, Didier-Érudition,
   1984, chapter 6. Charles Wells, The Wide Arch: Roman Values in
   Shakespeare is to be published by Bristol Classical Press in 1990. For
   some reflections on constancy in Shakespeare see T. McAlindon,
   English Renaissance Tragedy, Vancouver, University of British
   Columbia Press, 1986, pp. 10–25.
3. See e.g. Milton's introduction to Samson Agonistes: 'Of that sort of
   dramatic poem which is called tragedy'.
4. See Bullough, vol. 5, p. 90. Cf. Mark Sacharoff, 'Suicide and Brutus'
   philosophy in Julius Caesar', Journal of the History of Ideas, 1972,
   vol. 33, pp. 115–122; but contra see Roland Wymer, Suicide and
   Despair in the Jacobean Drama, Brighton, Harvester, 1986, pp. 151ff.
   Brutus' philosophical preference for the Academics is confirmed in
   Cicero (Brutus chapter 31.120; chapter 39.149). As Cato's son-in-law,
   Brutus was also familiar with the tenets of Stoicism, as Plutarch
   observes.
5. So e.g. John Anson, 'Julius Caesar: the politics of the hardened heart',
   Shakespeare Studies, 1966, vol. 2, pp. 11–33; Marvin L. Vawter,
   '"Division 'tween our souls": Shakespeare's Stoic Brutus',
   Shakespeare Studies, 1974, vol. 7, pp. 173–195.
6. The Latin version went through over eighty editions in the next three
   centuries, and was translated into all the major European languages.
   We quote from the 1594 translation: Two Books of Constancy
   Englished by Sir John Stradling, edited by Rudolf Kirk, New
   Brunswick, Rutgers University Press, 1939, with a useful
   introduction. For Lipsius' definition of constancy see p. 79. Another
   important vehicle for popular ideas of Stoicism was Guillaume Du
   Vair, La Philosophie Morale des Stoïques, c.1585. For Seneca's views
   on constancy see e.g. De Constantia Sapientis; in chapter 3.5 the

impregnable mind of the *sapiens* is compared to the hardness of stone and of adamant.

7. Lipsius (Stradling), *De Constantia*, p. 100.
8. See Thomas M. Greene, 'Ben Jonson and the centered self', *Studies in English Literature 1500–1900*, 1970, vol. 10, pp. 325–348. Jonson's 'round within himself' translates Horace's *totus teres atque rotundus* (*Satires* II.7.86).
9. Thomas Fuller, *The Worthies of England*, ed. John Freeman (1662), London, Allen & Unwin, 1952, p. 180.
10. Lipsius, however, had a remarkable knowledge of all aspects of ancient Stoicism, which he pursued in later and more technical publications. These were, however, less popular than the *De Constantia*. See Jason Lewis Saunders, *Justus Lipsius: The Philosophy of Renaissance Stoicism*, New York, Liberal Arts Press, 1955.
11. Lipsius (Stradling), op.cit., p. 85.
12. Thomas M. Greene, 'The flexibility of the self in Renaissance literature', in Peter Demetz, Thomas Greene, Lowry Nelson Jr. (eds), *The Disciplines of Criticism: Essays in Literary Theory, Interpretation, and History*, New Haven and London, Yale University Press, 1968, pp. 241–264.
13. Greene, 'The flexibility of the self', p. 258.
14. Anyone interested in pursuing the matter should consider, *inter alia*, *Lucrece* 48; *Lover's Complaint* 293, 315; *The Merchant of Venice*, II.ii.177; *All's Well That Ends Well*, I.i.103; III.vi.109; *Troilus and Cressida*, I.iii.228; *Julius Caesar*, III.i.213; *Antony and Cleopatra*, II.vi.120; *Pericles*, IV.i.5; IV.vi.139.
15. See the discussion in John Kerrigan (ed.), *William Shakespeare: The Sonnets and A Lover's Complaint*, Harmondsworth, Penguin Books, 1986, pp. 290–295, with the further literature cited in this edition, 68ff., in particular Stephen Booth, *An Essay on Shakespeare's Sonnets*, New Haven and London, Yale University Press, 1969, pp. 152–168 (162ff.); William Empson, *Some Versions of Pastoral*, London, Chatto & Windus, 1935, pp. 89–101.
16. See Benjamin Boyce, 'The Stoic *Consolatio* and Shakespeare', *PMLA*, 1949, vol. 64, pp. 771–780.
17. See Alan Sinfield, 'Hamlet's special providence', *Shakespeare Survey*, 1980, vol. 33, pp. 89–97.
18. Lipsius (Stradling), op.cit., p. 79.
19. Bullough, vol. 5, p. 279.
20. M.R. Ridley, *Antony and Cleopatra*, Arden Shakespeare, London, Methuen, 1954, p. 194.
21. See Baldwin, vol. 2, chapter 4, pp. 497ff.
22. The connection was first pointed out by P.D. Westbrook, 'Horace's influence on Shakespeare's *Antony and Cleopatra*', *PMLA*, 1947, vol. 62, pp. 392–398.
23. Our interpretation of this ode owes much to the following: Alex Hardie, 'Horace *Odes* 1,37 and Pindar *Dithyramb* 2', *Papers of the Liverpool Latin Seminar*, edited by Francis Cairns, 1976, pp. 113–140;

R.G.M. Nisbet and Margaret Hubbard, *A Commentary on Horace Odes Book I*, Oxford, Clarendon Press, 1970, pp. 406–421; Steele Commager, *The Odes of Horace: A Critical Study*, New Haven and London, Yale University Press, 1962, pp. 88–97.

# SELECTED BIBLIOGRAPHY
## (mainly for students)

For a full bibliography up to 1960 see J.W. Velz, *Shakespeare and the Classical Tradition: A Critical Guide to Commentary, 1660–1960*, Minneapolis, University of Minnesota Press, 1968. This can be supplemented by Hanne Carlsen, *A Bibliography to the Classical Tradition in English Literature*, Anglica et Americana 21, Copenhagen, 1985.

Barkan, L., *The Gods Made Flesh: Metamorphosis and the Pursuit of Paganism*, New Haven and London, Yale University Press, 1986.
Bolgar, R.R., *The Classical Heritage and its Beneficiaries*, Cambridge University Press, 1954.
Braden, G., *Renaissance Tragedy and the Senecan Tradition: Anger's Privilege*, New Haven and London, Yale University Press, 1985.
Bradshaw, G., *Shakespeare's Scepticism*, Brighton, Harvester, 1987 (chapter 4 on *Troilus*).
Brooks, H.F., Introduction to *A Midsummer Night's Dream*, Arden Shakespeare, London, Methuen, 1979.
Brower, R.A., *Hero and Saint: Shakespeare and the Graeco-Roman Heroic Tradition*, Oxford, Clarendon Press, 1971.
Clemen, W., *English Tragedy Before Shakespeare: The Development of Dramatic Speech*, trans. T.S. Dorsch, London, Methuen, 1961.
Donaldson, I., *The Rapes of Lucretia: A Myth and its Transformations*, Oxford, Clarendon Press, 1982.
Doran, M., *Endeavors of Art: A Study of Form in Elizabethan Drama*, Madison, University of Wisconsin Press, 1954.
Doran, M., '*A Midsummer Night's Dream*: a metamorphosis', *Rice Institute Pamphlets*, vol. 46, 1960, pp. 113–135.
Dutton, R., *William Shakespeare: A Literary Life*, Houndmills and London, Macmillan, 1989.
Erskine-Hill, H., *The Augustan Idea in English Literature*, London, Edward Arnold, 1983 (chapter 6 on Shakespeare).
Fender, S., *Shakespeare: A Midsummer Night's Dream*, Studies in English Literature, no.35, London, Edward Arnold, 1968.
Highet, G., *The Classical Tradition: Greek and Roman Influences on*

*Western Literature*, 1949, repr. Oxford University Press, 1987 (chapter 11 'Shakespeare's classics', pp. 194–218, 617–627).

Humphreys, A., Introduction to *Julius Caesar*, Oxford Shakespeare, Oxford, Clarendon Press, 1984.

Hunter, G.K., 'Seneca and the Elizabethans: a case-study in influence', *Shakespeare Survey*, vol. 20, 1967, pp. 17–26.

Hunter, G.K., 'Seneca and English tragedy', in C.D.N. Costa (ed.), *Seneca*, London and Boston, Routledge & Kegan Paul, 1974, pp. 166–204.

Hunter, G.K., '*Troilus and Cressida*: a tragic satire', *Shakespeare Studies (Tokyo)*, vol.13, 1974 (published 1977), pp. 1–23.

Hunter, G.K., 'A Roman thought: Renaissance attitudes to history exemplified in Shakespeare and Jonson', in Brian S. Lee (ed.), *An English Miscellany: Presented to W.S. Mackie*, Cape Town, London and New York, Oxford University Press, 1977, pp. 93–118.

Jones, F., *The Origins of Shakespeare*, Oxford, Clarendon Press, 1977.

Jones, E., Introduction to *Antony and Cleopatra*, New Penguin Shakespeare, Harmondsworth, Penguin, 1977.

Keach, W., *Elizabethan Erotic Narratives: Irony and Pathos in the Ovidian Poetry of Shakespeare, Marlowe and their Contemporaries*, Hassocks, Harvester, 1977.

Martindale, C., *John Milton and the Transformation of Ancient Epic*, London and Sydney, Croom Helm, 1986.

Martindale, C. (ed.), *Ovid Renewed: Ovidian Influences on Literature and Art from the Middle Ages to the Twentieth-Century*, Cambridge University Press, 1988.

Muir, K., *The Sources of Shakespeare's Plays*, London, Methuen, 1977.

Nuttall, A.D., *A New Mimesis: Shakespeare and the Representation of Reality*, London and New York, Methuen, 1983, chapter 3, pp. 99–120 (*Julius Caesar* and *Coriolanus*).

Palmer, K., Introduction to *Troilus and Cressida*, Arden Shakespeare, London and New York, Macmillan, 1982.

Spencer, T.J.B., 'Shakespeare and the Elizabethan Romans', *Shakespeare Survey*, vol.10, 1957, pp. 27–38.

Spencer, T.J.B., *Shakespeare: The Roman Plays*, London, Longmans, Green & Co. for the British Council, 1963.

Thomas, V., *Shakespeare's Roman Worlds*, London and New York, Routledge, 1989.

Thomson, J.A.K., *Shakespeare and the Classics*, London, George Allen & Unwin, 1952.

Velz, J.W., 'The ancient world in Shakespeare: authenticity or anachronism? A retrospect', *Shakespeare Survey*, vol. 31, 1978, pp. 1–12.

Vickers, B., *In Defence of Rhetoric*, Oxford, Clarendon Press, 1988 (especially chapters. 5 and 6)

Waith, E.M., 'The metamorphosis of violence in *Titus Andronicus*', *Shakespeare Survey*, vol. 10, 1957, pp. 39–49.

Waith, E.M., *The Herculean Hero: in Marlowe, Chapman, Shakespeare and Dryden*, London, Chatto & Windus, 1962.

Wells, S. (ed.), *The Cambridge Companion to Shakespeare Studies*, Cambridge University Press, 1986.
Wilkinson, L.P., *Ovid Recalled*, Cambridge University Press, 1955.

# INDEX

219

# INDEX OF PASSAGES